For Katie

Best of friends

With best of wishes.

I am excited for you to read the book.

Sincerely

Ken Brody

June 2.2011

The TRIAL of PIERRE LAVAL

The TRIAL of PIERRE LAVAL

*DEFINING
TREASON,
COLLABORATION
AND PATRIOTISM IN
WORLD WAR II FRANCE*

J. Kenneth Brody

Transaction Publishers
New Brunswick (U.S.A.) and London (U.K.)

Library of Congress Catalog Number: 2009043210
ISBN: 978-1-4128-1152-1
Printed in the United States of America

Library of Congress Cataloging-in-Publication Data

Brody, J. Kenneth.
  The trial of Pierre Laval : defining treason, collaboration, and patriotism in World War II France / J. Kenneth Brody.
      p. cm.
  Includes bibliographical references and index.
  ISBN 978-1-4128-1152-1 (alk. paper)
      1. Laval, Pierre, 1883-1945--Trials, litigation, etc. 2. Trials (Treason)--France--Paris. 3. France--Politics and government--1940-1945. I. Title.

KJV130.L38B76 2010
345.44'3610231--dc22

                                                                2009043210

In Loving Memory

Alton A. Johnson

and

Wineva E. Johnson

We shall never know what he spared us.
We shall never know what France would
have been without Vichy.

Albert Camus

Contents

Acknowledgments

The basic document for the study of *The Trial of Pierre Laval* is the trial transcript published in 1946 by Albin Michel, Paris, and extensively used herein with the generous permission of the publisher.

Of prime importance is the account by Yves Frédéric Jaffré of his prison visits to Laval as junior member of the defense team. It was published in 1953 by Andre Bonne, Paris, under the title *Les Derniers Propos de Pierre Laval*. The copyright having since reverted to the author, extensive excerpts are here made with the kind permission of Maitre Jaffré who has given extensive interviews and read and critiqued the manuscript.

The late Comte René de Chambrun was the son-in-law of Pierre Laval. He figures prominently in this narrative. Over a long life he accumulated a vast archive of documents, artifacts and memorabilia of Pierre Laval all of which, in addition to many interviews, he made available to the author. The many books he published on Pierre Laval are cited in the text and listed in the Bibliography. M. de Chambrun also reviewed and commented on the manuscript. I am profoundly grateful to Maitre Jaffré and M. de Chambrun for their signal contributions to this work and to Ambassador Walter J. P. Curley for introducing me to M. de Chambrun.

For her able assistance throughout this project I am deeply indebted to Mme. Isabelle-Sophie Grivet of the Foundation Josée et René de Chambrun. Oral historian Michael Takiff and Anne Ekstrom made valuable contributions to the work. Richard Abel, Alison Brody, and Arthur Levinson also read and commented meaningfully on the manuscript and merit my profound thanks. Rebecca Peer of Peer Project Management prepared and maintained the manuscript over a long gestation period.

I am grateful to these libraries which furnished important materials: Bibliotheque Nationale Mitterand, Paris, Portland State University Library and Multnomah County Library, Portland, Oregon.

Sandra Brody not only read and critiqued the manuscript, but also gave her loving support to the work from its inception.

Introduction

Pierre Laval was born in humble circumstances in the village of Chateldon in France's Auvergne region on June 28, 1883. He studied and practiced law, entered politics and in 1914 was elected mayor of Aubervilliers, a Paris suburb. In the same year, he became the youngest member of the French Chamber of Deputies.

He held several ministerial posts in the 1920s and in the 1930s was three times prime minister of France and *Time* magazine's 1931 Man of the Year. He was foreign minister and then prime minister in 1934-1936. Alert to the rapidly growing threat of Adolf Hitler's Nazi Germany, he attempted to align Benito Mussolini's Italy with Britain, France, and the Soviet Union in a defensive front to contain that threat. Italy's 1935 aggression in Abyssinia complicated matters. In December 1935, Laval entered into an agreement with British Foreign Secretary Sir Samuel Hoare to settle Italy's aggression in Abyssinia and at the same time to retain Italy as an ally against Hitler's Germany. That agreement was derailed by hostile British opinion. Laval resigned and a disappointed Italy in time became Germany's partner in the Rome-Berlin Axis and its World War II ally.

The German attack on Poland on September 1, 1939 signaled the start of the Second World War. France collapsed under the German attack in May, 1940 and signed an armistice in which Laval played no part. But he was a leader in Parliament in the transfer of power in July, 1940 from the Third Republic to the Vichy French regime headed by World War I hero Marshal Philippe Pétain. Laval served in that government as vice premier and minister without portfolio from July to December 13, 1940 when he was dismissed.

He returned to government in April, 1942 as prime minister of the Vichy regime and continued to serve during Allied campaigns in North Africa, Italy, and finally France. During that period he was widely seen, both in France and abroad, as the leading proponent of collaboration with Germany. The persecution and deportation of Jews in France, German

1

demands for labor and military assistance, and the fate of Alsace-Lorraine were prominent among the issues in which he was involved as Vichy prime minister.

As the Allies approached Paris in August, 1944, he tried and failed with former Prime Minister Edouard Herriot to reconvene Parliament. Instead, he resigned all governmental functions when taken into captivity in Germany in August, 1944 where he remained until the war ended in May, 1945.

After seeking refuge in Spain, he returned to France on August 1, 1945. He was promptly arrested and charged with treason and intelligence with the enemy. Both charges carried the death penalty.

His trial began on October 4, 1945. What Laval did at Vichy and why he did it would be the basic issues of the trial. This book is, as the title indicates, the story of the trial of Pierre Laval. It considers the pre-trial proceedings, or lack thereof, all of the evidence adduced and all of the arguments made by the prosecution and Pierre Laval's vigorous defense in the first days of the trial. Because of grave irregularities in the preliminary proceedings, Laval's defense counsel declined from the outset to participate in the trial. For those reasons and because of the prejudicial conduct of the prosecution, the judge, and the jury, on the third day of the trial Pierre Laval declined to participate further. What his defense would have been both in a regular pre-trial proceeding and in a fair trial are today matters of conjecture. Nevertheless, this book presents the defense that might have been but never was made and then relates the final judgment, its execution and its aftermath.

Prologue: The Black Plane

July 31, 1945. The JU 88 aircraft which took off from the Prats de Lobregal Airport in Barcelona headed for Innsbruck in the American zone of Austria was a remnant of the defeated Luftwaffe, the German Air Force of the Second World War. That conflict had recently ended in Europe with the unconditional surrender on May 5 of Nazi Germany, but it still raged on against Japan in the Pacific.

The plane was painted all black. It bore no distinctive markings or national insignia. But the civilian-clad crew were German: the pilot, Sergeant Gerhard Boehm and navigator Helmut Sunk. They had brought the same plane to Barcelona on May 2 from Feldkirche, Germany in the rapidly expiring Third Reich. On both journeys the principal passengers aboard the black plane were Pierre Laval, often dubbed Pierre le Noir or Black Peter, and his wife Jeanne.[1]

Who was Pierre Laval? As the youthful Prime Minister of France in 1931, *Time* magazine reported that he "loomed calm, masterful and popular as the Man of the Year who...rose from obscurity to world prominence, steered a Great Power safely through 1931, (and) closed the year on a peak of popularity among his countrymen."[2] Today this sometime Man of the Year was the most hated man in France.

As prime minister again in 1935-36, Laval had labored diligently with Italian dictator Benito Mussolini to construct a defensive alliance against the growing and chilling menace of Nazi Germany, only to be frustrated by British reluctance.

That same Nazi Germany ignited the Second World War on August 1, 1939. With the total defeat and disintegration in 1940 of the French armed forces and the French government, Laval had been a driving force in replacing the defunct Third Republic with a new government which took its name from the small spa city of Vichy in central France where Parliament met to effect the necessary constitutional changes and where the seat of the new government of France came to rest.

The head of the new French state was Marshal Philippe Pétain, the deeply revered hero of Verdun and of the victorious World War of 1914-1918. Pierre Laval served from July 1940 to December 1940 as one of two vice premiers under Pétain and returned to Vichy in April, 1942 as Prime Minister of the Vichy regime. Had Laval retired in 1940 to his beloved farm and fields in the Auvergne village of Chateldon, his name would have been no more than a footnote in French history. Instead he took center stage during France's darkest years.

No two men could have been more different: the taut, spare, erect, handsome octogenarian soldier, his rosy complexion set off by his white hair and moustache and his cerulean eyes, jarringly contrasted with the squat, swarthy, dark-eyed, rumpled scion of Auvergnat peasants. The contrast extended to their manner – Pétain so reserved, laconic, distant, Laval so vigorous, voluble, expressive. Pétain was seen as an icon of rectitude, of old fashioned virtues, of patriotism and of duty. He liked to say that he had made a gift of his person to France. Laval was widely perceived as flexible to the point of slipperiness – did not his name spell the same forward and backward? – a fixer, a dealer in the corridors of power. Pétain was respected, he was admired, he was loved. Laval, sturdily independent, never courted popularity and never, after 1931 attained it.

As the armies of liberation approached Paris in August 1944 both Pétain and Laval refused to serve further in a government of what was left of Vichy France. They were taken by the Germans into captivity, first in a Hohenzollern Castle at Sigmaringen, then in the village of Willflingen. During this time Laval toiled arduously in collecting documents and preparing his defense for the trial he knew he must face. Amid the chaos of the collapsing Third Reich, he sought and failed to find refuge in Switzerland. He had had ties with Spain and it was there that the black plane took him on May 2, 1945. He received a frigid welcome. On landing, he was asked if he would not prefer to continue his journey to Ireland in which case the plane was fueled and ready. Declining this offer, Laval and his wife were interned in the fortress of Montjuich.[3]

The Spanish dictator, Franco, had been close to Nazi Germany which had supported him in the Spanish Civil War. He had contributed troops to the German assault on the Soviet Union. In the hour of the German surrender he needed to seek the favor of the victors. Laval was an embarrassment and his welcome expired after three months. The black plane stood by on July 31. Laval was asked if he would prefer to seek refuge in Portugal or Ireland. "A Prime Minister of France," he replied icily, "is not a traveling salesman."[4] Marshal Pétain had earlier crossed over into France. His trial was then in progress. He would be found guilty of treason, but with the death sentence commuted to life imprisonment. Laval's enormous self-confidence buoyed his hopes that once back in France he could persuade his fellow citizens in general and a jury in particular that all he had done at Vichy was for the protection, for the benefit and for the well-being of France and the French.

A captive in Germany, a fugitive in Spain, Pierre Laval was returning to France to face an accounting for his role in these tumultuous years. Whether that accounting would be a process of justice or of revenge remained to be seen.

When the black plane landed at Innsbruck, a crowd of military police and newspaper correspondents surged forward to catch their first glance of the famous (or infamous) passenger. Laval emerged wearing a rumpled grey suit and his trademark white tie. He tried to smile. U.S. Brigadier General John Copeland was crisp and brief. Turning to Laval he said, "I have the duty of arresting you and turning you over to the French authorities."

Laval's attempt at humor was ill-timed: "I would have preferred to go to New York," he replied, "but I wasn't given the choice." He proceeded to field the journalist's questions as if he were a prime minister conducting a press conference. His wife, pale and seemingly ill, was more somber. "I don't believe in justice anymore," she said, mustering the faintest of smiles for the photographer.[5]

While these discussions were going on, Laval's voluminous baggage was unloaded from the black plane. Contained in it were not only the clothing and personal effects of the Lavals. Far more precious were the documents Laval had collected and the materials he had so laboriously prepared in the long months of his detention in Germany. They would constitute the basis for his defense in the trial he knew he must soon face. The fate of the documents and the fate of Pierre Laval would be intertwined.[6]

The next day the Lavals left for Paris at 3:40 P.M. At an intermediate stop they boarded a Beechcraft wearing French colors. It arrived at Le Bourget, Paris, at 7:30 P.M. A crowd of about 300 had gathered to meet them. The pilot and a French officer emerged from the plane followed by Madame Laval. Where was Laval? After a few tentative steps forward, he momentarily retreated back into the plane. Only when a police vehicle pulled up alongside did he, for the first time in a year, set foot on French soil. Observers noted how emaciated Laval was, his clothes hanging limply about him, his dark skin further bronzed by the sun of Spain, his fleshy lips trembling, his dewlaps unrestrained by the collar of his white shirt. He clutched close to him a briefcase containing his most important documents and carried his ever present cane.[7]

Was this the much photographed, well-remembered image of France's premier, the president of the Council of State? Or was this simply an old man, an uneasy, an apprehensive old man? Positive identification was not difficult. It was what in its report *Les Nouvelles Du Matin* called the "supreme *coquetterie*," the ultimate signal, his perennial white tie.[8]

Laval had reason to be apprehensive. As he appeared there were raucous shouts, many from the police: "*Salaud*," "Down with Laval," a manifestation which the *New York Times* primly called "unprofessional."[9] Pierre Beteille, one of the members of the commission that would take part in the trial of Pierre Laval, stepped forward. "In the name of the law, I arrest you," he said. Laval seemed not to notice him and embraced his wife. Over his vigorous protests, Beteille then confiscated the seventeen valises containing the results of Laval's arduous labors in the castle at Sigmaringen, and at Willflingen. They were now, for the moment, lost to Laval and if and when they would reappear no one could tell.[10]

The Lavals were escorted to a waiting car which would take them to the Fresnes prison. At the gates of the airport a crowd had been waiting for two hours to see Laval. When they saw him, slouched in the rear of the car, there were angry shouts of "Death to Laval." Attended by two outriders, the car took back streets to avoid crowds and traffic. When they arrived at the prison, the Lavals were taken to separate cells.[11]

Charges would promptly be lodged against Pierre Laval. They would be plotting against the security of the state and intelligence with the enemy. The single word to comprehend both charges is treason. For each charge the penalty was death.

France had been liberated, more by the efforts and sacrifices of others than by its own. France had suffered large losses of life, military and civilian. France had sustained grievous damage to its fabric, both by the action of the invaders and of the liberators. France had suffered hunger. France had suffered cold. France had suffered the shame of defeat, its armies reduced to two million prisoners languishing in German camps. France had suffered the daily humiliation of occupation. France was now among the victors. For all that France had suffered, there had to be someone to blame. France did not turn an accusatory gaze upon its statesman who had averted their eyes from the clear and present danger of Nazi Germany and who had blundered into war, nor upon the generals who had so assiduously prepared to fight the wrong war. It was Pierre

Laval, who had met with Hitler, who had close ties to the Germans, who had pursued the policy of collaboration, who had drafted French labor for German factories, whose police had harried resistants and deported Jews, at whom all fingers were now pointed. What indeed had he done and why and to what end and to what effect? These were the issues that a trial could, but not inevitably would, illuminate.

Unlike Pétain, who chose to remain mute at his trial, Pierre Laval would address the issues and contest the charges against him with a confidence born of his years of holding the highest offices of France, with fervor, with skills developed over his long career in law and politics, and with all of the immense physical and moral energy he possessed.

1

Pierre Laval

The mule knew the way as it pulled the mail cart down the leafy country road from the ancient Auvergne village of Chateldon to neighboring Puy-Guillaume. This intelligent animal allowed the driver, twelve-year-old Pierre Laval, to give his undivided attention to his Latin grammar. He was, as he would always be, squat, dark-skinned, and hardly prepossessing. But the black locks that fell over his forehead could not obscure the lively black eyes nor detract from the warmth of his smile.

The year was 1895. The old century was drawing to a quiet close in rural France. The Third Republic, which had arisen from the ashes of total defeat by German arms in the Franco-Prussian War of 1870 would face the German challenge and another German invasion not once but twice in the new century so close at hand.

Young Pierre was a likely lad, bright and ambitious. And even at that early age, he had charm. He attracted a circle of sponsors, the priest, the magistrate, his teachers, and above all Dr. Claussat, the local notable and political eminence.

Their help was welcome. Young Pierre's father, in addition to being postmaster, was also an innkeeper, a café owner, a butcher, and the proprietor of several vineyards. He had done well according to his lights and it pleased him to think Pierre would join him in these enterprises. This didn't please Pierre, who was eager to continue his education and eager, too, for broader vistas than Chateldon had to offer. He was persuasive and he succeeded, enrolling at the Lycée Saint Louis in Paris at fifteen. He continued his education while working as a *pion* or monitor at a series of provincial schools. He had intended to study zoology, but it became clear to him that the law offered broader vistas, especially for one so personable and self-confident as young Pierre Laval.[1]

Three decades later, Pierre Laval was indeed enjoying broader vistas. He was, in 1931, the prime minister of France and at that moment at the center of a classic tickertape parade up New York's Broadway. He was seated in an open touring car, crowned by an unlikely and uncomfortable high silk hat. At one side His Honor, Mayor James J. Walker, wore his own topper with an ease and insouciance Pierre Laval could never match. On his other side sat New York's perennial greeter and chief of protocol, Grover Whelan, whose pince-nez dignity, his silk hat jammed squarely fore and aft over his ears, contrasted to Jimmy Walker's nonchalance.

The tickertape drifted down, the crowds cheered and a large volume of those cheers was for Mlle. Josée Laval, the prime minister's nineteen-year-old daughter. Her mother, Mme. Laval, had no taste for the limelight and Josée was accompanying her father on his state visit to America and to President Herbert Hoover.

She was petite, exceedingly pretty, with black hair and eyes as dark and sparkling as her father's. The staid *New York Times* was moved to report that "...she proved captivating by her charm of expression, her lively eyes and graceful carriage—an arresting girl of the distinctly Latin type."

Her costume was, the *Times* added, "at least six months ahead of New York," and it supplied the details: a blue ensemble of wool corduroy, a blue angora hat of the modified beret type, light colored stockings, brown shoes and brown gauntlet type gloves. "A cluster of orchids adorned the shoulder and she admitted that an unknown admirer had sent her flowers every day during the voyage."

On landing she had been mobbed by reporters who asked her views on marriage, on domestic life and for her impressions of New York to which she could only reply "C'est formidable."

If she was pretty, if she was fashionable, she had a serious side, too. She was a law student at the University of Paris who was said to be her father's "right hand man" and would "unhesitatingly leave a dance to help her father with his speeches or work."[2]

If she captivated the Broadway crowd, there was one young Frenchman on whom she made a lasting impression. He was spending an apprenticeship in a famous News York law firm. He saw her from afar. He couldn't forget her. He clipped her newspaper picture and pasted it on his mirror where he could see it every day when he shaved. He was the young René de Chambrun, vivacious, irrepressible, known to his intimates as Bunny. He was heir to two great traditions, on the paternal side descendant of Lafayette and on his American mother's side nephew to Alice Roosevelt

Longworth and godson to President William Howard Taft. One day he would marry Josée Laval.[3]

Father and daughter proceeded to Washington where Josée's youth and style contrasted to Mrs. Hoover's matronly frumpery. With what pleasure the sometime butcher's boy from Chateldon must have looked upon his daughter as guest of honor at the Washington dinner given by France's ambassador and Mme. Claudel. And what delight he must have taken in the ball which followed the dinner party. It was attended, the *Times* reported, by one hundred of the "younger set," and "Miss Laval's dinner partner, with whom she opened the ball afterward, was Count François Buisseret of the Belgian Embassy staff."

Pierre Laval made a solid impression. Henry Stimson, the secretary of state, said, "Laval stands in a class by himself for frankness and direct-ness and simplicity and he is different from all other Frenchmen with whom I have negotiated in these respects."[4] That echoed the opinion of the British Foreign Secretary, Sir John Simon, who praised Laval's directness and stability of mind.[5]

Father and daughter attended ceremonies at the Arlington National Cemetery with Stimson. The military was represented by the Iron Com-mander of the American Expeditionary Force, General of the Armies John J. Pershing and by France's General Count Adelbert de Chambrun. Coincidence again, he would one day become Josée's father-in-law.

It had been an exhilarating experience for Pierre Laval and his daughter. It gave her a large view of the world of affairs and it strengthened, if that were possible, the bond between them. Across the years no one would fight harder for Pierre Laval than his devoted daughter Josée.

Pierre Laval had clearly come a long way from Chateldon and in rapid stages. What were the personal qualities and what were the paths by which he had engineered this vertiginous ascent?

He was, as has been said, far from handsome. His broad brow and squat physique were those of an Auvergnat peasant. He was swarthy of complexion and his expressive eyes were black. He was totally disinter-ested in dress and style.

But he was persuasive. He had charm. He married well: his bride was the daughter of his Chateldon sponsor, Dr. Claussat. He opened his first law office in Paris in the industrial area of the Faubourg St. Martin. It was in an old house dating from the reign of Louis Philippe. It had on the one side a tripe shop and on the other a cobbler. Up the narrow, twisting stairs, his neighbors were a midwife, a three-franc dentist and a disbarred notary who functioned from time to time as a pawnbroker.

Laval sometimes borrowed the notary's white tie.[6] In his political ascent, he was shrewd enough to recognize the value of a trademark which is what Pierre Laval's habitual white necktie became.

Laval's practice was at first modest: petty clients, criminals, small affairs. He was, unsurprisingly, like most of his clients, an ardent socialist. Representation of labor unions brought him larger issues and more remunerative clients. His persuasiveness and his incisive intellect began to produce notable results. He frequented political clubs and debating societies where his gregarious nature and ready wit won him friends and supporters.

He was, in the language of the sporting world, a natural in politics. He became the perennially popular mayor of the blue-collar Paris suburb of Aubervilliers, and Aubervilliers gave him its loyal support until the day of his death. In 1914, at thirty-one, he became the youngest member of Parliament.[7]

Over the years, he traveled from the left to the right emerging as an independent member of Parliament. But he never lost the friendship and often retained the support of the friends of his socialist youth, a phase of his political life which he was always proud to recall. He held ministerial posts in the twenties and in January, 1931, he became prime minister at the age of forty-seven. He introduced social insurance, he settled labor strikes, always on the basis of man-to-man, head-to-head negotiations where his innate human qualities were at maximum advantage.

The social insurance bill was typical of his methods. It had been debated and tabled year after year. Laval was unimpressed with the statistics, the tables, the drafts, and the proposals. He knew the language and the psychology of the workers. "Look," he said, "Suppose I'm a worker who pays four francs a month and the boss pays the same. What do I get when I'm sixty?" He arranged a plan of employer-worker contributions with the state contributing its share. The program passed Parliament with a minimum of debate. Get to a broad agreement, that was his method, and the details, he called them "honorable amendments," could be worked out over time in the mutual self-interest of the parties.

In settling a major textile strike, he was again a realist. "You can't talk to workers in Marxist slogans," he advised. "If you don't know the language of the working man you're not a Socialist."[8]

A contemporary said, "He believed stoutly in himself and in his genius. He distrusted conventional diplomacy. He proposed that the only prompt and fruitful method lay in direct conversation, in personal contacts, man-to-man.... A free exchange of ideas, in tête-à-tête, stripped of the elaborate terminologies and of such childish timidity as inspires professional diplomats, must surely lead to solutions of the most complex problems."[9] It was in such a characteristic tête-à-tête that Prime Minister Pierre Laval met the Italian dictator Benito Mussolini in Rome in January, 1935. The issue of supreme importance to them was the menace of Adolf Hitler's rapidly rearming and expansion-minded Nazi Germany. Mussolini had been the champion and defender of Austria in 1934 when Nazi thugs assassinated the Austrian chancellor Dollfuss in an attempted takeover that was to be the first step in Hitler's program of European domination. Mussolini's troops on the Austrian border and Mussolini's declaration that he would defend the independence and integrity of Austria had forced Hitler to back down. The warning Mussolini sent to his British and French allies was chilling: "Hitler will create an army. Hitler will arm the Germans and make war, possibly even in two or three years. I cannot stand up to him all alone. We must do something..." and he added for emphasis, "we must do something quickly."[10]

Pierre Laval needed no urging. Italy was not only the champion of Austrian independence but it was the guarantor, under the Locarno Treaty, of the demilitarization of the Rhineland, the German territory bordering France. The demilitarized Rhineland was France's greatest safeguard against another German invasion like those of 1870 and 1914. To Pierre Laval, Mussolini's Italy was the linchpin of the containment of Nazi Germany.

Pierre Laval sensed immediately that he could do business with Mussolini. They were country boys, born in the same year, youthful socialists, now heads of state. After the formal ceremonies, the exchange of declarations, the public functions, they retired to a more personal talk, one-on-one. They emerged with a broad series of agreements safeguarding Austria and the Rhineland and laying the foundations for military cooperation. Laval later met with Stalin in Moscow after bringing the Soviet Union, on May 2, 1935 into a treaty of friendship and mutual assistance with France. The combined strength and determination of France, Italy, the Soviets, and France's Polish, Czech, and Yugoslav allies, plus Great Britain were in Pierre Laval's mind the vital counterbalance to the looming threat of Hitler's Germany. This was his goal, and this was the program in which he nearly succeeded.

Laval's path was strewn with obstacles. Great Britain was loath to join in the efforts to contain Germany, preferring instead its own direct dealings with Germany. Moreover, the Italian dictator made a disastrous decision to create a new Roman Empire in Africa by his attack on the

Abyssinian realm of the Emperor Haile Selassie. This, Mussolini thought, he could accomplish in time to concentrate his attention on Europe and the Nazi menace.

Adolf Hitler had long ago proclaimed that he would never go to war without an ally and his chosen ally was Italy, both for strategic and ideological reasons. There was enormous opposition, especially in Britain, to Italy's act of aggression against a fellow member of the League of Nations, led by supporters of the League of Nations and the powerful peace movement.

Pierre Laval knew what was vital lay not in Africa, but on the borders of Austria and in the Rhineland. He knew that League sanctions and anti-Italian policies could drive Mussolini into Hitler's welcoming arms. It fell to Pierre Laval and Sir Samuel Hoare, the British Foreign Secretary, to work out a solution acceptable to Mussolini that provided significant rewards for his Abyssinian aggression in order to preserve him as the vital ally against Nazi Germany. This was the celebrated Hoare-Laval agreement of December, 1935.[11]

When it learned of the agreement, the moral indignation of the British public was immediate and furious. It saw Hoare-Laval as an immoral reward to aggression. That was not how Pierre Laval saw it. "Morals are one thing," he had earlier said, "The interests of the nation quite another."[12]

The British government yielded to the popular outcry. The Hoare-Laval agreement was withdrawn. Left stranded by his allies, Mussolini persisted in and won his Abyssinian war and, disconsolate, looked for a friend. The friend he found was Adolf Hitler and the understandings they arrived at resulted not long after in the German reoccupation of the Rhineland, the German takeover of Austria, the Rome-Berlin Axis, the Second World War, and the total frustration of Laval's strategy of containing Nazi Germany. This sad chapter is epitomized by the observation of Sir Eric Drummond at the time British ambassador to Rome, that it is easy to choose between good and evil, but that there are however, some situations in which one is only offered a choice of two evils, one greater and one less. Laval had concluded that it was in the nation's interest to embrace the lesser evil.

France collapsed under the German assault of 1940 and British forces were routed from the continent. France lay prostrate at the conqueror's feet. How France would live, how France would survive until the day of liberation were excruciating questions since, for all but the smallest number of French, how to live and how to survive in occupied France were not theoretical questions but a daily reality.

The fading government of the Third Republic concluded an armistice with Germany in which Laval had no part. But he was a leader in forming the Vichy French government of Marshal Philippe Pétain as head of state in which he served as a minister from July until December, 1940 when he was dismissed. Recalled to government in April, 1942, he served under Petain, with increasing powers, as prime minister of the Vichy regime until the liberation of Paris in August, 1944.

There fell to him during these years the task of governing a conquered and occupied France and defending its people as best he could.

In October, 1945, on the morrow of victory the same man now stood arraigned before the High Court in Paris. He was charged as a minister and then prime minister of the Vichy regime with crimes against the security of the state and with intelligence with the enemy, or, in popular parlance, collaboration. The simpler word to comprehend these charges is treason.

The penalty was death.

2

Preliminary Proceedings

The youthful lawyer was twenty-three that August evening when the telephone call came that changed his life. His name was Yves-Frederic Jaffré. He was of medium height, slim, clear-eyed and, with his chiseled features, undeniably handsome. His dark hair curved down over his collar in a length distinctly longer than the style of the time.

His caller was the celebrated lawyer Jacques Baraduc: "Come see me tomorrow morning. I have something important for you."

Jaffré had only met Baraduc once or twice. He had no idea what the important matter might be. He found Baraduc the next day in his bathroom, his face covered with lather. "The Batonnier has appointed me and Naud to defend Pierre Laval. I'd like to have you on our team. Do you accept?"

Jaffré's response was immediate. "I accept."[1]

Baraduc was surprised. Not many in this time of turmoil wanted to take on controversial and unpopular causes. Many of Jaffré's colleagues questioned not only his alacrity but his judgment. "You're crazy," they said, "to put your family at risk. Pierre Laval will be convicted and shot. Any defense is hopeless, even if you succeed in proving he wasn't a traitor."

Jaffré was not to be deterred. He was twenty-three and his ideals were intact. He later reflected,

> When I came to the bar, confident in what my professors had taught, I knew that perfect justice didn't exist in this world. But still there were principles, codes of law assuring every citizen minimal guarantees: that individual liberty is not an empty word, and that, if human practice is not infallible, still in our country it is founded on these grand concepts, objectivity, impartiality, serenity.[2]

That faith was to be sorely tested in the weeks to come. But for the moment, he knew the task ahead. Pierre Laval's life was at risk. It was the task of his defenders to save him.

17

That same afternoon Baraduc and Jaffré called on Pierre Bouchardon, the president of the Commission of Inquiry of the High Court, which was that court's supervisory body.

Bouchardon was aged and bald, his voice halting and nasal. He was a relic of the 1914-1918 War when he had become something of a celebrity for his participation in notable treason cases including the trial of Mata Hari. Had the government chosen him for his reputation and the infamy that attached to the traitors he had prosecuted? It occurred to Jaffré that this passionate hunter viewed Pierre Laval as another exotic trophy to add to his collection. But Bouchardon was gracious in arranging the formalities of representation. On that hot August afternoon Baraduc and Jaffré left a cordial interview with the impression that the preliminary examination would be as complete as counsel wanted, that Pierre Laval would be afforded every opportunity to answer the charges against him, explain his policies, present witnesses, indeed, make out all the elements of his defense.

Bouchardon noted especially that Marshal Pétain, the head of the Vichy French State, had chosen to remain silent at his recently concluded trial, refusing to reply to the magistrates. He had been convicted and sentenced to life imprisonment.

Pierre Laval was not only ready but eager to present his case. This time the High Court would have an ample opportunity to hear and assess the reality of France in the tragic years of 1940 to 1945.

Baraduc and Jaffré departed optimists, optimists that the defendant would have an adequate preliminary examination before impartial judges. A hope, Jaffré later mused, too beautiful to be true.[3]

In her home across the square from the Palais Bourbon, the seat of the French Chamber of Deputies, Baraduc and Jaffré met Laval's daughter, Josée de Chambrun. Jaffré was struck by her courage, by her keen intelligence, by her determined will as well as by her eyes, the astonishing jet black eyes of her father. She shared with her father not only her black hair and her olive skin but also an intimacy both intellectual and emotional. She would prove tireless in his defense. She accompanied the lawyers that day to the prison at Fresnes outside Paris where they would meet Pierre Laval.[4]

He had been isolated from the other prisoners. Cell 170 was on the second floor. It was humid. The prison had been built over an ancient swamp. The high-profile prisoners were not allowed to use the conference room where lawyers commonly met with their clients. Instead an empty cell on each floor, bare and whitewashed, furnished only with a wooden table, served the same purpose.

A guard was sent to fetch Laval. He appeared in the corridor. Laval smiled. It was a curious smile, a smile that was his alone, at the same time affable, ironic, and not a little mysterious. He had papers in his hand. His clothes hung loosely over his emaciated frame. His cheeks were sunken. But he seemed perfectly at ease.

Jaffré was strangely moved. Naud had felt the same way when he first met Laval. "I was drawn to him.... I immediately felt linked to the strange, dark-skinned individual, whose hands resembled old ivory, and who, like Georges Clemenceau, had inherited those slanted, Celtic eyes."[5]

They repaired to the reception cell. Laval put his papers on the table, then leaned against the window to warm himself in the sun. Baraduc introduced Jaffré. They shook hands. Laval's first words were to inquire about his wife and daughter. At the thought that Josée was at the gates of the prison and he could not embrace her, his face clouded in a moment of sadness. He worried about his wife. She, too, had been imprisoned and he had no news of her.

He lit a cigarette and dragged heavily on it. His fingers were tobacco stained. He had fine hands. His gestures were measured, calm, elegant as arabesques. His tie was loose and his collar too large. His eyes were extraordinarily bright.

Why, he asked, had they detained Madame Laval? Everybody knew she had nothing to do with politics. She had never wanted him to return to government. She knew instinctively it would cause trouble. It was absurd to jail her.

Laval only knew she had been taken in secret. When she was asked to choose a lawyer, she had declined. She had nothing to defend, she said, and with or without a lawyer, she expected justice.

On Jaffré's every visit, his family was always Laval's first concern. And when Laval was being examined at the Palais Bourbon, he would look across the square where the de Chambruns lived and say, "Everything I love most in the world is there, in that house."

The two lawyers reported to Laval on their interview with Bouchardon. He was not surprised but he welcomed the news. "Surely they can't treat my case like a holdup," he said. The history of France under the German occupation was more complicated than people imagined. Petain didn't want to talk. But me, Laval said, I'll explain everything, if only they'll give me the chance.

His voice was composed, tranquil, modulated with his characteristic accent. There was no trace of fear.

He asked Jaffré where he came from. "A Breton," Jaffré replied. "Ah," said Laval, "a great race. Like the Auvergnats." He wanted to know Jaffré's age, and who his parents were. He asked if he had suffered stage fright when he pleaded his first case, and whether he had won it. "To the first, affirmative," Jaffré, replied. "To the second, negative." Laval laughed. But himself, he had never had stage fright.

This was Laval's way—to know a man, to establish a bond of intimacy. This came easily to Laval because at the bottom, he loved people and delighted in their individuality.

They chatted gaily as if they were not in a prison. Jaffré was deeply affected. Laval's appeal was undeniable.

They examined Laval's papers. Laval turned serious. He explained them with masterful clarity and precision. Little by little Jaffré felt seduced.

Laval chain smoked. He asked for a doctor's certificate that he was addicted to tobacco and incapable of thinking, writing, talking without it. That wish was fulfilled.

The hour passed quickly. The lawyers took their leave. The first interview was over.[6]

The first session of the preliminary examination of Pierre Laval took place in the Chamber of Deputies on August 23, 1945. Security was heavy. Laval rode in a classic paddy wagon with the guards fingering their machine guns. What need was there to treat a man who had been three times prime minister of France as a common criminal? En route, Laval's car passed De Gaulle's motorcade. Laval was philosophical: "Look," he said, "The guard mounts; the guard changes."[7]

He waited in an anteroom for the examination to commence. Jaffré thought that the atmosphere resembled that of a doctor or a dentist's waiting room. Laval chatted amiably with the others there and with a police inspector. He betrayed neither apprehension nor fear, but instead a faculty for living in the moment, for passing in the twinkling of an eye from pleasantries to seriousness.

Laval told the police inspector what he had so often said to his lawyers: that he would be content to be judged by the first hundred Frenchmen picked out at random in the street. That would be an authentic jury, he said, representing all tendencies, all opinions. He would have nothing to fear from them. To the contrary, he had profound faith in their common sense. Gloomily he added, "But I will be judged by partisans."

President Bouchardon inaugurated the first two sessions, supported by M. Beteille. They were courteous and Beteille smiled freely.

The examination quickly became a monologue. Laval was precise and scrupulous in his answers. He simplified tangled facts. It was, to Jaffré, history being revealed. When a further question was posed, Laval reflected briefly and continued in the same vein.

As Jaffré saw him, Laval was perfectly at ease, objective, direct, devoid of ego, haughtiness or humility. To Jaffré he projected the confidence of a man who knows he is innocent facing judges whom he believes to represent justice. He aimed not to seduce his judges but to convince them and when the examination was over, he read the clerk's record attentively, striking out a passage here and there and amending the transcript to reflect his statements with greater precision.

At the end of the first session, with Bouchardon's authorization, he joyfully saw his daughter Josée. Once more he looked through the window across the Place Palais Bourbon at her home and repeated, "Everything I hold dear in this world is there."[8]

The preliminary examination continued. There would be two or three examinations in August and September, Beteille said. The Petain trial had exhausted the lawyers and the court. Like Laval himself, they needed a respite. They would take up the matter again in October.[9]

The magistrates prepared a written plan for preliminary examinations and gave it to defense counsel. It referred to five different files, each with a number of subdivisions, each comprehending one of the charges against Laval. It seemed to the defense counsel that this was a rational, organized scheme of trial preparation, implying a measure of collaboration with the defense.

And the examination proceeded in an atmosphere of courtesy and objectivity. Beteille seemed to take pleasure in examining Laval on his relations with Pétain. Recounting a clash of opinions, Laval observed that Pétain had been in his dotage. But he was loyal to his old chief. "Of course it's true," he said, "but I would never sign a sworn document that said so."[10]

Laval stuck stubbornly to the truth as he saw it. He was critical of Batonnier Payen who, in defending Pétain, had leveled charges of military collaboration with Germany against Laval. The examining magistrates reproved him. Didn't he know that they had a great affection for Payen. Laval could see the chagrin in their faces. He stood firm.

"Whether you permit me or not," he replied, "you cannot stop me from saying what I think about these charges."[11]

One question lurked always in the background. It was the proverbial elephant in the room. What role had all these functionaries, the Presiding

Judge, the Attorney General, the examining magistrates, played under the German occupation? Laval bluntly observed that some of these very magistrates had sat on Vichy's High Court of Justice at Riom which, during the Occupation, had prosecuted notable figures of the Third Republic including Léon Blum, Edouard Daladier, Paul Reynaud, all former prime ministers, and General Gamelin, head of the army in 1940.

The shaft struck home. It was true.

"But at Riom," Beteille protested, "I was imposed upon."

"I hope," Laval replied, "You won't be imposed upon here."[12]

Thus, at the outset, there was revealed the underlying irony of the trial of Pierre Laval. He was being tried for his service to the Vichy regime of Marshal Pétain by examining magistrates and later by prosecutors and judges who had themselves been faithful servants of the same regime. The reason was not hard to find. The whole French administration, including the justice system, had continued to function during the years of the Occupation. Where then did duty lie? And where justice?

There was passion, there was anger from time to time. But in the main, the interrogation proceeded courteously, correctly. After the examination Laval would see Josée for a few precious moments before he was returned to Fresnes.

Things might have gone on this way and the preliminary examination might have proceeded to full term. One day all this changed. Messieurs Chazette and Max André had been delegated by the Commission of Inquiry to participate and report. They were neither lawyers nor magistrates familiar with the procedures of the court. The program would, they said, be accelerated. They were curt and they were dismissive. There was to be no delay in judging Laval. The protests of defense counsel were in vain.[13]

"What," cried Laval, "is my examination to be closed before it is opened? How will I get the documents, the witnesses to defend me?" Across his face fell the look of a beast of prey who awaits death at the hands of the hunter.

The examination continued in this charged and changed atmosphere. Laval proceeded with his lengthy, organized, and detailed responses. André and Chazette cut him off. He protested that the questions were far from simple, that he had the right to answer. Beteille tried to calm the storm. Max André persisted: "I'll have no red herring to delay the trial," he thundered. "Answer precisely."[14]

But that, said Laval, in tones more of astonishment than anger, was precisely his aim. He had been concerned about partisanship by his judges but he had never imagined a sweeping denial of the most elemental rights of the defendant.

What Max André now said told everything about the partisan spirit of the judges of the High Court: "There is no need for an examination for you."[15]

From that instant, the whole affair was flagrantly tainted with error of the most fundamental stripe. Defense counsel could not believe their ears. They protested with all the vigor at their command. Beteille was visibly bothered by this extraordinary turn of events. But he did not respond. He remained silent, impassive.

Laval threw up his arms. This was no examination. "Do you think things are better in France since you've been in power?" he demanded.

"France occupies a better place," André replied, "than when you were there."

"If I hadn't been there," Laval retorted, "a great many Frenchmen would be dead who are alive today."[16]

Little by little calm returned and Laval continued to explain to examiners who were not interested in what he had to say. By the time the session closed, it was clear to defense counsel that Laval would be tried as soon as possible, indeed before the national elections set for October 21. They wanted to be done with Laval before then.

On September 12, Beteille consulted his watch and instructed the clerk in the traditional words: "By reason of the late hour, the examination is continued to a later date."[17]

There never was a later date.

Two days later defense counsel learned from the newspapers that the Laval trial would open at the beginning of October. What could the lawyers do but protest? But they were prevented from even that recourse because they had no official notice of the trial date. It was evident to them that the press knew more than they did. Something was about to happen.[18]

The rule was that when the examining magistrates forwarded a case to the court for trial, the defense counsel would be immediately notified by registered letter. Under the Penal Code, a proceeding could be nullified for failure to observe the prescribed procedure. And that was so even in so small an affair as the theft of a bicycle.

There was a more serious concern. The law of November 18, 1944 establishing the High Court made no provision for an appeal.

On September 19 defense counsel were advised by Counselor Schnedecker that the presiding judge had asked for a supplemental examination.[19] This then, was the first official notice that the preliminary examination was closed. At least now a protest could be lodged with Bouchardon. Laval's lawyers protested the closure of an examination which had only just started. Their protest enumerated the charges contained in the indictment that had never been the subjects of a preliminary examination. It alluded to the press reports concerning the opening date of the trial. It recounted the assurances that had been given to the defense. It pointed to the historical importance of the trial.[20]

The appeal was in vain. Now the newspapers reported the exact date of the trial: October 4. If true, it seemed clear that men in high places wanted the whole affair liquidated before the elections.[21]

There was another grave problem. It was vital for the defense to examine the prosecution's files and documents. But when Baraduc asked to see them Examining Magistrate Schnedecker replied, "The dossier is in M. Beteille's locked file cabinet and he's gone on holiday with the keys.[22]

Counsel did not give up hope. They continued up to the last moment to look for some change of course. Such a denial of justice seemed to them inconceivable.

The subjects of the new examination were exotic. The disappearance of a painting called *L'Agneau Mystique*; German overflights of the Unoccupied Zone; and the disposition of a small part of the French gold stored in Martinique. But these were only minor issues compared to those that had never been examined: neither the proceedings of the National Assembly in July 1940 when the Pétain government was formed; nor the meeting with Hitler at Montoire in August, 1940; nor German requisitions of French labor; nor the life and fate of France under the German Occupation.

Jaffré found an angry Laval in his cell. He had been shocked by the imminence of the trial. But he soon rallied. The net result was to whip up his energy and spur his own efforts tenfold.[23]

He only had a few days to prepare his defense. In the supplemental examination, he said, he was being toyed with in the paws of interlocutors with irrelevant questions and irrelevant tales. It was hard enough to assemble the materials of the defense on the real issues. They came to see him he thought, like an exotic beast. The only thing they accomplished was to prevent him from doing his own work.

A smile lightened his face. "But do you think," he asked Jaffré, "that I am rude to them? I love company. I love conversation. I don't get much of it here. Do you know, yesterday a magistrate came with his clerk who had a bad eye. He looked crossways at me. He takes me for a traitor, I thought. Well, whatever it was we talked about, when they left he stuck out his hand to me and said, 'Farewell, Monsieur le President.'"

His complaints remained the same. Why, he asked, did they continue to question him about *L'Agneau Mystique*? What did they want him to say? In the matter of the overflights, how could he have stopped the Germans? Sure, the Armistice forbade such flights, but France was powerless. He had protested. He knew how little such protests availed. But he said he had other cares and concerns whether the French would eat, and how they would survive.[24]

Then there was Martinique. It wasn't all that simple he told Jaffré. There were his inveterate enemies in Paris, Marcel Deat and Jacques Doriot. They were outspokenly pro-Nazi, insistent on full collaboration with Germany. A formal refusal and France would have been in the hands of extremists like that.

So, he said he had given mixed orders to Admiral Robert. He had congratulated him on his return to France, and in the end hadn't the gold in the admiral's care been saved? What then? Did they prefer, he asked, for the gold to be lost in order to ratchet up the charges against him?

Laval never ceased working. A shadow crossed his visage when he spoke of the trial date. "They want it before the elections so they can throw my cadaver in the face of France."[25]

Laval composed a letter to the Garde des Sceaux, the French title for the minister of justice. It was a post Laval had once occupied. In his letter he recounted the promises, the denials of the rights that should be afforded to the pettiest criminal. And this did not concern him alone. It concerned, as he always insisted, history. What he wanted, he said in a lapidary phrase, was for "toute la lumiere," all the light to be shone on his life and acts. The Garde des Sceaux was the custodian of justice. Laval could, he wrote, prove his case if only they would let him.[26]

But, Laval told Jaffré, they refused to listen. They would condemn him before he could speak. Would not history one day ask what had really happened and who was responsible? "What I really was," he compressed it into a single phrase, "was a trustee in bankruptcy," the bankruptcy of French policy of the 1930s.[27]

Once more he counted off the vital issues on which there had been no preliminary inquiry: his negotiations with the Germans; his return to power in April, 1942; the origins of his fortune which seemed to interest them so much; the German requisitions of food and manpower; his meeting with Hitler at Montoire; the National Assembly, which set up the Vichy State; his meetings with Herriot in 1944; his captivity in Germany.

He had not been examined on these nor so much else of importance that had happened during the Occupation.

"It would take months and months," he told Jaffré, "to prepare a case like mine. Do you imagine it could be done in twenty-five interrogations? Wouldn't you need documents, witnesses?"

"I challenge you, Jaffré, to show me any French statesman before the war who did more to put France on guard against the perils she faced and tried to avoid them."[28]

The accusation of treason was to him monstrous. "It is my honor, above all, that I wish to defend. They can't refuse me that. I want France to know that it has no reason to be ashamed of me. But how can they judge me in an atmosphere of passion and hate."[29]

He had written to the Garde des Sceaux on September 22 upon learning that the preliminary examination was officially closed. His protest was in vain. The trial would start on October 4.

Early in the morning of October 3, Laval was transferred, again under heavy guard to a prison in Paris. He was lodged in a sordid cell in the women's division under the watchful eyes of the guards.

When Jaffré arrived, a cigarette dangled from Laval's lips. His briefcase was under his arm. The dank and gloomy cell was even more depressing than Fresnes. Laval sat down. His somber and thoughtful mood was tinged with disgust.[30]

A mournful chant reached the cell. The women prisoners were walking their rounds:

> Sur l'pont du Nord, un bal y est donné
> Sur l'pont du Nord, un bal y est donné
> Adele demande a sa mere d'y aller.

> On the north bridge a ball is held
> On the north bridge a ball is held
> Adele asks her mother if she can go.

"It seems my prisons are all bathed in song" Laval observed. "I prefer the kids at Fresnes. They're gayer."[31]

Had a jury been impanelled, he asked? There had been no indication. But Laval was ready and he continued to work over the arguments he would press.

He asked his lawyers if he should exercise his peremptory right to dismiss or recuse jurors. And had the lawyers seen the jury lists?

What, also, of defense witnesses? He had hastily jotted down a series of names. Many addresses were unknown. Many had moved or had been moved by events. Many were affected by the postwar semi-terror that reigned in the land; and they found excuses not to respond. There were those Pierre Laval had saved from deportation or death. There were thirty who had the courage to reply and present themselves when the court opened.

What was to be done in the brief interlude between jury selection and the commencement of the trial? The defense counsel allocated tasks among themselves. Baraduc would handle international affairs, Naud domestic. Jaffré, the youngest, would cover Laval's youth, his rise and plead the issues of the prisoners of war and the German labor drafts.

Jaffré' was sick at heart. How could a trial proceed under such conditions. Laval, sensing his discomfort raised his arms again and told the young lawyer, "This is the new justice."[32]

The jury selection was to take place at 1:30 P.M. on the same day, October 3 in the vast civil chamber of the Court of Cassation. Its windows looked out over the placid Seine. Laval was in the midst of a group of police inspectors. He chatted with them.

"It's curious," one said. "You look like my father."

"Send your father here," Laval joked. "I'll change places with him. Is he an Auvergnat?"

"No, a Normand."

"What does he do?"

"He has a bistro."

"A fine métier," Laval said. His father had been an innkeeper. "A more advantageous position than mine." He told another policeman that if he had not been deported, that if he had been able to join the police, it was probably thanks to him, Laval. A beefy policeman, red in the face, turned to his colleagues, his voiced tinged in sarcasm, "Are you going to thank him?" he asked. Pierre Laval's reply was instantaneous. "I don't know where you were and what you were doing during the Occupation. But me, I saved lots of guys like you when I was in the government."[33]

Jaffré scouted out the large hall where the jury selection was to take place. Not many prospective jurors were there. Those who were were impatient. "They asked us to be here at 1:30. They're mocking us." This was a perennial complaint of jurors and it seemed to Jaffré a favorable omen.

Judge Paul Mongibeaux, who would preside over the trial of Pierre Laval, now made his entrance, accompanied by the Judge Donat-Gigue of the Court of Cassation, and two other magistrates. Mongibeaux thanked the jurors present. He declared that he would not be intimidated and that he would not allow witnesses whose testimony had nothing to do with the affair. He added, "We aren't at the Chateldon fair. Come what may, Laval's trial will be finished before the elections."[34]

Jaffré was dumbstruck. How could such words be uttered by the highest magistrate of France? How, he wondered, could Mongibeaux talk of intimidation in the face of a defense almost totally disarmed?

The jury selection proceeded. The rules of the court required twenty-four jurors, twelve from Parliament and twelve selected from the Resistance. For each category there were to be four substitutes. This meant thirty-two jurors in all. The jurors were to be selected by lot from a list of fifty members of the 1940 Parliament and fifty others.[35] But how could they be selected by lot when there were only thirty-two present? The selection normally discriminated between jurors and substitutes. And suppose the defendant chose to recuse or challenge one or more jurors? Under the law, both the prosecution and the defense could recuse six. Under these conditions the jury selection descended into farce.

The character of the jury could only discourage the defense. Half were parliamentarians, men of 1940 and uniformly of the left, many of them Communists, that is to say Laval's political enemies. The other half were members of the Resistance including again many Communists. When Jaffré looked back fifty-five years later, what he remembered was the hatred the jurors bore for Laval. The memory still wounded and his voice rose as he cried out again and again: "La haine, la haine, la haine," "the hate, the hate, the hate."

Defense counsel had labored the evening before to prepare a plan of challenging those jurors they deemed most hostile, those who had demonstrated in one way or another their desire and their will to condemn Laval to death. But Laval leaned toward his lawyers. "I recuse no one," he said. Later he told Jaffré that he asked only for a fair hearing but that he cherished no illusions. He returned to his cell. Now that the trial date was fixed his spirits rose. Jaffré had never seen him, so combative.[36]

Many days before defense counsel had concluded that they could not participate under the conditions of the trial. They suggested that Jaffré accompany Laval to court. "You're the youngest," Laval told him. "You can help me and besides, I'll have your company." Jaffré was touched. On reflection he thought that he should remain together with his colleagues. Laval agreed. They addressed a letter to the court, explaining the reasons they would not appear in court the next day. They were sound reasons: the abbreviated preliminary examination, the declarations Mongibeaux himself had made in open court. They would ask the Batonnier to release them from their charge. They did not despair of justice.[37]

3

The Trial, October 4, 1945[1]

The trial of Pierre Laval took place in a lofty courtroom in the Palace of Justice in the Ile de la Cité, which is the heart of Paris which is in the heart of France. The courtroom lay under the shadows of Notre Dame, and through an upper window could be glimpsed the lacy spire of the Sainte-Chapelle.

This was a special court. It had been established on November 18, 1944 by the government of General de Gaulle under the name of High Court of Justice. Its purpose was to judge members of the Vichy regime—Petain, the head of state, Laval, the head of government—and other high functionaries and officers of the regime.

There would be a panel of three judges of whom the first and foremost was M. Mongibeaux, First President of the Court of Cassation, a final appeals court. There would be a prosecutor, M. Mornet. There would be a jury of twenty-four chosen by lot from a panel of fifty of whom half would be members of Parliament in September, 1939, and the other half members of political parties or of the Resistance. There was provision for the preliminary investigation of the case by examining magistrates.

The final decision would be made by the judges deliberating in common with the jurors. One aspect of the High Court would be particularly ominous for Pierre Laval. There was no provision, at any stage, for any appeal from the rulings or indeed the judgment of the High Court. Whatever the judgment, it would then and there be final. No claim of error would be heard.

It was the fourth of October, 1945. Presiding Judge Mongibeaux took his place on the bench. The jurors were seated. Attorney General Mornet occupied the place assigned to the prosecution.

The defendant now made his entry. Gasps of shock and surprise echoed through the courtroom packed with the press and the public, the curious and the concerned. Pierre Laval, was alone. The defense counsels' bench was empty.[2]

Presiding Judge Mongibeaux proceeded as if it were all as planned. He peered down at the accused. His crimson cloak was trimmed with squirrel fur. With his neatly trimmed and pointed beard, he struck one observer as a D'Artignan, one of Dumas' Three Musketeers, now grown aged and respectable, while Laval's biographer Fred Kupferman found him reminiscent of a bearded lady in a fur coat.[3] He was said to be good natured but the trial that was about to unfold would severely strain the equanimity of participants and spectators alike.

"Your name is Pierre Laval?"

"Jean Marie," the defendant responded, embellishing the record with his middle names.[4]

He had been fourteen times a minister of state, three times prime minister of France. As the Allied forces approached Paris in August, 1944, still prime minister of the collapsing Vichy regime, Laval had tried in partnership with Edouard Herriott to reconvene the Parliament of the Third Republic as a bridge to the government of a liberated France. Instead he had been carried off into German captivity. With the final surrender of Germany he had sought refuge in neutral Spain. But Spain's welcome was cool and short lived. On August 1, 1945 Laval returned to France, to be met at the airport with an indictment for treason and had ever since, together with his wife, been lodged in Fresnes prison.

France had collapsed in May and June 1940, under the German assault. France had been overwhelmingly defeated. France had been occupied. France had lived four black years under the German jackboot, the German knife at its throat. France had been plundered. France had been cold. France had been hungry. France had been humiliated. This same France now found itself among the victors. For its failings, for its sufferings, for its shame, France demanded its victims. France looked for guilty men. And all the fingers, it seemed, were pointing at Pierre Laval.

Today Pierre Laval was pale and emaciated, his blue suit hanging loosely about him, his white tie falling from a collar now far too big. The stresses of captivity and flight had left their marks. Laval was habitually careless of his appearance, but for this day his gray hair and his suit had been lovingly brushed by his devoted wife. He was far from handsome. Yet there was an intensity in his dark eyes and the force of his personality would be revealed when he spoke.

"I will soon open your interrogation," the Presiding Judge announced, "but I must tell you that I have just received a letter from your lawyers. I shall read it, because nothing should be hidden in an affair of justice."

He adjusted his steel-rimmed spectacles and started to read:

"Monsieur Le Premier President"

He paused and then continued.

"My colleagues, Jacques Baraduc and I regret to inform you that we have asked our Batonnier to discharge us from our appointment. We must declare the absolute impossibility of an effective defense for our client in this proceeding."

The *batonnier* is in France the presiding officer of the local bar, responsible for both the guidance and the discipline of its lawyer members.

"A preliminary examination was necessary," the letter continued, "indeed indispensable. It was announced and promised to us. But it was broken off over our protests."

Defense counsel was referring to the fundamental basis of French criminal procedure. It is called the instruction, or preliminary examination. The so-called judges of instruction, the examining magistrates, investigate the case. They take the testimony of principals and witnesses, examine documents and review the evidence. This is the step in the proceedings where the prosecution and the defense lay out their cases. And it is only upon completion of this step, only after a full investigation of the case that the examining magistrates may determine whether and what charges to bring against the defendant. Any such charges are then heard in a second proceeding in the trial court. What defense counsel here said was that this procedure had not been followed in the case of Pierre Laval and instead the preliminary examination had been cut off prematurely, denying to Laval the opportunity to present his case.

"We fear," the letter continued, "that the haste to open this trial was inspired, not by judicial concerns, but was instead motivated by political reasons.

"The declarations that you made yesterday, which the press reported, leave us in no doubt. In effect, you said that you were prepared to sit morning, noon, and night to end the trial before the November elections.

"We have never intended to use dilatory tactics, as the press reported, and to which you have lent credence.

"Permit us to say, with the greatest respect, that we have been profoundly wounded, both of us, by the accusation of blackmail which you described as a defense tactic. That was never our intention.

"It is with sadness that we renounce the charge entrusted to us. We tender to you our regrets that we cannot bring to the work of justice the contribution which would confirm the tradition of our order.

"Our colleague, Jaffré, having been officially appointed, agrees."[5]

The letter closed with the usual courtesies.

Mongibeaux paused and pondered. The charges that he had made intemperate and unjudicial remarks the day before clearly had to be answered.

"I will comment on that letter. It was never my intention to make any imputation, whether regarding the defendant or his counsel."

Pierre Laval leapt to his feet, his eyes blazing. "That's not what the papers said."

"I'm not responsible for what the papers say," Mongibeaux retorted. "What I said, and I'll say it again, I won't yield to pressure. I don't deny having used the term "blackmail." If there is any, I won't stand for it. That's all I said. My honor and the honor of my career are at stake. I will never bow to intimidation."

"You talked about shady dealings at the Chateldon Fair," Laval replied. "Well, there hasn't been one there for a long time."

The Presiding Judge was on the defensive. He wanted to put all this behind him as quickly as possible.

"I'll say it for the first and I hope for the last time. As much as I respect the rights of the defense, I have no intention of being manipulated." "Or," he added, "intimidated."

"Your honor," Laval interjected.

The Presiding Judge cut him off: "You will have the word when I give it to you."

"That said, I've addressed the Batonnier. He isn't here. I don't want to leave you without counsel. Mr. Mornet, what are your conclusions?"[6]

Attorney General Mornet, with his beaked nose and bristling beard, his red robe trimmed in ermine, called to the mind of one observer a red feathered bird of prey. "When I look into his eyes," another said, "I can see his teeth." Fred Kupferman found a less threatening image – a department store Pere-Noel.[7]

Mornet was indignant. He protested the assertion of the defense that the trial was politically inspired. He was astonished that such charges should be adopted by two lawyers who knew the court and who knew him. He protested, too, the claim that the preliminary examination had been brusquely cut off.

"No, the examination wasn't cut off, and I'll tell you why."

"What is the basis of the indictment of Pierre Laval?" he asked. "It rests on incontestable facts. And what are those facts? They are the governmental acts in which Pierre Laval participated even if he didn't perform them. It is the policy which was followed for four years of which this unhappy country was the victim. What else is there to discuss?

"You talk of an examination that was broken off. Pierre Laval has been in France two months. For six weeks his counsel had available all of the acts and all of the declarations imputed to him as well as his policies of which an unhappy country has been the victim."

"What promises were made to the defense? Who made them? In whose name? By a magistrate authorized to make them?"

"Indeed," he went on, "the case of Pierre Laval doesn't need any preliminary examination. The examination started the day Pétain came to power with Laval as his second. It continued through the coup d'état of July 10 when the Republic and its essential laws were suppressed."

"It continued with the abominable racial laws. It continued at Montoire, where Pétain and Laval met Hitler. And when Pierre Laval was removed from power in December 1940, there was the most intense press campaign in the history of France in his favor by the journals of the Axis because he was always Germany's favorite."

"The instruction continued," Mornet went on, "with the recall of Laval to power on German bayonets and machine guns. And, since 1942, what were the other elements of an instruction?" Mornet catalogued the answers: the massive drafts of workers to Germany, the attitude of Laval's government to the events in North Africa, the pursuit of patriots, the court martials.[8]

This tirade goaded Pierre Laval to a thunderous reply: "But you were all working for the Pétain government then. The whole lot of you. The magistrates. And you too, Mr. Attorney General."[9]

A stunned silence fell over the courtroom. It showed how well they all understood. It was true. It was undeniable. Indeed, the Presiding Judge and the Attorney General had worked for, had been functionaries of the very Pétain and Laval governments whose acts were now imputed as crimes and not worthy of the safeguards afforded to any common criminal.

The Presiding Judge struggled to deflect a blow he could not answer. "I repeat, one more time..." he began. But Pierre Laval, his indignation and his voice rising, cut him off: "You can condemn me, you can kill me, but you have no right to outrage me."[10]

"If you say anything that constitutes an outrage," Mongibeaux retorted, "you are overruled."

"I'm a Frenchman," Pierre said proudly, "I love my country. I serve no other."

The court room erupted in hostile cries and catcalls.

Laval stood firm. "And I'll prove it," he said.

"You have an attitude," Mongibeaux roared.

"A little more modesty, you scoundrel," a juror cried out.

"You'll see when I've spoken, all of you. I'll prove it,"

Mornet thrust himself forward. "I will not tolerate this improper attitude. Guard, remove the defendant."[11]

Laval made an effort to regain his composure. He asked to be excused and that the court accept his apologies.

The Presiding Judge lectured the defendant. It was a singular thing, he said, to commence a defense by outraging the judges.

"Happily," he said, "we are above outrage. We are above invective. We will not be prejudiced by your attitude. It is lucky for you that we don't represent that peculiar form of justice that you organized. We represent justice and we warn you once more—we will not be intimidated."

Mornet addressed the jury. "I beg of you," he insinuated, "to master your indignation. Rise above it."[12]

Again, he told them, no preliminary examination was needed. The examination had opened five years ago, in 1940, and it closed the day of the Liberation, the day when Pierre Laval had sought refuge in Germany, refusing to put himself at the disposal of French justice.

No, the preliminary examination hadn't been broken off. It had lasted for five years. Mornet now addressed Mongibeaux. He would not allow Laval to suffer for want of defense counsel. That was his right. He had designated three and if the defense counsels' table was empty, well, that wasn't the Court's fault.

The Presiding Judge looked down at the accused, "Monsieur Pierre Laval, what have you to say?"

Pierre Laval was by nature a compromiser and conciliator. There was a time for anger and indignation. There was a time for a gentler approach. That time was now.

"My emotions have betrayed me, Your Honor," he said. He had not been surprised by his lawyers' decision. He had been a lawyer for many years. He understood their unwillingness to defend him under such adverse conditions.

As he spoke, he gained confidence. He spoke softly. He was persuasive. That had been his stock in trade. He had charm and it had never failed him. He knew how to create intimacy, the feeling in each juror that Laval was addressing all of his thoughts and all of his feelings to him alone. He knew how to cast a spell. Now was the time.

"My case is important. I am accused of a plot against the security of the state. But I was never examined about my role in the 1940 National Assembly, nor my internal policies, nor about the return of President Herriot to Paris. Nor about any of the questions which could interest the jury in a case like this which is at heart not criminal but political.

"I am accused of intelligence with the enemy. But I was never examined about my meeting with Hitler at Montoire, nor about my negotiations with the Germans. And never about the German demands for food and labor. I was never asked about my foreign policy before the war, but that's nevertheless one of the charges against me.

"I hope you will tell me that here at this trial I can present my case. What does a trial gain, a trial less of a man than of a policy, by rudely shutting it off? That would be the negation of all of the principles of criminal law.

"If I didn't have my honor to defend, and if I didn't have to justify my policy and cover for those who honestly and out of patriotism obeyed my orders, I would be tempted by weariness or disgust to yield to injustice and cruelty. But that would be an act of weakness on my part. I know how to be strong and brave in adversity.

"I will not yield to the arbitrary procedure you would impose upon me. I don't despair because you are Frenchmen. I hope that I won't regret my confidence in the justice of my country. I've shown you that. I've recused no juror because each of you has the right to judge me.

"Hear me and you will understand. In accusing me, you wish to defend France. When you hear me, you will know it is France that I have served.

"I appear before you as an accused. But if my body is in chains, my soul is free. I will show you how I have suffered for my country."[13]

The Presiding Judge was eager to cut off the flow of the defendant's words. He again raised the question of the absence of defense counsel.

Pierre Laval was ready to address that issue, too. His lawyers had shared their concerns with him and he understood. The Attorney General had asked who had promised a complete preliminary examination. It was, he replied, Judge Beteille who had drawn up an overall plan of twenty five interrogations. He had completed only five, or to be more accurate four and a half, and Laval had been told that he could continue his explanations at the next session. But there never was a next session.

His lawyers, Laval told the court, lacked the files, the documents essential to the defense.

This wasn't a simple case. Pierre Laval enumerated his leading roles in the French State: three times prime minister, not counting the Occupation, fourteen times a minister. How could he defend his policies without a complete examination?

"I will answer everything," he said. "There will be no tactics, no maneuvers. I'll give you written answers. The jurors can read them. I will put in a complete defense."

He asked the Presiding Judge, who knew law and lawyers, how his defense counsel, who were not political men, could master and prepare a case so short of time and materials. It had been suggested that he, a lawyer could defend himself but, he observed, a doctor doesn't treat himself.[14]

That plea did not prevent Laval's ably arguing the critical issue of timing. The High Court before which he was appearing was a special court established in June, 1944, by the provisional government of de Gaulle to try crimes of officeholders between the French collapse of 1940 and the Allied victory of 1945. Elections were scheduled for October 21, 1945. They could result in a new Parliament and the case would then be remitted to the Senate as the High Court. No one was more familiar with the men and mores of the Senate than Pierre Laval who had served there as well as in the Chamber of Deputies. It was in Parliament that he had burnished his powers of persuasion.

Perhaps this critical date, October 21, was why the trial was planned to last only fourteen or fifteen sessions. But if longer were needed, would the Court refuse? Was this why the pre-trial examination had been so abruptly cut off?

Laval had seized the initiative. He was not about to yield it. What he now argued was a profound statement of the fundamental nature of the case against him: "As a private person, I have the right to defend myself. But I have a higher duty. It is imposed on me by the high offices I have held. This isn't a case about shoplifting in a department store."[15]

He had been asked, in preliminary proceedings, if he had signed a certain circular of January 13, 1943 concerning the drafting of manpower. He explained that if he had signed it, he would freely say so.

But that was hardly the question. "The real reason," he told the jurors, "is more complicated. You should inquire as to the circumstances. Why did I sign it? You should ask how I defended France against German labor requisitions. For that, you need a real examination."

So in the case of an order concerning the Commissariat of Jewish Affairs: "I don't contest the materiality of it. But do you want to know the reason? I could have told you in a real preliminary examination."

He appealed to reason and common sense: "Why not give me and my counsel eight days to examine the files, to copy essential documents. Without them a real defense is impossible. What inconvenience would that be?"[16] "How will you answer me, you who are wise, if you have no preoccupation other than justice, real justice."[17]

Mongibeaux was exasperated. "I've given you more than enough time," he said.

"But you said you would sit morning, noon and night," Laval retorted.

The Attorney General was anxious to be heard. But instead the Presiding Judge once again expressed his concern at the absence of defense counsel. Laval was acquitting himself very well indeed he observed but there were limits to the latitude he could be granted.

The Attorney General again clamored to be heard on the subject of the competence of the court which, he said, Laval had questioned.

"Without contesting it," Laval shot back.

But the Attorney General persisted. The court had jurisdiction under the existing law. No change of regime or constitution could disempower it. As to the promises of a preliminary examination which Laval claimed to have been made, well, if they had indeed been made, the examining magistrate had exceeded his authority. And the defense, he asserted, had been given all of the documents to which they were entitled under the Penal Code.[18]

Pierre Laval was eager to respond. "Your honor, please..."

"You have talked long enough," Mongibeaux responded.

"But the accused has the right to reply to the prosecution. It's in the Code."

"But you have already spoken."

"I haven't spoken. I haven't said anything about all this."

Mongibeaux was curt. "You just spoke. In my opinion you've talked long enough."

Laval's response was drenched in sarcasm. "Thank you, your Honor."

"This incident is closed," Mongibeaux ruled. "All the explanations necessary have been heard. After all, we're only trying to identify the accused."

Laval struggled to maintain his composure. "But if I can't answer the Attorney General..." Mongibeaux looked past Pierre Laval to the clerk of the Court. "Be so good," he said, "as to read the indictment."

Laval thrust himself forward in a paroxysm of frustration. "It's pathetic that I can't respond..." "Maybe it's pathetic," Mongibeaux replied, "And if it is I take full responsibility." After reading the indictment he would recess the hearing to confer with the Batonnier on the matter of defense counsel.

There was an uproar in the courtroom. It came from lawyers of the Paris bar. A juror asked Mongibeaux to silence them. Did they have a right to demonstrate, he asked.

"Certainly not," the Presiding Judge replied. And to put an end to such demonstrations he would confer with the Batonnier.

He adjourned the session. But the demonstration went on. The lawyers of Paris were concerned about the absence of defense counsel. It was a matter of principle. They expected to see defense counsel in their places when the hearing resumed, as it did at 2:30 P.M.

But when the court again convened the defense counsel's table was still empty.[19]

The Court's first session had brought out the fundamental issues of the trial – the accusation against Laval, the defects of the preliminary proceedings, the absence of defense counsel and the roles played by the leading actors, defendant, prosecutor and judge, during the Vichy years.

"Why was Laval there?" historian Fred Kupferman asked. His answer: If France wouldn't pardon Laval, it was because he never said "No." And against him, to interrogate him, were two men who had said "Yes" all their lives. So the trial of Laval never really took place. Instead, it was a family affair, a Grand Guignol played by bad actors, except the accused.[20]

4

The Accusation[1]

Mongibeaux again gaveled the court to order at 2:30 P.M. "I see," he observed, "that defense counsel are not present at the bar." He now addressed a stern warning to Laval.

"Accused, I am telling you for the last time: these hearings will proceed with calm and dignity. If you make any trouble, any kind of outrage against me or against the High Court I won't hesitate to expel you and carry on without you. We have the power to judge you in your absence. Consider this a warning."[2]

Laval was conciliatory. "The public offices I've held, my respect for the legal system, and indeed, my own self-interest will be the guarantees of correctness on my part, you may be sure."

Mongibeaux once more asked Mornet his opinion on the absence of defense counsel. "Nothing new," Mornet replied.

Mongibeaux now turned to Laval. "Do you have something more to say?"

"With respect," Laval replied, "I only ask, in the interests of justice, a continuance of my case for so long as you may fix, so that my lawyers can lend me their effective assistance. Without a continuance, they cannot."

"The court," Mongibeaux announced, "will retire to deliberate."

When the hearing resumed, it did not appear that any consideration had been given to Pierre Laval's plea. Without further ado Mongibeaux asked the clerk to read the indictment.[3]

Here, at last and at length, were the charges on which Pierre Laval would be tried for his life. The clerk's words were sonorous: The defendant was charged with plotting against the security of the state and intelligence with the enemy. That is to say treason.

The clerk now read the lengthy document. Pierre Laval's pre-war political career had begun it said, at the extreme left which he later disavowed. He had been a minister many times and twice prime minister. The growth of his private fortune had paralleled his political ascent.

The indictment turned to matters of foreign policy. As a result of the failure of his policy in the Abyssinian affair, Laval had been turned out of office in 1936. His hatred of England was born then. He lost the confidence of the French people.

The reference here was to Laval's efforts, as foreign minister and prime minister in 1934 and 1935, to find a compromise solution to Mussolini's aggression in Abyssinia that would uphold, as best it could, the League of Nations and at the same time preserve Italy as an ally against the clear and present danger of Nazi Germany.

At the beginning of the Second World War in 1939, the indictment continued, Laval pretended that his intimacy with Mussolini could provide the basis for a negotiated peace. He wanted a change of regime of which he would be the beneficiary, with the concurrence of Pétain, in a system that aped Mussolini's fascist state.[4]

Then there were the tragic events of the fall of France in 1940. With the collapse of French arms, Laval, the indictment charged, had been one of the first to demand an armistice with the victorious Germans. His name was on the ministerial list Marshal Pétain presented to Prime Minister Reynaud and from then on Laval played a role in the events that led to July 10, 1940 when the powers of the Third Republic were conferred upon Pétain and the Vichy regime.

It was Laval, the clerk went on, who by his intrigues and menaces had prevented the president of the republic, the Chamber of Deputies and the Senate from going to North Africa where the government of the Third Republic could have carried on the fight and upheld the honor and sovereignty of France.[5]

It was by similar intrigues, the indictment continued, that he had imposed upon Parliament on July 10, 1940 to confer extraordinary powers on Marshal Pétain with himself as successor, a veritable coup d'état ending the Third Republic. Had he not himself once said that his most important accomplishment had been the suppression of the Republic and the placing of power in the hands of Pétain?

It was, the indictment continued, an absolutist regime such as France had never before seen, copying the methods of the invader, putting the Jews outside the law.

More charges followed. The October 24, 1940 meeting of Laval
and Pétain with Hitler at Montoire aimed at placing France at the
disposal of Germany, a policy in the interests of Germany only and
thus criminal.

A palace revolution had turned Laval out in December, 1940. The
Germans then mounted a violent campaign to recall him and Laval was
content to be seen as the man in whom the Germans had confidence
above all others. And he did, the indictment read, in fact return to power
in April, 1942 with German support.[6]

The jury listened intently as accusations were heaped upon accusations.
Laval's policy, the indictment charged, was all German: persecution of
Jews, Freemasons, Communists, and resistants. The police put at the
service of the Gestapo, 22,000 Jews arrested in Paris on the nights of
July 15 and 16, 1943.

And then there was his famous declaration of June 22, 1942: "I wish
for a German victory."[7]

Mornet knew the value of first impressions on a jury and the indictment
was the first summary of the prosecution's case that the jury would hear.
Laval, it charged, wanted military aid for the Germans and manpower for
German factories. Then there was the scam of the Releve where French
prisoners of war would be returned home in exchange for laborers for
German industry. The indictment alleged that Laval had said, "The hour
of the liberation of our prisoners, will be the hour of the German victory."
It charged that he had instigated an obligatory labor draft with ration
cards denied to refusers. The circular of July 12, 1943 had demanded
220,000 workers for Germany. It was those who would not go who had
joined the Maquis, the resistance.[8]

The indictment now cited the Anglo-American landings in North
Africa in November, 1942. Pétain and Laval had chosen to scuttle the
fleet at Toulon rather than see it play a role to the benefit of France. The
indictment charged that the Vichy government had facilitated the German
defense of North Africa, that some French had betrayed France. But others
had taken up arms for France, who did not think Germany invincible.[9]

The clerk finished his reading.

Attorney General Mornet now took the floor.

"It would be superfluous to say more. It was political treason, it was
moral treason, delivering France to the invader."

The facts, the documents and the witnesses, Mornet assured the jury,
would amply support the charges of a plot against the security of the
state and intelligence with the enemy.[10]

This was a remarkable catalogue of accusations of historical events in a turbulent time of war, in a France which had lain supine and helpless at the feet of a vicious enemy. But was it all true? Was there another side to the case? Would the trial be a search for the truth or a sham trial producing a predestined verdict?

The clerk now read a supplemental charge.[11] It referred to a M. de Lapommeraye, who would testify to Laval's statements in July, 1940, concerning the overthrow of the Republic and his desire for the new French government to imitate the Nazi model.

Laval had not, the clerk read on, protected Alsace-Lorraine against an annexation contrary to the terms of the armistice. He had allowed the Germans to expropriate the French-owned Bor copper mines in Yugoslavia; and he had ordered Admiral Robert to destroy his ships and planes at Martinique rather than let them fall into American hands.

In November 1942, he had put North African airports at the disposal of the Germans facing the Anglo-American invasion. He was charged with offering French military assistance to Germany in North Africa.

The clerk now turned to the defenses which Laval might raise. He would say that no man of sense could in 1940 have doubted a German victory. Under those conditions, the only course was to cooperate with the conqueror.

He would say that the Germans had imposed on him by force what he would not have otherwise done and that a skilled statesman could, by the appearances of collaboration, obtain real benefits for France.

If I had not been there, he would say, the situation of my countrymen would have been infinitely worse. "He will tell you that France owes him thanks."

The prosecution took the other view. Without denying the claim of advantages and pretended advantages, the clerk declaimed, there was only one undeniable conclusion: It was a degrading policy, an unpardonable policy that reflected the character of its author. It had caused great moral and material damage, of which France, its immense sacrifices and its contribution to victory notwithstanding, still bore the tragic consequences.[12]

The prosecution now moved in for the kill. They knew, the indictment said, the claims the defense would make, they forewarned the jury which would not be taken in. The final appeal was flattering to the hearts and minds of the jury. Their verdict they were told, would honor and ennoble them. The words of the indictment were chosen with care. There had been a collaboration with the enemy "which...without the resistance of the immense majority of Frenchmen together with the martyrdom, the heroism of all those who had fallen, would have left an ineffaceable stain on the saddest page of the history of France."

As a final flourish, the clerk read the name subscribed to the indictment: "Attorney General Mornet, Paris, September 26, 1945."[13]

So that was it. They were all heroes, and where there are heroes there must be a villain. The villain stood in the dock. He was Pierre Laval.

No matter that all France had greeted the armistice with relief and approval. No matter that the number of resistants, heroic as they were, was minuscule in the early years of the Vichy regime. No matter that an immense majority of the French, to use the words of the indictment, tried to carry on as normal lives as their circumstances would permit, passively awaiting the turn of events for which they hoped.

No matter that the Paris masses had rapturously welcomed Pétain in Paris only two months before the Allied forces stormed the Normandy beaches.

France had collapsed ignominiously in the total disaster of 1940. The French Army, into which the French people had poured so much service, so much treasure, had been routed into a panic-stricken mob, herded off, two million strong, to German captivity. The vaunted fortifications of the Maginot Line had been bypassed and taken from the rear. The Occupation had lasted four years.

But they were heroes, all of them. France demanded that they be heroes. It was the only decent, acceptable position for France, in its defeat, in its shame, to maintain.

Who was to blame? It must be the accused. But what part had he really played in the events that brought about the debacle of 1940? Had he played any meaningful role in those events at all? What had been his purpose during the Occupation? Was it to advance the German cause or to protect, defend, and shelter the captive people, the very future of France? And would this trial, this inquest of history, illuminate these issues; would it even seek to do so?

In Pierre Laval's own mind, he had labored mightily, as foreign minister and prime minister in 1934, 1935, and 1936 to avert the disaster, to contain the ever growing menace of Nazi Germany. But a policy of inaction and appeasement had brought about the debacle of 1940. He had then become, he said, the trustee in the bankruptcy he had tried so hard to forestall. And in the end, he was in the dock and he mused bitterly: "*Il faut que j'aie tort por qu'ils aient raison.*" "I have to be wrong so they can be right."

Let us look carefully at the indictment. Leaving aside the allegations arising from the pre-war period, as the court was indeed to rule, the first substantive charge was that Laval had been among the leaders of those who sought the armistice of 1940.

This raises, first of all, the factual question what, if anything, Laval had to do with the armistice. The next question must be whether it was a crime, under the prevailing circumstances, to be in favor of an armistice. In that case, the bulk of the French government, not to mention the overwhelming majority of the French were complicit in the same crime. Had Pierre Laval thrust an unwanted armistice upon an unwilling and stoutly resisting French people?

The next charge was that by "intrigues and menaces," Laval had prevented the French government from transferring its seat to North Africa, there to carry on the war. Again, the first inquiry must be factual: was this true? Did Laval have the capacity and did he accomplish it? In the end, the French government declined to move and how many and who were to be criminally implicated in that decision? And had the decision not to remove the government of France to North Africa been a sound and good decision and what would have been the strategic consequences had it been decided otherwise?

The indictment charged that by intrigues and menaces, bribes and promises, Laval had foisted the Pétain government upon Parliament, establishing the Vichy regime and suppressing the Republic. Could one man have done this? Who and how many and by what process and procedures had Parliament voted extraordinary powers to Pétain and why? These were questions for history; but what was the responsibility of those who followed Laval's lead and freely voted with him and were those votes, freely given, crimes?

The indictment charged that at Montoire, Laval and Pétain had betrayed the interests of France in favor of those of the enemy. But what had really happened at Montoire, and was it to the benefit or detriment of France? The generalized language of the indictment offered neither facts nor conclusions based on facts.

The indictment spoke of the persecution of the Jews. What was the truth? What was the accounting, how many lost, how many saved, under what circumstances?

What, too, were the facts of the drafts of French labor for German factories; and had Pierre Laval in his dealings with the enemy advanced the interests of France or defended those interests to the extent within his power.

In the bitter aftermath of war and defeat, occupation and liberation, these were difficult issues to weigh and to balance and the only verity must be that the answers were neither all black nor all white. The vague and general charges of the indictment, in a developed and fair system of justice, must be supported by pertinent and material facts, certainly not by rumor and innuendo; and supported, too, by a preponderance of the evidence as a basis for the severest of sanctions—the death penalty.

And in any developed and fair system of justice, the defendant must be protected against passion and prejudice and must be accorded every opportunity to make out his defense. That had not happened so far in the pre-trial proceedings. Whether justice would be honored and served in the High Court remained to be seen.

5

Pierre Laval, Prisoner[1]

It had been early agreed that Jaffré would be the chief intermediary between Laval and his lawyers. His regular visits to the prison were also a boon to Laval, not only in advancing defense preparations but also in offering to Laval, alone in his cell, the human contact he craved.

In the course of these visits, Laval talked freely on a wide variety of topics: his early life, his fortune, his political convictions and sentiments, why and how he collaborated with the Germans, some of his public utterances and other topics that had been the subject of testimony during the course of the trial. All such statements were of course self-serving, and the statements of a man defending himself against a verdict he sees as inevitable and which will end in the silence of death.

Pierre Laval's voice was stilled by the execution of the judgment imposed upon him. He left few written records and no formal autobiography or memoir. His prison conversations with Jaffré are worthy of consideration in any assessment of his life and deeds. The question would seem to be not so much their admissibility into the historic record but the weight to be accorded them. Were we to have a record of the prison conversations of Charles I or of Marie Antoinette or of Captain Dreyfus, who was innocent, or of Julius and Ethel Rosenberg, who were found guilty, we would read them with fascination and ponder upon their significance. But we would not wish those voices to be forever extinguished.

When Jaffré looked back years later on his visits to Laval in prison, he was struck by Laval's evenness of temper. He seemed always the same. "His courage, his serenity, his lucidity never for a moment abandoned him," Jaffré later wrote. There was the normal apprehension of a man who knows his fate is sealed. But he never let down and this seemed to Jaffré admirable in a man who loved life so much.[2]

Jaffré most often met Laval in the reception cell, but from time to time he visited Laval's own cell. Like all the cells at Fresnes, the walls were bare. It was humid, a narrow cell, some sixteen feet long and eight feet wide. The sun never reached inside. Jaffré was struck by the neatness and the good order of Laval's arrangements. The bed was tautly made. His coat hung in a corner. On the shelf were his cooking utensils and on a table his files were carefully arranged.[3]

Jaffré once remarked that the cells of the other detainees were not nearly so well arranged. That was no great merit, Laval replied. He liked things in their proper places. He hated disorder. When things were disorderly, he thought, it affected his spirits.[4]

He was proud to point to his casserole, his little cuisine. "Does it amuse you that I'm a cook? Don't think I don't know how. An oxtail en croute, for example, an old Auvergnat specialty. But I can't do the big things here. An egg. But it's not all that bad. Look at my hot plate. Magnifique."

He smiled. "It's too bad I can't have you to lunch. What harm can there be in having my lawyer to lunch? If I'm ever Garde des Sceaux again, that's a little reform I'll initiate."

When Jaffré complained of Laval's conditions, Laval deprecated his concerns. "I went without too long in my early years to have forgotten the taste of misery"[5]

Laval was under constant surveillance. He saw only his lawyers and the guards when they delivered meals. For a man so intensely sociable, so avid of human contact, this was deprivation indeed. Jaffré asked him about this.

It was hard, Laval replied. It was hard to be badly lodged and badly fed. But what weighed most upon him was the injustice of the accusations against him. "The world must know," he said, "who I am, what I have done, and why I did it."

His sole diversion was a half-hour walk in the courtyard. Not everyone in the prison was his friend. There were those who wished him ill. He had to be on his guard, to avoid any incidents.[6]

There were other prisoners at Fresnes who had been his political adversaries. He didn't want to talk about them, he said, and certainly not to denounce any of them. If they were accused of being in German pay, let it be proved. Some were crazy. Some were fanatics. But they had all thought they were serving France.

He paused to reflect. Everyone thought he was serving France. You had to examine the facts to see who served France better, in its immediate interests and in the long run. "I'm not concerned about such an inquiry," he would say, "so long as it's honestly made."[7]

Pierre Laval was treated correctly by the prison staff, never molested in deed or word. From the director to the lowliest sweeper, he was always addressed and referred to as M. le President or M. Laval.

Was it the high places he had held, or the thought that he might return to power? Or was it his dignity, his simplicity, his courage, and his ability to meet them on their own level while remaining himself. Their conduct was, Jaffré thought, unconsciously affected by Laval and his manner.

He loved to talk to the guards when he could. He thought of them as his own people, like the peasants and the workmen of Chateldon. He preferred them to the bourgeois.

He would ask them where they were from, how many children they had, if they were well housed, how long they had been guards. There was no artifice in the interest he showed. He always found something in common with them. He made them laugh. He made them cry.

He would pose a political problem to them: "What would you have done if you were in my place," he would ask. And when the answer came, he would say: "Exactly what I would have done. And it's for that that I'm here."[8]

"You govern a country as you govern a family," he liked to say. "A little more complicated, but basically the same thing." He read his memos and notes to the guards and asked their opinions. If Jaffré disagreed with him, he would ask a guard for his opinion and Jaffré remembered that, at least in retrospect, the guard was often right.

There was, Jaffré thought, neither affectation nor artifice in all of this. It was simply the nature of the man.

"The guards," Laval said, "they're only men like the others. Maybe it's not an attractive calling. But somebody has to do it. Everyone can't be an academician or a Counselor of State. So long as there are societies, there have to be prisons and guards to guard the prisoners." The guards weren't idiots. They weren't insensible. Some were even kind. They understood what he told them. "The High Court," he mused, "it's well enough. But at the end of the day, it's by men like these that I would like to be judged." And that, he added, is the judgment that counts, whether he lived or died.[9]

"Ah," he would say, "If only I could talk to the French one at a time and explain to them what I've done!"[10]

One evening Jaffré and Laval were hard at work when a young and sympathetic guard appeared. He was affable but inflexible. Time had expired. Jaffré must leave.

"Five more minutes," Laval pleaded. The guard was sorry but stood on the rules.

"Where do you live," Laval inquired.

"Paris, Monsieur le President."

"And you've told me that you're engaged to be married?"

"Yes, indeed."

"And you see her every evening, your fiancée?"

"Of course, Monsieur le President."

"And she loves you."

"For sure." " And I love her."

"You're right. It's the best moment of your life. And you'll have a happy family," said the man whose happiness in his family was the foundation of his life.

The guard looked at his watch. This did not escape Laval. "What time is your train?"

"A quarter of an hour."

"Jaffré, can't you take him in your car?" And so it happened that Jaffré would thereafter spend a precious extra half-hour of work with Laval.[11]

There came another day when another guard—he was young and debonaire—left Laval and Jaffré in the reception cell when the time had passed to leave. Jaffré accompanied Laval back to his own cell. They found the door locked. Laval stayed in the corridor while Jaffré went in search of a guard to open the door. Jaffré then left Laval amiably chatting with the jailer who had let him back into his cell.

The next day the rumor circulated in the Paris press that Pierre Laval had attempted to escape.

The report tickled Laval's fancy. "What, me try to escape? What an idea. I don't know how. It's not so easy to get out of Fresnes. Do they think I'd jump over the walls? Where would I go? I have a face that's pretty well known. How would I disguise myself? Oh, as a gypsy; that's the ticket. They always said I looked like one. With a horse and a caravan, a scarf around my neck, espadrilles, I'd be a pretty passable gypsy. But who would I fool? They'd all say, 'Aha, there's a Bohemian who looks suspiciously like Pierre Laval.' Oh, it wouldn't be a bad life. I'd see the country and I'd like that. But not for long. Me, I'm attached to my own place. I like to have a roof over my head. But if I do escape, look for me in a gypsy caravan."[12]

One day as they talked, there was a loud and raucous stir above their heads that ended up in song. "Just the guys above us," Laval reassured Jaffré. Their repertoire was, to say the least, inclusive: the "Internationale," with its call for world revolution, the fierce nationalism of the "Marseillaise", "Madelon" with its echoes of the First World War and even that hymn of praise of the Vichy years, "Marechal, Nous Voila."

They interfered with his work, Laval said, and the noise was often painful to his ears. But he had gotten used to it. The director had told Laval he would give the order for silence, according to the rules. But Laval had dissuaded him. "Look," he said, "while they're singing they forget for the moment that they're your guests."

He returned to a familiar theme. "My case isn't like the others. All I'm asking for is the right to defend myself. They can't refuse me that." But they did. The refusal, Jaffré and Laval suspected, came not from the prison director but from higher quarters.[13]

One day after Laval's walk, while talking to the guard, Jaffré learned that Joseph Darnand, shunned by all, was suffering from hunger. Darnand had been the head of the Milice, a ferociously repressive special French police organization in the service of the Germans.

Jaffré reported this to Laval who put together a box of food from his own stores. "Take this to Darnand," he asked the guard. "He needs it more than I."

He was reflective when the guard had left: "When I think of all the trouble Darnand caused me. He is an unconscionable brute. But he was a brave soldier in the First War. When I heard he had taken an oath to Hitler I asked if he wasn't ashamed. But he didn't seem to be at all. What troubles he made for me. And I had to take it. And if they won't listen to me, if my trial turns out badly, well, it will be in good part thanks to Darnand. But that's still no reason why he should go hungry."[14]

Laval shrugged his shoulders and lit another cigarette.

6

The Trial, October 4, 1945[1]

The Presiding Judge now ordered the examination of Pierre Laval. It commenced not with questions to the accused but with a statement delivered by the judge who relished the spotlight and the opportunity to put his stamp on the trial.

He had, Mongibeaux said, examined the origins and early life of Pierre Laval. They were extremely honorable. He had started at the bottom of society, then excelled at his studies, first in science, then in law.

He had risen rapidly at the bar, too. Laval, he said, had begun with those generous ideals common to intelligent youth of his era. That is to say, he was a militant Socialist, not to mention, a bit of an extremist. He had been in politics in the ranks of the far Left and all that was perfectly honorable.

"You became a deputy, marked for success by your talent for words, by your assiduous committee work and, having caught the eye of the leadership, you were many times awarded a ministerial portfolio."

"You have yourself pointed out an error in the indictment. You were not twice, but in fact three times prime minister and fourteen times a minister."

"I like fourteen better," Laval bantered. "Thirteen was never my lucky number."[2]

The Presiding Judge plunged ahead. Contact with the realities of power, he said, had changed Laval. He was less and less moved by the generous sentiments which had animated his debut. Mongibeaux did not say that Laval had disavowed those concepts, but that he had become a "realist." His personal ideals had to be compromised in the interest of the country and—what the presiding judge now said would alert the jury to what was to follow—not forgetting his personal interests.

"I don't understand," Pierre Laval interrupted.

The Presiding Judge once more summed up. "Your political views adapted to the realities of power and of personal life. I don't say you disavowed your earlier views. Only that you conformed them to the interests of the nation and to your personal interests, as the head of a family." He paused. "Well, there's nothing dishonorable about that. Perhaps, each of us tries to improve his own situation." Laval had faced up to Parliamentary realities and gained a reputation as an able man, Mongibeaux observed, but one who wasn't above slipping a banana peel in the path of a political opponent.

"You have frequented the corridors of Parliament too often to say that," Laval shot back.[3]

"I haven't," Mongibeaux protested.

"You were chef de cabinet of Raoul Perret," retorted Laval. Perret was a former finance minister over whom there lingered a reputation for dishonesty.

The Presiding Judge was unmoved. Perhaps, he continued, this was all hearsay, but nevertheless it had been so widely current that he could hardly ignore it. Laval's rise both in Parliament and at the bar had aroused the enmity of those who observed it. So he had faced covetousness, jealousy, malice and all of these had affected him. "You learned," Mongibeaux said, "that it was not only in the Scriptures that man was a wolf to man and, when you arrived at power, you weren't always surrounded by an atmosphere of cordiality."

So, Mongibeaux continued, the rivalries, the jealousies Laval had encountered in domestic policy he had also found in foreign affairs. There he had played a great part as foreign minister and as prime minister. In domestic policy, Mongibeaux conceded that Laval had made financial reforms, that he had cleaned things up.

"From which France benefits today," Laval interjected.[4]

Mongibeaux now reviewed Laval's foreign policy. He had clashed with countries that could have been allies. He had clashed often with the country that was not only France's great friend but also France's great rival, Great Britain. He had seen Hitler raise Germany up from the nadir to the first rank of the nations of Europe. He had observed the rise of Mussolini. Had it not entered his head that the authoritarian regimes were not without advantages?

Mongibeaux now concluded this remarkably vague series of assertions and statements as yet unsupported by tangible evidence by observing: "My summary was a bit long."

"And a bit inexact," Laval replied, "but that only makes it more picturesque."[5]

The Presiding Judge reasserted his authority. "I said at the start that you could speak as long as you wished. I am a magistrate of the old school. In the clash between the interests of the accused and the interests of society I will always put the interests of the defendant first. I neither know nor recognize Reasons of State." This was as significant as it was cryptic. Was Mongibeaux not here telegraphing what his response would be to any claim that Laval had acted out of necessity or duress?

Mongibeaux once more proclaimed that he recognized all the rights of the accused. But his final observation would cause concern to any defendant. It was a warning, even a threat. He would not permit the accused to upset the court and its proceedings, an observation made, he said, for the benefit of the accused.

Laval's response was conciliatory. Perhaps, in his replies, he said, he had been swayed by a natural wave of emotion. Mongibeaux carried on with his resume.

Laval, he said, had had contact with Germany in the early thirties. He had had contacts with Mussolini. He had seen the rise of Mussolini and Hitler and that their countries had benefitted.

"I saw Stalin, too," Laval interjected. "You forgot to mention that."[6]

The Presiding Judge forged ahead, repeating his charge that Laval had changed, had become a man of state who wondered if dictatorial regimes were not more advantageous than republican regimes. He had begun to believe that the country needed a führer, a duce, or at least a guide. "You changed your opinion," he insisted. "Well it's only natural. Things look different when you've become chief."

The Presiding Judge now congratulated himself. "I don't believe I've made many errors so far and, if so, they were more of opinion than fact."

"They are errors of understanding," Laval replied.

Laval could challenge them, Mongibeaux said, when he had finished his exposition. He now moved on to Laval's private affairs and the large fortune he was alleged to have accumulated in his political ascent.

"I can explain everything," Laval stoutly maintained. "What a pity that all this was never looked into during the pre-trial examination. That would have exposed all of this hateful rumormongering. Why refuse it?"[7]

Mongibeaux retreated. "You can explain later. But it's only a matter of secondary importance."

"But not for me," cried Laval. "I have to defend myself against a crime while I'm being spattered with mud. I want to wash it off, and in public."

Laval's private fortune, Mongibeaux alleged, was estimated by experts, at 58 to 60 million francs, and the rumor was that that was only a fraction of the whole.

"Right now I have a thousand francs on deposit at Fresnes," Laval observed bitterly.

"An almost vertical decline," Mongibeaux said.

"A total loss," Laval corrected him.[8]

Mongibeaux's next comments were generous. As prime minister in 1935-36 Laval had faced financial crises. He had shown courage in the face of desperate circumstances, a courage which was rare in parliamentary governments, the courage to accept unpopularity.

Laval pounced upon this opening. "That is exactly what I'll show you during the Occupation." That was the heart of his defense; that what he had done, popular or unpopular, had been in the interests of France and the French. "I'm surprised," he added, "to hear you say at the beginning of the trial what will be even more self-evident at the end."

Mongibeaux now reached the critical year 1939, the year that Hitler invaded Poland starting the Second World War. He accused Laval of having failed to support the necessary preparations for war. "You were always anti-war, always hostile to the appeal to arms. Honorable, yes, but it was pacifism and it enervated the will and the potential of France."[9]

Here was a topic on which Laval was anxious to talk. "I was for peace, sure," he began. "But I knew Hitler was the real danger. I knew he would put Europe to the torch. And I knew there was only one way to stop him. And that's precisely what I tried to do."[10]

"And if my policy had been followed, we would never have known the shame of Munich, the Hitler-Stalin pact. No, it could all have been avoided."[11]

He had the documents, documents he had carefully protected from the Germans.

"You will see that the man before you, in chains, is not the guilty man. If France has suffered, if France has known war, it could all have been avoided if only we had stopped Hitler long ago. We should never have gone to war, after the Hitler-Stalin pact, to defend Poland when we wouldn't defend Austria, and when we wouldn't lift a finger for Czechoslovakia..."

This was close to the heart of Laval's case: his pre-war policy, the entente with Mussolini that he had signed in January, 1935 and the agreement that he had signed in December, 1935 with Sir Samuel Hoare to end Mussolini's war in Abyssinia and above all to keep Mussolini's

Italy as an ally, the defender of the independence and integrity of Austria, the guarantor of the demilitarization of the Rhineland. These two, Austria and the Rhineland, were Hitler's critical targets in his drive for the hegemony of Europe. And it was Mussolini's Italy that was the ally without whom Hitler proclaimed he would not go to war. But in a startling about-face Britain had disowned the Hoare-Laval agreement which Italy was standing by to accept. This action had in turn spurred Italy's own about-face and its turnaround from France's ally, England's friend, to Hitler's soon-to-be partner in the Rome-Berlin Axis. It was the betrayal by Britain of Pierre Laval's policy that had pushed Mussolini into the waiting arms of Hitler, that had frustrated the diplomacy of Pierre Laval to the tragic detriment of France.

Courts are not well designed for expositions of foreign policy and Pierre Laval's presentation was limited and interrupted by time and circumstances. He had, he explained, told all this to the Senate Committee on Foreign Affairs in March, 1939. He assured the court that he had nothing to hide. He would answer any questions. He would not propose theories. Instead he would present facts. He wanted above all to tell his story.

The Presiding Judge's response was tinged with exasperation. "For the third time," he said, "you can explain everything. But we're not here to discuss the origins of the war."

Laval persisted. "There are those who are glorified and there are those who are crucified," he cried out. "I don't want to wait for history to assign me my true place."[12]

Mongibeaux now made a critical concession. "There was a climate in which your personality developed and it's good to know it. But the charges against you are plotting against the security of the state and intelligence with the enemy. They don't involve the pre-war period. You can talk as long as you like about those years and your policies in those years, but that's not the crime with which you are charged."[13]

An observer of the proceedings might ask this question: Why had the indictment charged that Laval had disavowed his sometime associations on the political Left? Why had it made allusions that could only be pejorative to his personal fortune? Why had it referred to his plan to end the Abyssinian War, the purpose of which had been to preserve Italy as France's ally in containing the clear and present danger of Nazi Germany? Why had the indictment charged that after the failure of that plan, Laval had lost and never could again regain the confidence of Parliament? Why, if none of these accusations were germane to the principal charges against Laval of plotting against the security of the state and intelligence with the enemy, had the prosecution made them? They could only sow prejudice and distrust in the jury which would consider quite different issues if it were squarely to address the indictment.

Mongibeaux now arrived at the war years. There was, he continued the Drole de Guerre, the Phony War, when Pierre Laval had had "an attitude." Again and again in the course of the proceedings, an accusing finger would be pointed at an attitude, as if the attitude were in itself a crime. Well, there were those, Laval replied, who thought a real war would never be fought. "And there you have it," he explained, "the intelligence and the experience of those who led us."[14]

"Did you," Mongibeaux asked, "like Clemenceau say 'I'll fight on the Somme?'" This was a vivid appeal to the veterans and to the Resistant members of the jury. "No," he accused, "you were a pacifist; you didn't provide France with the invincible arms she needed, both material and moral."

"Are you talking about when I was in the government?" Laval asked.

"No," Mongibeaux admitted, "you weren't in the government then."

"And when I was," Laval replied, "I always got the military appropriations passed."

Mongibeaux retreated. He had only talked in generalities. But, he added, in the corridors of Parliament, Laval had not been one of those who tried to explain the gravity of the situation. "No," Laval thundered, "what I tried to do was to prevent the war."

Once more Laval took the floor, dominating the court and the courtroom. He told how he had tried to speak in the Senate on September 3, 1939, its last session before the declaration of war. But he had been refused. The Constitution clearly provided that only Parliament could declare a war. But it never did, and here he was, accused with trifling with the security of the state.

No, he said, he hadn't been for the war which had been brought on by the faults, by the errors of certain men.[15]

Laval warmed to his theme. "I am accused of secret envy of Hitler and Mussolini, a dream of dictatorship. Well, I didn't know Hitler until I met him during the war, to my great misfortune, to the misfortune of France. Of course I met Mussolini in 1935. Because Mussolini was a fascist? No, because I wanted a pact of alliance with Italy. Mussolini was head of government and Italy was France's neighbor. In 1931 I visited the German Chancellor Bruning. I never asked if Bruning were a Catholic. In 1935 I saw Mussolini and three days later I saw the Pope, and after that Stalin, and on my return from Moscow, Goering. How's that for variety?"[16]

"If I had known the address of the Devil," he paused now and repeated the phrase, "If I had known the address of the Devil, I would have tried to find him to make peace, because I know that war is murder and, the victory and the Liberation notwithstanding, you gentlemen of the jury can see the irreparable ruins everywhere about you."[17]

Pierre Laval was fighting for his life. "We could have avoided those ruins. France was once first among nations, at the head, with Great Britain, at international conferences. And today I suffer in my cell that they deny to France its natural place. I am in a desperate situation today. But I suffer happily because I suffer for my country. I have faith in it. It will regain its premier place, of that you may be sure.... And when I see the authors of the defeat coming forward to accuse me. The audacity..."[18]

He stopped, struggling to swallow his anger, his shame. "You have to understand me," he told the judge. "After what my life has been, to find myself here, before you, well it revolts me."

"You say that I contributed to losing the war," he continued. But, he warned the court, they would see the truth when he was done.

Take, he said, for instance, the case of the Jews. That was an article of the indictment. Did they know how he had concluded his own memorandum on this subject? He would tell them.

"I would wish to be judged only by the French Jews because when they knew the facts, they would congratulate me for my presence in power and they would thank me for the protection I gave them. Those words might shock you; but when people understand the truth, they will no longer be shocked."[19]

And it was the same, he said, with the Freemasons and the secret societies. Even the Communists. It was not he who had imprisoned them, who had deported them. He had not been responsible for brutality. His voice rose. "No, I will show you that when our country was sick and unhappy and occupied, I used all the forces at my command to defend it, to serve it, and that's why I'm here."[20]

"Will you permit me," the Presiding Judge asked, "to have the floor for a personal incident?" With exaggerated courtesy Laval turned to Mongibeaux. "I give you the floor, your Honor." The courtroom erupted in laughter.[21]

The accused, Mongibeaux now said, had pronounced himself ready to dine with the Devil to bring peace. The war came from those men Laval had characterized as the Devil and the accused had had some sympathy for them. The real cause of the war was the totalitarian countries, Germany and Italy, Germany most of all.

That, Laval reminded the Presiding Judge, wasn't the issue. But the war could have been prevented. He would show how.

"You have the habit," Mongibeaux said, "of furnishing solutions to difficult problems. I hope you have the solution to this one."[22]

When Laval wanted to tell about his statement to the Senate Committee on Foreign Affairs on March 16, 1939, Mongibeaux was dismissive. It was all very interesting but... "But," and here he said it again, "We have to remember the real issue here—a plot against the security of the state."

Laval disagreed. "This isn't just a trial," he said. "We're writing history."

The court wasn't interested. The war had happened. Who was responsible? That wasn't the issue, though the personal attitude of Pierre Laval was. There had been a climate of opinion then, Mongibeaux said, and Laval had been at the side of those whose *attitude* wasn't conducive to preparing for war. It was morale that counted, the morale of an undivided people; indeed morale was an armor as potent as tanks.

Laval, Mongibeaux said, had been in contact with dubious politicians and with certain soldiers who were against war. It was a paradox, but the soldiers were in the camp of the pacifists.

"I didn't know them," Laval replied.

"There was one in particular," Mongibeaux continued, "and that was Marshal Pétain. You were in contact with him."

"At the beginning of the war," Mornet added.

"No, no," Laval cried out.

"And it was at that moment," Mornet chimed in, "that this trial began." Once more, it was said, as it would be said so many times by the Presiding Judge and by the Attorney General, that Laval's pre-war activities and pre-war issues formed no part of this trial. The narrowing of the real issues had begun.[23]

Did the court have police reports, Laval challenged, of his contacts with Pétain? He denied them. It was a legend. To the contrary, Mongibeaux replied, there were documents, there was the testimony of Commandant Loustanau Lacau who had served on Pétain's staff in the 1930s and had kept in close touch with him.

"I was mistaken about Pétain," Laval mused, "and I humbly confess it." He thought of another soldier who had in his own lifetime epitomized French glory and ruled over France's African Empire. "When we needed a Marshal Lyautey, instead we got Marshal Pétain."

The Presiding Judge continued his narration. At the beginning of the war, he charged, Laval had engaged in operations looking to a coup d'état. He needed a cover and he said that cover would be a Marshal's baton.

Laval vigorously denied having said what was now fatally attributed to him. He would never have used such language. It would have been offensive to the Marshal and, even had he had such an intent, a phrase like that would have backfired.

When Mongibeaux insisted on the report of Loustanau Lacau, Laval was incredulous. "You take him as a witness. You'd better be careful." Laval related how Loustanau Lacau, at the beginning of the war, had made charges of lying and treason against a minister he would not name, and when challenged, he had no proof. Loustanau Lacau had called on Laval uninvited. He had been received with courtesy. Nothing more.[24]

"We have yet to come to the accusations against you," Mongibeaux said. But Laval persisted. In his mind, the trial was root and branch a political trial, a trial not so much of a man as of his policy. He had to seize the opportunity to explain his policy and the moment was now.

"I was the one who raised the alarm of Hitler." Charlemagne was a great man, a very great man, but he believed in God. The new Charlemagne didn't believe in God. He took himself for God. It was without precedent in history. Those who were to be the victims of Hitler had to join together. If they had succeeded they could have saved the peace; if not they risked exposing the country to the tragedy that befell it. [25]

The solution, Laval insisted, had been to go back to his policy as prime minister in 1935 and 1936. That is to say, the alliance with Italy, the Franco-Soviet Pact.[26]

"Italy wasn't Mussolini and only Mussolini, he explained. Italy was a place in the geography of Europe. Italy was a fleet, an army. Italy was, above all, a passageway for the French army to the hundred divisions of the Little Entente, it was the passageway, across Eastern Europe to Moscow, to the Soviet Army. And Hitler would have been crazy to go to war, and he wasn't that crazy, if that chain had been wrapped about him."

Laval staked out his claim to history with a succinct phrase:

"I practiced the policy of encirclement."[27]

When war was declared, the fate of Poland was sealed. He understood why Stalin, who had seen Britain and France abandon Poland, had then entered into his fatal pact with Germany.

Here Laval was curiously wrong. The pact between Stalin and Hitler had preceded, indeed signaled the start of the war. But the charge that the passivity of Britain and France at Munich and after had swayed Stalin's policy was undeniable.

"In foreign policy," Laval continued, "I was always like a peasant. I looked at the land. I looked at the maps. If I hadn't made the pact with Stalin in 1935, it would have encouraged him to deal with Germany. When Stalin treated with Germany in 1939 and 1940, he was only following an old Georgian proverb: 'Better to embrace your enemy out of fear than let him eat you.'"[28]

Mongibeaux intervened. It was useless, he said, to tell of what might have been. In May 1940, the Phony War had become the tragic war. Mornet agreed. Laval could be a hundred times right about his foreign policy, but that—he said it again—was not the case before the court.

"Then why," Laval shot back, "why is it in the indictment?" Mornet insisted that there was no charge or acts or crimes before the war. The trial, he said, commenced only in September, 1939.[29]

But, Laval protested, the indictment spoke of his foreign policy, of his hatred for England. It was all untrue. "But," he added, "Now you're beating a retreat. And I'm glad."

"I'm not," Mornet replied. "But there is no charge based on foreign policy before the war. Only since the war."

Laval thanked the attorney general and went on. "How could I explain my policy during the war without explaining my policy before the war? Of course my policy was peace." But a policy of peace, he added, was best only when it was based on a strong army, solid alliances, and an international organization.

He had had difficulties with Great Britain. But he admired the English. He admired the vigor with which they defended their interests, their pride in their race, their Empire. He only wished that French statesman would have the same psychology, the same methods, the same ambitions.[30]

They said he didn't like England. He had always sought unity with Britain, but only on the basis of equality and never of dependence.

Again, the Attorney General interjected that this wasn't the issue before the court. Mongibeaux concurred. The charge was not insufficient preparation for war. The charge was that when war came, that instead of waging the all-out defense of a Clemenceau, he had tried to have intelligence with the enemy, to work for the victory of the enemy—Germany.

"No, no," cried Laval.[31]

"And Italy," Mongibeaux added.

Mongibeaux again dismissed consideration of what might or should have been done. Whether the accused had prepared the debacle of 1940 wasn't the issue. But there were those who after the defeat tried to profit from their country's misfortune.

"You were," Mongibeaux accused, "one of those who spread defeatist propaganda, one of the most active agents of Pétain, favorable to an armistice. In Bordeaux you were a leader of those who were in favor of an armistice with Germany." And, he concluded, Laval was among those who stopped a movement which could have maintained French independence, that is to say, the movement of the government to French North Africa, there to carry on the fight. The testimony of Albert Lebrun, the last president of the Third Republic, would show all this and more—how Laval had prepared to enter the new government.[32]

Whatever the indictment might have said, both the Presiding Judge and the Attorney General had in the course of this colloquy wiped the slate clean of any charges antedating the onset of the war in September, 1939, except insofar as prejudice may have lingered in the minds of the jurors who had been attentive to the reading of the indictment.

Now, at long last, came the substantive charges: that he had borne major, not to say capital, responsibility for the armistice of June 1940 and equal responsibility for preventing the transfer of the French government to North Africa.

Whether these charges were true or not it was the duty of the prosecution to prove, and if indeed proven, whether they constituted capital crimes or instead were well within the scope of that action and opinion which were a part of the duties and responsibilities of political figures.

These were genuine issues. The trial of Pierre Laval, at this moment, had truly begun.

7

Pierre Laval: A Life[1]

Of the three defense lawyers it was young Jaffré who had the most frequent contact with Pierre Laval. He visited him regularly in prison, carrying communications to him and retrieving Laval's assiduous notes and trial preparations for himself and his colleagues.

These meetings soon took on a special quality. Pierre Laval craved human contact. Isolation was a heavy burden for him. And so it happened that amidst discussions of the case and then the progress of the trial, conversations between the two soon acquired an intimacy, an exchange of lives and of thoughts on the most personal level. Laval derived immense pleasure from these meetings. He saw in young Jaffré, who had also risen from modest antecedents, something of himself at the outset of his career. His regard for Jaffré took on a paternal air. And Jaffré watched with keen interest the life and character of Pierre Laval unfold before him in these bleak surroundings. Jaffré found Laval at different times lively, simple, direct, familiar, witty, droll, and at other times grave, vehement, moving, persuasive, and always, Jaffré thought, himself.

"When I was your age...," Laval would often say to Jaffré. Jaffré knew he was about to hear some anecdote of Laval's early years. He joyfully recalled his fights in the village square—he had a scar to show for one of them. He had been more stubborn than the mule that pulled the cart in which the youthful Laval had carried the mail. When the mule once refused to move, he lit a fistful of straw under the mule's belly. Problem solved. Thereafter, the sight of a handful of straw would set the mule in motion.

Laval smiled at the memory. An old teacher had watched the spectacle. She threw up her hands and said to Pierre: "You'll end up either a minister—or on the scaffold."[2]

Laval's smile turned wry. "You see," he told Jaffré, "sometimes things really do come true. Maybe both of them."

He told of coming to blows at sixteen or seventeen with a teacher over the affections of another pretty, youthful teacher who was Pierre's English tutor. The bloody combatants ended up in court where Laval had pleaded his own case with the happy result that he was acquitted and his adversary fined sixteen francs.

With added pleasure, Laval told Jaffré, the batonnier who was present at the hearing had asked Laval about his future plans. "You ought to be a lawyer," he said. "You have what it takes." Maybe, Laval mused, this had set him on the path to his career.[3]

But it was, his own village, Chateldon, that moved him most.

"Do you know Chateldon? It's a place like no other in the world. It's my country and for me, it's always the most beautiful. It's a village in a valley with hills all around it, and vineyards on the hills. They make good wine there! Sure, it's not burgundy. But it's good. And I love it. An old village, Chateldon, with buildings from the Middle Ages. There's a high hill with an old chateau on top. That's where I live."[4]

"It was for sale. You mustn't think it was a palace. It was an old wreck from the thirteenth century and hardly any of the rooms were livable. Well, it pleases me to live there, in the heart of my village and it pleases my wife because she's from Chateldon, too. And so we live there."

He turned pensive, reflective.

"I regret Chateldon more than I regret power. You can love power. You can love it because it gives you the chance to serve. I never thought of it any other way. Power, it comes, it goes. Others take your place who think they can do better. That's how it goes. But a home, a family, that's where you really live."[5]

But he could not forget the ongoing trial and the fate that loomed up before him. He was exasperated by the implications of dishonesty in the indictment. "Read the indictment," he demanded of Jaffré. "Did you ever see anything like it? How could a magistrate allow those snide phrases in the indictment with nothing more than gossip I wouldn't dignify with a reply if I were a free man?"[6]

And that's all it was—only gossip about the personal fortune. Why had they put those phrases in the indictment? "Because they reinforce the charges of treason, the worst of crimes. How much harder it would be to prove an honest man had committed treason. But if a man had enriched himself unjustly, how much easier to say that he sold out France."

He defied them to prove that he had been dishonest. Before the war, when his political enemies were in power, they had had every opportunity to prove any such charges. They said he had been bought by Mussolini. What did they take him for? Did they think that the head of the French government would offer his services to Italy for money? Did they see Mussolini slipping an envelope to him? Well, he said, all the records of the Italian government and of the Italian banks were available. And anyway, he asked, why would Mussolini have to pay him for an agreement that was advantageous to France, that reinforced French security.[7]

His anger passed, replaced by that welcoming smile that prefaced another chapter of personal history.

Did Jaffré want to know how he had accumulated a fortune? There were guards nearby. Laval motioned them to join him. He had nothing to conceal, he said. He wanted the people, ordinary people, to know. And to him the guards represented the people and, what is more, the justice of the people.

He asked them, "If you had the chance to improve your situation, would you take it? Doesn't a man have a natural desire to acquire a competence and independence, especially if he has children?" They agreed.

"Where was it written that it was against the law for a politician to make an honest fortune?" he demanded. As long, he argued, as riches were gained by work, tenacity, ability, perseverance, they were a benefit to society. Why were the results of talent and energy suspect today? He had worked incessantly since he was young. He had worked to gain an education. He had risen early, retired late, hadn't taken vacations. He didn't go to the theater. He had seen perhaps ten movies in his life.

The guards looked on, absorbed. "I started out," Laval said, "as a lawyer representing little people, unions. And I never stopped pleading for them. That certainly didn't make me rich.

"But I was ambitious. I took on bigger cases. I didn't do all that badly." A sense of compromise had come in handy. His practice allowed him to buy Villa Said, his Paris home. "Was I the first to succeed at the bar?" he asked.[8] He then offered to share with Jaffré the secret of success. "It's simple," he said, "and it's free."[9]

"When you buy a business, don't buy a successful business. Buy a failing business and turn it around. That's what I did with the *Moniteur* newspaper of Clermont-Ferrand. I rescued it. I was interested in everything, advertising, accounting, sales. I even picked out the serial romances." He emphasized sports. He ran the print shop as an adjunct. "I wanted to be a good boss. I paid good wages. I got on well with the union." The first duty of management to the workers, he said, was to make the business a success.

It was the same story with Radio Lyon. He had found it mired in problems. One didn't need to look far for the source. It was run by a retired colonel. He and his staff knew nothing about the business. Laval found an experienced manager. The station, like the newspaper, flourished.

He told Jaffré how he had bought the sawmill at Chateldon and exploited mineral water springs. Was that a crime? The municipal water had exceptional qualities. He lovingly related giving some of it to an American friend who promptly spit it out. Laval intimated to him that the water had aphrodisiac qualities whereupon, Laval claimed, his friend had ordered a full case.

But, he insisted, he had never been a speculator. Whatever he did he insisted that it be concrete, solid. His affairs, he told Jaffré, were open to all, "au soleil," to the sun and its probing rays. They could examine his affairs with a magnifying glass. And what fantastic rumors there had been. That he was as rich as Aga Khan, as rich as the Rothschilds. That he had given his daughter a sensational dowry when in fact, because both the bride and groom were only children, there had been none.[10]

"They said I was a miser because I was an Auvergnat. I wasn't a miser but I was economical." In his economy, as in all things, he wanted order, tenacity, the same will to succeed he had applied to the affairs of state.

It was all a mystery to him. "I was once minister of justice. I could have commanded big fees after that. All my predecessors did." "But," he went on, "I couldn't accept to profit because of the office I had held. So I never tried a case again." Was that the action of a dishonest man he demanded of the guards? "Never," they replied. And yet, Jaffré reflected, to support the charges of the indictment there had been no proofs offered and the charge itself had been declared outside the scope of the trial, leaving only the implication of the stain, the injury, in the jurors' minds.[11]

Why, Laval wondered, would anyone accept the responsibility of power if not to serve his country? His anger arose at the thought that he had acted under any other motive. This phrase continually passed his lips: "Il faut que j'aie tort pour qui'ls aient raison." "I have to be wrong so they can be right."[12]

"After all, my family pleaded with me not to return to power at Vichy. My friends, too. Why would I do it? Certainly not for money. I had enough. To satisfy ambition? I had already held the highest posts, achieved the highest honors. And I was no longer young.

"But I had had experience of public affairs, of negotiations. I thought I could serve my country at the moment when it suffered the most. If I had an ambition, it was that my country should suffer less and survive its torment with the least damage. For that I would do what was necessary, even if it were unpopular." But, and this animated all his thoughts, when the drama was done and France delivered, was he not entitled to be judged on what he had obtained and what he had saved?[13]

"When I was young," he told Jaffré, "I had ambitions, to be a deputy, then a minister, then head of government. I was proud to represent France in happier days. But when the German labor chief, Sauckel, wanted to drain France of manpower, when Hitler demanded that France go to war at Germany's side, I didn't think of ambition. I thought of the types in Aubervilliers I knew so well, the peasants, all those whose fate was going to depend upon what I might say or might not say."[14]

"But I'm content." he told the young lawyer. "History will see what can't be seen today."[15]

In another of those lightning changes that Jaffré by now knew so well, he asked: "Do you know what I miss most?" Jaffré knew that another chapter of personal history was about to unfold.

He missed his family. But his family apart, what he missed wasn't politics. He missed his beasts, his fields. He thought of his farm at Chateldon. Yes he had had political ambitions. But at heart, he was and would always be a peasant.

"The land, that's what I love. Because it's the source of everything. Do you know, Jaffré, anything more beautiful than a bountiful harvest? I've done various things in my life. I haven't done all that badly. I've told you how I earned my fortune. But nothing gives me as much pleasure as to harvest my own wine, my own potatoes."

"I could be a good farm manager. It isn't easy." Almost as hard as governing a country. You need the same qualities. Keep your feet firmly planted on the ground. Don't mistake a cabbage for a tomato." He was he said, no amateur. "I learned from childhood to love the land, to respect it. I know cattle, I can tell the virtues and faults of a horse at a glance. When I hold a clump of soil in my hand, I can tell you if it's rich or poor and what crops it will grow best." He brightened. Such talk gave him infinite pleasure. If only he had spent the Occupation tending to his vineyards and to his cattle.[16]

"But I regret nothing... and even if I had it to do over again, I would."

He thought the peasants would understand, the mayors of the Auvergne would understand. "You have to understand," he said, "how the work of the world is done. The political class is interested only in politics. But I knew what work was, what it required, the spirit of those who did it. I didn't know it all. But I know about print shops and newspapers; I know about radio and sawmills. I know about wood, about farming. How can you govern a country if you don't know how it works? The working class, they're intelligent. Their heads aren't in the clouds."[17] What always interested him, he told Jaffré, was the living, the solid, the useful. A man with a métier, a trade, could always teach you something. A candidate for office ought to learn these things before he orated about them.

He recalled a market gardener, the best in France, maybe in the world. He was up and about at four in the morning, never flagging in his researches. What extraordinary products he raised up! What asparagus! Magnificent! "I decorated him," Laval said. And another with his giant chrysanthemums that won prizes across Europe. With men like that France would soon recover.[18]

When he was chief of government at Vichy, he had envisioned a project for a national school of gardening at a chateau in Touraine. "I thought of it as a mother thinks of a child she awaits. When I was locked in battle with Sauckel, the thought of it refreshed me, the fruits, the flowers, the young, passionate in their work there." "Talk is one thing," he told Jaffré, "but to plant a tree, to build a house, to open a school, that's better." Jaffré listened, transfixed. A guard signified that the time had come to leave. Laval extended his hand to Jaffré. "If you ever become Minister of Agriculture," he smiled, "think of my project."[19]

When Pierre Laval was alone in his cell, he worked incessantly on his brief, or perhaps better, his memoirs. When Jaffré was present, he would discuss it with him. That was his way, by talking to someone, to sharpen his ideas, to weigh them, to try them out on his listeners. He was a master improviser, as much with the pen as with the spoken word. And when he wrote, it was with clarity and precision, and almost without smudges and erasures.

It was the work of a man terribly pressed by time if his brief were not to be posthumous. Pen in hand, he had a passion for precision, for correct grammar. He hated sloppy work. "Have I put it right?" he would ask Jaffré, then asking him to bring more paper, always more paper. More, he said, than a member of the Academy. He had never written so much in his life.

If he had never been in prison, if he had never been on trial, he wouldn't have written a memoir. He would have been more interested in his beasts, his fields. And what he wrote wasn't really a legal defense brief, but more properly the outline of a brief given that he had neither the time nor the documents and the evidence at hand. He worked only from his memory, which seldom betrayed him.

Jaffré was certain that the purpose of this memoir was to show the judges the need for a full inquiry, to gain time, surely a legitimate tactic. But underneath it all, Jaffré thought, it was the sincere desire to throw as much light as possible on his case. Laval was convinced he could win over the jurors, even the most partisan. Again and again he would say to Jaffré: "I have nothing to fear from objective justice. I have nothing to hide. This is what I've done and these are the reasons why."[20]

It was only after he had been brought to Paris and knew how near the trial date was that he understood the need for haste. But, why he would ask? "They want to finish with me. They want to be rid of me," he said. Jaffré saw the unease in his eyes. But as Jaffré saw him, his courage never failed. He now knew they would cut off his defense. Up until the day of the trial he did not despair of persuading the court of the need of an extended inquiry. And it was only after the day of condemnation that he was able to finish his memoir. He edited and reedited, now for the sake of posterity, for history, for the revision that he was sure would one day come.[21]

"Do they know what they are doing?" he would often ask. How could they take his affair so lightly. He didn't know the new men of the Liberation. But he expected they would observe the elementary rules of justice.

"It isn't as if I had shot my mother-in-law," he would say.

It was a political trial. He understood why he had to be before the High Court. But his trial was about what had happened in France in the four years of the Occupation. There had to be evidence, documents, such as you could find in Germany.

One day Jaffré confided to Laval that he had heard talk in certain circles that he would be condemned for Reasons of State. This was the ancient thesis that the needs or the state trumped the demands of justice. "Reasons of State," Laval exploded. "They dare to raise Reasons of State. They wish to make us believe that France asks, not justice, but a sordid revenge and that they're obliged to satisfy it."

There were he admitted, times when Reasons of State could properly be invoked. The interests of the nation sometimes overcame those of individuals. Such measures could be justified in time of war, even unjust, cruel measures for the common good. So, during the Occupation, he had had, he said, to pronounce certain words, take certain decisions. Reasons of State, indeed. But the Germans were on the back of France. How else, he asked, to defend the interests of his country?[22]

But today? Where was the menace, he asked? Those who were thought enemies of the Republic were in prison. The electors would have their chance. They needed calm. They wanted peace, they wanted to eat, they wanted to settle their affairs.

But in the end, he still believed that the new men might render justice. Even if they were, he thought, little men who wanted to be rewarded for their heroism in London and Algiers. Well, to make speeches in London was one thing; to govern an occupied country another.

He had studied the ancients. He had observed and learned from Clemenceau, from Poincaré and from his old friend, Briand. "Government," he said, "is like cuisine. There are recipes that are worth repeating."[23]

He believed in continuity. He believed men who had had the experience of power had much to teach. His great error, Jaffré later concluded, was that he didn't see the difference between the new men and the men of the Third Republic he had known so well.[24]

He thought the new men intelligent, possessed of a certain political sense, solicitous of the interests of France, not vindictive, not bloodthirsty. He believed up to the last minute that his trial, if hasty, would nevertheless be a real trial and that historical objectivity would conquer passion.

But he was wrong.

Laval spoke often to Jaffré about the prewar years that had figured in the indictment, even though the Court had ruled them outside the charges of treason.

"We need to know who was really responsible for our misfortunes," he told Jaffré. "Aren't the really responsible ones those who led us to defeat in 1940? It would be formidable indeed to condemn me and place a crown on their brows."[25]

He wasn't talking about the Armistice. The history of France hadn't begun in June, 1940, he said. If France, had, in the aftermath of the victory of 1918, suffered the most crushing of defeats in a war that France herself had declared, that wasn't the work of the Holy Spirit.

This was a favorite theme. It was easy to say that the chances of war had been adverse. He knew the French were brave. They were good soldiers. But they had lacked the modern means to defend themselves against an enemy, armed to the teeth, disciplined, fanatic.

If there was a crime, Laval said, it was in the years before the war. The wisdom would have been to forge a chain around Germany.[26] He enumerated his policies: the policy of the January, 1935, pact with Italy, the policy of the Franco-Soviet Pact, of Stresa and of the Hoare-Laval accords.

"You don't go to war for ideologies," Laval said. "That would be a crime against the nation. You defend yourself when you are attacked." That was a sacred duty. He had always said that. And there was the duty to prepare. He had always acted, he said, to protect the security of France without ideological concerns. "Germany was the danger. I warned of it, not because Germany was Nazi, but because it was armed and dangerous. I went to see Mussolini. I went to see Stalin. Nobody complained of that. And I would deal with Hitler, too. When a peasant wants to sell a cow, he doesn't ask if the buyer is a Radical or a Socialist."

"I saw," Laval said, "Germany's intentions. I wanted to forge a defensive bloc so strong that Germany would find peace more profitable than war. Well, let the gentlemen of the High Court look at the record, and see what French statesman had better serve France."[27]

Other French statesmen, he complained, had sabotaged his policy of making war more difficult for Germany. They had gone to Munich. He asked Jaffré to recall the sectarian strife in France in the days of the Popular Front when all the while Germany was arming, when France needed production and discipline to back up its diplomacy. France, he said, deserved better than the leaders it had been given. France had believed their fine words. They spoke of peace. They promised bread and liberty. And they produced war, misery, slavery. The true crime had been to precipitate France into the abyss.[28]

He told Jaffré at his meeting with the German commander Brautchisch in 1940 after the debacle. Brautchisch had remarked how unjust it was that the burdens of defeat should have fallen to Laval. But someone, Laval told Jaffré, had to do it. Preferably someone who had been broken into the stresses and the ardors of such negotiations.

He remarked on the curious fact that in his newspaper, *Le Moniteur*, he had been the first in France to publish *Mein Kampf*. "The shameful page in our history, if there is one, wasn't the Occupation where we were overcome and had to survive. It was in the years before. I'll say that to my dying day because it's the truth. But they want to judge me. They say I betrayed France. But the ones really responsible, they aren't at Fresnes, and they ought to be."[29]

He didn't believe in political trials. Let history judge.

Laval returned to the theme that ran like a thread through all of his thought, all of his discourse. He had returned to power amid the ruins others had created.

"*J'etais le syndic d'une faillite*." "I was the trustee in bankruptcy."[30] It was the most ungrateful task that could face a public figure. "I did anything I could so that France should suffer the least. And it's me who's here in these four walls. Merde, alors."

8

The Trial, October 4, 1945[1]

The court had touched upon Pierre Laval's pre-war political career, his rapid rise, his personal fortune, not without insinuations that the two had been linked. All this Laval had vigorously countered and the Court had quickly conceded that none of these issues formed any part of the charges of treason and intelligence with the enemy that were before it.

This had hardly satisfied Laval. His aim throughout the trial was to examine exhaustively all of the issues. He was buoyed by the belief that if he had that chance, he could win the jurors over from prejudice and partiality to objectivity. His task still was to overcome the insinuations of infidelity and disloyalty to his political origins and dishonesty in high offices that could fatally infect the other charges.

But the Presiding Judge wanted to be done with the case as soon as he could, surely before the impending elections. He pressed on to those issues that were indeed at the heart of the case against Pierre Laval.

These revolved around the key events of June and July, 1940, the Armistice by which, after the total rout of the French and British armies, hostilities were suspended; the decision of the French government to remain in metropolitan France rather than move to French North Africa; and, finally, the proceedings whereby a new government was formed and the powers of the Third Republic placed in the hands of the new regime under Marshal Pétain and based at Vichy.

What part had Pierre Laval played in these events? What part had he played in the Armistice? What part in the decision of the government to remain at home in France? What part in the formation of the new regime? And, if he had played a role in any of these events, as certainly many other members of the French Parliament, and of the government, not to mention any number of citizens had, what was his right, and what was his obligation as a senator and as a citizen, and did any such action rise to the level of a capital crime?

All of this the presiding judge now summarized.[2] Laval, he pronounced, had been an active agent of defeatist propaganda tending to an armistice with Germany. And it was he who in contact with various members of Parliament had stopped the departure of the government to North Africa. He had prepared to enter the new Vichy government and though he had not been a member at its debut, he had soon after demanded the portfolio of foreign affairs. But there was objection. Such an appointment would not sit well with Britain.

Laval: "Baudouin wanted to keep the job."

Mongibeaux: "But not long after, you became a minister."[3]

Laval: "Will you permit me to reply to the question of the armistice?"

"You'll have time soon enough," Mongibeaux replied. But he would first finish his summary. At Tours, he said, at Clermont-Ferrand and then at Vichy, at the sitting of the National Assembly, Laval had shown hostility to Britain. In the transcript of its proceedings were Laval's statements that Britain would be defeated. And Mongibeaux recited the tragic events at Mers-el-Kebir in June 1940, when the French fleet had been attacked with bloody losses by the British fleet.

Laval was quick to penetrate this opening. "What did you think of Mers-el-Kebir then?" he asked. What could Mongibeaux say? That the British had been right to attack the French fleet?

Mongibeaux evaded Laval's question. "I don't have to answer, I'm not the defendant. I'm examining you."[4] But what would his answer have been?

The Presiding Judge continued his summary. He depicted Laval's central role in what he called the secret assembly. This was in fact an extraordinary session of the National Assembly composed of both the Senate and the Chamber of Deputies. He alluded to Laval's strong support for the transfer of power from the Third Republic to Marshal Pétain.[5]

Mongibeaux now said he would yield the floor to Laval. It would be an historic inquiry and one, he complimented himself, which would proceed in an atmosphere of serenity and independence. Here, then, were the questions that he would put to the accused: first his activities before the war, because it would clarify his actions during the war; then what Mongibeaux called his intrigues and maneuvers while he was at Bordeaux; next the affair of the Massilia (which was to say the issue of the departure of the government for North Africa); and finally the menaces and maneuvers at the National Assembly at Vichy which resulted in the transfer of powers by the National Assembly to Marshal Pétain's new regime.

This was a very large order, a ramified assortment of issues, events and personalities. What Mongibeaux called Laval's intrigues, his menaces and his maneuvers had been in fact expressions of opinion which were, in that desperate time, widely shared and the actions he urged were at the same time widely approved.

Pierre Laval was eager to respond. He wanted to make it clear that the answers he had given in the pretrial examination had not been definitive. It had been the custom of the M. Bouchardon to ask some questions concerning the charges and then announce: "I have interrogated you and you have responded."[6]

Laval said that he had not answered as completely as it was his right to do. But, he wanted there to be no misunderstanding. The answers he had heretofore given should in no event deprive him of the right in open court of a full reply, including questions about his political career and his private fortune and the connection between them.

Mornet: "That's not the charge against you."

Laval: "But it's worse than a charge. It's the poisonous atmosphere you want to surround me with."[7]

Mornet: "But these are allegations pure and simple."

Laval: "But why? M. Caujolle has been commissioned to make a complete report on my private fortune."

Mornet: "I didn't ask for it."

Laval: "How can you make allegations against a former head of government and then rest silent? Maybe they're only allegations. But they have consequences. I'm here before a jury. They're naturally curious. They want to know about my private fortune and how I got it." The prosecution might say this didn't constitute a formal charge against him. Well, to the contrary, the truth could serve him as a defense.

Yes, Laval admitted, he had been an ardent socialist in his youth. But he was never a renegade. He could tell how he had left the Socialist Party if he were allowed to answer fully.

Laval: "You say to me, you intrigued at Bordeaux. You intrigued for the Armistice, you intrigued for the convocation of the National Assembly, and you have menaced—that's what the indictment says—there were intrigues and menaces, there were promises, there were all the elements of a swindle."[8]

Laval went for the jugular. "Your Honor, when I arrived at Bordeaux, the Armistice had already been decided upon. Was it that the military commanders, was it that the government, was it that the president of the Republic were all forced to make an Armistice because Pierre Laval, who was isolated, who headed no party, had an opinion contrary to theirs? No, gentlemen, it was they who ought to appear here before you as defendants. It was they who should have safeguarded the interests of France." "But in fact," he repeated and it was literally true, "the Armistice had been already decided."[9]

Did they want his opinion of the Armistice? "I will tell you frankly what ninety-nine percent of the French won't tell you today: that ninety-nine percent of the French were then convinced that France could no longer resist. That's what the members of Parliament thought. En route to Bordeaux and Vichy, they had traveled through cities and countryside, they had seen the army cut to pieces, they had seen the long, sad columns of refugees on the roads."

And then there was the opinion of the commander-in-chief, General Weygand. What Laval had said as clearly as possible was that the Armistice, whether France could continue the fight, was a question for its military commanders.

"You knew the military chiefs were partisans of the Armistice," Mongibeaux said, as if it were Laval's duty to convince them to the contrary. He had not, Laval replied, advised Pétain against an Armistice for the simple reason that he was convinced of the necessity of an Armistice. "And if you brought here all the French who were convinced of the need for an Armistice, you'd need a lot bigger courtroom." No, all of the French were convinced, and if there were some who weren't, they quickly learned that France couldn't carry on.[10]

These were plain truths, unpleasant to hear in 1945. Laval pressed on. "When the Armistice was signed, I didn't have to resort to polemics; the vast majority of France thought it indispensable, that they couldn't go on."[11]

Laval paused to reflect. "The trouble wasn't the fact of the Armistice, but how it was bungled. And I paid for that when I was head of the government." There were those who said that the Armistice was imposed, that the Germans wouldn't discuss the terms. "But I know something about the Germans. I've learned it since. You can't get everything you want. But you can get a protocol, which lets you reopen some questions about the Armistice."

Laval summed up once more.[12] He had exercised no influence on the Armistice, which had already been decided and arranged by Petain and Weygand and, into the bargain, he had never been a member of the government that asked for and signed the Armistice. And that said, he would move on to the National Assembly.

In accordance with the Constitution, the National Assembly had to be preceded by meetings of the Senate and the Chamber of Deputies. These were open sessions where everyone had the right to speak.

"M. Jeanneney spoke. He was the President of the Senate. What did he say?" Laval paused. "Well, he eulogized Marshal Pétain. M. Herriot spoke. He was the leader of the Chamber of Deputies. What did he say? He eulogized Marshal Pétain."

"How did they vote? Excepting only three deputies in the Chamber and one vote only in the Senate, they all voted to convene the National Assembly the next day."

"How can you talk of intrigues, of menaces, of promises?" Laval thundered. "Are you serious?"[13]

So the National Assembly had convened on July 10, 1940, over 700 strong, despite the difficulties of travel and communications. There had been a question of the proper quorum, but in the end, there were more than enough present. And how had they voted? The president of the Republic had resigned. Out of 649 members of Parliament, 569 had voted for the transfer of power from the Republic to Marshal Pétain, thus inaugurating the Vichy regime, and only 80 voted against.

Pierre Laval's indignation reached new heights as he faced his accusers. "Do you really believe, Your Honor, that I am capable of seducing 569 deputies and senators? Do you think I have such powers? Suppose I had that power. I wish I did. It would never be more useful to me than right now."[14]

"And there's something else. Why has everyone waited until today to raise a protest against the proceedings of 1940. It would have been better if they had protested then. But Jeanneney said nothing. Herriot said nothing. Nobody said the Republic had been strangled. No one raised the least protest nor made the least reservation."[15]

How could they sustain this charge? "I remember it as if it were yesterday. There were no protests, no reservations, not even an allusion. No, nothing that could cast doubt on the absolute necessity of an Armistice. Nothing at all."

There had been special commissions appointed. It was the same with them. "Never, at any moment, in any form, did I hear a protest about the Armistice at the session of the National Assembly."

Laval returned to his theme: "How could you say I menaced, I intrigued, I promised. If I'd been chief of some big party, you could blame me for having the votes at my disposal." But, this was his defense in three words: "I was alone."[16]

He now made his appeal to the jury: "What was the real reason for the vote of the National Assembly? It was a patriotic reason, never doubt it. An elevated patriotic sentiment, you may be sure, because all of the representatives of the country understood that France had to be put in the least onerous position to bear the German Occupation. That was the issue."[17]

A juror interrupted with a question. Laval had been Pétain's chief spokesman in the July 10 meeting of the National Assembly. Why had the Deputy Vincent Badie been denied the right to speak. Laval disagreed. Badie had not been denied and, had he insisted, he could have spoken.

The presiding judge had mentioned the remarks of Boivin-Champeaux, reporter to the committee charged with preparing the report to the National Assembly, that it had all been a swindle.

"He wasn't altogether wrong," Laval replied. It was a swindle, he said, in the sense that the Marshal used his powers to ends that had not been foreseen: the dissolution of many of the established organs of democracy—the General Councils, the elected mayors, certain Municipal Councils. And he had created the Legion, an umbrella organization of veterans to replace political parties. What Laval was signaling here was the deep gulf between his own democratic philosophy and the more authoritarian views of the Marshal.[18]

Mongibeaux: "But you had a high position, you were a minister."

Laval: "So high that I was summarily dismissed from the government by the Marshal on December 13, 1940."

Mongibeaux: "You were a minister, you were the heir presumptive."

"Vice president of the Council," Mornet chimed in.

Laval: "I can't answer everyone at once."

The deadlock was broken by a juror's question about the Massilia and whether the members of Parliament who had boarded ship for North Africa could vote by correspondence. It was all, Laval said, in the record of the session of the National Assembly. And they would find in the record his response to Vincent Badie.[19]

All that was, Mornet observed, of no importance. Laval was charged only with this: his influence on the July 10 Assembly, and his threats, which stopped the departure of the government to North Africa.

Laval: "The charges against me are even severer on my supposed victims. How could M. Lebrun, the president of the Republic, on a simple protest that I made..."[20]

Mornet: "We will hear M. Lebrun as a witness."

Laval: "Well, at Bordeaux I exercised my rights as a member of Parliament. I gave my opinion. I told Lebrun exactly what I had told Jeanneney and Herriot—if they wanted to go to North Africa, if they thought it was best for the country, then they should convoke the Deputies and Senators and so advise them. I had a different opinion. But I might have yielded to a better argument."

"You make it a crime not to go to North Africa," he declaimed. "But in the end it was the best thing that could have happened that we didn't."[21]

He proceeded to tell why. Britain had been defeated. Had the French government gone to North Africa, Hitler could have pursued them through a friendly Spain, itself unable to resist. Nor were there means to resist in North Africa. The Germans in Africa! The Germans in Suez! What a complete reversal! Perhaps, then, the rupture with the Soviets wouldn't have happened. And the Americans wouldn't have had North Africa as a platform for the liberation of France. Nobody had asked his advice. But he had given it because he thought that to go to North Africa was madness.[22]

He once again insisted. He had exercised his right, the same right as all of the others. "How could the government collapse before the protest of a single Senator—even if there had been a dozen. What kind of an argument is that?"[23]

He returned to the National Assembly. The vote had been perfectly regular and President Lebrun had said so. If Lebrun had resigned as president, which was a charge in the indictment, he had resigned not because of Laval's pressure but because he thought it was incumbent upon him. Lebrun had departed, Laval added, after the vote of the National Assembly and not a single deputy or senator had written to express regret that he had.[24]

"And at the National Assembly," Laval said. "I never thought the Occupation would last four years. I thought that when we voted the laws of July 10, the Marshal could make a new Constitution. And that Constitution couldn't be reactionary, because the country wouldn't have it, wouldn't return to the past. That's what I said and it was under those terms that I served."[25] He had not only spoken but, he said, he had worked for a Constitution that respected republican laws and the control of public spending. No, he was not embarrassed by this inquiry. They would see, when they inquired, the injustice of the charge.

These were vital issues. In paving the way for the new Vichy regime, while serving from July to December, 1940 as a Minister without portfolio, what kind of a regime, what kind of a government had he envisioned and sought? If it were essentially a republican regime, or only a temporary regime to accommodate a brutal necessity that would revert to its republican antecedents as soon as possible, then the charge of a coup d'état would lose its force.

Mornet: "You participated in a government that made a coup d'état."

Mongibeaux: "M. de Lapommeraye would testify that Laval had said to him of the vote of July 10, "'And that's how you overturn a republic.'" And that several days later, speaking to teachers at Mayet-de-Montagne, Laval had declared himself the initiator of the National Revolution. And that he had later said to M. de Lapommeraye...

Laval: "What a memory!"

Mongibeaux asserted that Laval had told de Lapommeraye that Britain was beaten and that if France wanted to survive, to be reborn, it could only be reborn if it adapted its institutions to those of Germany.

Laval: "I can't take him seriously. If he comes, let me call another witness. I don't ask for the indictment of de Lapommeraye." He paused and smiled. "I'm on principle opposed to such indictments." The court room rocked with laughter. But he stoutly denied what de Lapommeraye had said.

No, Laval continued, he didn't think that de Lapommeraye would bear false witness. But what he had said was only a *plaisanterie*, a joke, a passing comment—he did it from time to time and jokes sometimes turn out badly. Maybe it was in bad taste and he regretted it. But it was his acts that were more important than his words.[26]

Mornet: "But your address to the teachers that wasn't a joke."

Laval: "Are you sure I said it?"

Mongibeaux: "Yes."

Laval: "You weren't there."

Mongibeaux: "But it's in your dossier."

Laval: "I was suspicious when I heard the charges, when I saw the documents that weren't typed and didn't have my signature. There were words in those documents to which I never put my name. At Compiegne you said I declared that the hour of liberation of the French prisoners wouldn't sound until the hour of German victory. Well, I have the printed speech. I asked myself, how could I have said such a thing. I read the speech. I said nothing of the kind."

At Mayet-de-Montagne, the audience hadn't been teachers but Pétain supporters and spokesmen. The presiding judge read a phrase: "The country liberated from its fatal institutions."

Laval: "You weren't there and you can't authenticate those words."

Mongibeaux: "But they were printed in *Le Petit Parisien.*"

Laval: "But that paper was printed in Paris, and I was in Vichy, and when I read it, it was too late to object."[27]

Laval recalled what he had said at Mayet-de-Montagne: "Everybody talks about a National Revolution and no one defines it." Everyone had his own desires, his own ideals, his own definition. But the regime had never defined the National Revolution.[28]

How many times had he spoken to teachers, to other delegations, always ironic about the National Revolution to which he contrasted the Republic. "You can never," he told the jurors, "deprive the French of their right to vote, except in the most troubled periods. I knew that. I had some small experience of politics. I was always at odds with the Marshal, with the Germans and with the Paris press. And there were rivalries among the Germans which could work to benefit France."

This was Laval, the practical politician seeking support when he could find it. All Germans, he observed, didn't have the same agenda. There was the Army, there was the Embassy in Paris, there was the SS, there was the Todt organization and each had its own goals and its programs to attain them. In the tensions among them, were there not gains to be gotten for France?

But everybody knew his republican sentiments, even if they didn't appreciate his sturdy parliamentarism. He named names. Albert Sarraut, a former prime minister tragically assassinated. He could have vouched for Laval. And Herriot, with whom, on the eve of liberation Laval had sought to revive Parliament.

The juror Biondi: "Didn't you say in the Petit Salle of the Casino at Vichy that Britain would be defeated in a few weeks, that the victory of Germany wasn't in doubt, and that France would have to align its institutions with those of the victors?"[29]

Laval: "At the Casino I said Britain would be defeated. That's what I believed. After our defeat, I didn't think that England could hold out. That was my opinion. I was wrong." But, he added bristling with indignation, arms raised high: "That's not a crime—only an opinion."

Laval: He had drawn a conclusion from the defeat: Align our institutions with those of Germany. But he never intended to install Nazism or Fascism in France. "At the height of the Occupation, head to head, nose to beard, with the Germans, I said just the opposite. I told them France would never accept the domination of another country in its internal affairs." [30]

The Presiding Judge was ready with another quote: "France must collaborate with Germany. There can be no collaboration if our regimes are divergent. Democracy cannot survive our defeat. We must support the principles of authority of National Socialism."

Laval: "But no, that phrase is surely wrong. If you had stopped at 'principles of authority,' I might agree. But when you added 'National Socialism' the whole phrase was false.

Mongibeaux: "And collaboration with Germany?"

Laval: "That's the heart of the whole trial."

Mongibeaux: "Collaboration and reversal of alliances."

Laval: "I never spoke of reversal of alliances. Not only that, but I fought against it."[31]

It was now clear to everyone in the court room that Pierre Laval, his face ashen, was shaking with fatigue. He wanted to continue. He had been speaking since one in the afternoon. He asked that the session be terminated for the day. The presiding judge suggested a recess of a half hour.[32] Laval spoke with effort. "I am alone in the presence of charges so grave I have to weigh my words. I have no lawyer to consult files. I am, I fear to say it, trapped. And I'm very tired."

"I have to prove my willingness to respond to examination. But," and this was a continuing theme, "this isn't only the trial of a man, but of a whole policy, of a tragic period of history and it needs a whole examination. We are in fact editing pages of history."[33]

"What do you have to fear?" He recovered his physical forces. "My body is in chains, but my soul is free. I love my country, I want to prove it, not for my sake alone but for yours, too."[34]

The Presiding Judge was unyielding. The preliminary examination was over. The trial must continue. The Court would lend an attentive ear but he must carry on, again suggesting a half-hour recess.

He could not, Laval said. He referred to the difficult circumstances of his cell.

A juror. "Lots of patriots knew cells like yours under your government."[35]

Laval: "I will explain everything. But I am without a lawyer."

Mongibeaux: "That isn't any fault of the Court." Nor was the Court responsible, for the raucous demonstrations that were then taking place in the courtroom. Laval assured the Court that he had no part in them.

He was deferential. He didn't want to raise his voice. He wanted to be polite. But he understood the position of his lawyers. They could be present, as a matter of form. But what difference would it make? He needed them. He needed witnesses. He was alone in his cell, cut off from the world, unable to prepare his case, to summon witnesses.

He issued a challenge: "Will France render justice or will France treat me as the Germans treated us under the Occupation? Why do you fear the truth?[36]

The Presiding Judge cut him off. He called a recess, he said for reasons of humanity. But he charged that the defendant was speaking at far greater length than the questions required. Laval insisted that he hadn't wanted to inflame. He had represented his country. And now France was free.

A juror: "No thanks to you."

Laval: "I'll show you it wasn't in spite of me."

Mongibeaux: "Will you let me speak?"

Laval: "I can't stop you."[37]

The Presiding Judge had reached the limit of his patience. He had warned the accused twice. He reflected for only a moment and then ordered: "Guard take away the accused."

"Vive Laval," a young man in the courtroom cried. Amid pandemonium, the presiding judge ordered him arrested and above the din a juror cried out: "He deserves twelve bullets, just like Laval."[38]

This was an extraordinary conclusion to an extraordinary day. What, at this moment was the posture of the case against Pierre Laval? The Court had dropped from consideration anything related to his prewar political activities and his private fortune. Further, neither the Presiding Judge nor the Attorney General had disputed that he had not been a member of the government that had signed the Armistice with the Germans nor that he had had any influence on what was primarily a military decision. He had, it was clear, expressed vigorous opinions against the transfer of the government to North Africa. That was his right as a senator and he was far from the only one to share that opinion. He had said it in 1940 and again in 1945, and history has validated his view that drawing Germany into North Africa in 1940 in the train of the French government's moving there could have had tremendously adverse consequences on the whole course of the war. It was, on the contrary, one of Hitler's prime strategic errors not to have done so.

He had also vigorously promoted and advocated the transfer of the governmental powers of the Third Republic to the new regime of Marshal Pétain. But so had 569 other members of Parliament, whom he was capable of controlling and directing no more than he was capable of controlling and directing the military chiefs. Those 569, like Laval, had the right and the duty to take a stand on the vital issues that faced the nation and that was exactly what he and they had done.

He had been accused of making certain statements. Some he forcefully denied, others he sought to put into context. Was he being tried for his opinions, for his words, or for his acts?

All this leads us to consider two remarkable aspects of the trial as it had so far unfolded. The entire case had consisted of the unsupported assertions of the Presiding Judge and the Attorney General. No witnesses had been heard, no documents presented. From the standpoint of Anglo-American jurisprudence, no admissible evidence had been presented or heard. What the Court and prosecutor had presented and what the jury had heard was supported by neither authentication nor cross-examination.

To compound these substantial shortcomings, there had been an abbreviated preliminary examination, assumed to be conducted to the end of determining what, if any, charges should be brought. But this examination had been radically truncated and the jurors had not been apprized of these attenuated proceedings. The jurors had heard only what had transpired in the court room, nothing more.

There was another remarkable aspect of the day's hearing. It was the naked hostility to the defendant displayed time and time again by the jurors and all of this without a word of warning or reproof by the Court. Such outbursts, in an Anglo-Saxon courtroom, would call for the immediate dismissal of the juror (in which case the Laval jury would have been insufficient in numbers) and very probably the declaration of a mistrial. But the trial of Pierre Laval saw no such action, certainly no such recognition by the Court of the manifest bias on display.

Readers of the Paris press the next day would find a reasonably comprehensive report of the proceedings in *Figaro*, the newspaper of the business community, in *Combat*, the Gaullist organ and in *Le Croix*, the Catholic newspaper. All of them focused on Laval's denunciation: "You were all under the orders of my government."

Figaro added detail not to be found in the austere reporting of the trial transcript. Thus:

Laval entered the courtroom shaking with an ill-concealed rage beneath a somber visage. From his salt and pepper hair there fell a wayward lock of yellowing hair. Behind him, the bench of the defense remained empty. He set down several thick dossiers and demanded a glass of water. When he sat down, it was to deliberately turn his back to the Attorney General with whom from time to time he exchanged scornful sideways glances. From the start he adopted an arrogant attitude.[39]

During the session *Combat* noted that "in the back of the room the lawyers protested." Protests by members of the bar who were attending the trial will become a continuing theme in newspaper reportage. Thus, when the defendant pleaded for a continuance, *Combat* reported:

The court retired to deliberate. It returned five minutes later and resumed the trial. All of the lawyers who were a part of the public left the courtroom as a sign of protest.[40]

L'Humanité presented a more vivid picture of the day's proceedings. Its headline screamed:

NO! THE LAVAL TRIAL MUST NOT SERVE
LIKE THAT OF PÉTAIN
AS A SPRINGBOARD FOR REACTION
YESTERDAY AT THE FIRST SESSION
SCANDALOUS MANIFESTATIONS OF THE FIFTH COLUMN
TO AID THE MANOEUVERS OF THE TRAITOR

The Communist organ further reported:

Yesterday afternoon at 13:25 the first session of the Laval trial commenced before the High Court of Justice. As we have explained in yesterday's edition, the scandalous attitudes of the accused and his provocations which echoed among the lawyers in the audience indicated the intention of the fascist reaction to make this trial a springboard. We must add that the lack of firmness on the part of President Mongibeaux has not made for an appropriate atmosphere.

L'Humanité also described Laval's entry into the court:

"A tired old man, the face gaunt, his hair a dirty grey, the moustache half brown. When he is in top form with his infallible memory, he remains master of himself, in his feigned indignation a shameful comedian, a provocateur—thus appears the traitor Laval.

And when Laval challenged the court to "condemn me right now" the newspaper reported: "He acted like a wild beast in a cage and cried at the top of his rage."[41]

What was missing from *L'Humanité* story was any reference to Laval's challenge to court, prosecutor and indeed all who had been associated with the Vichy regime.

9

Pierre Laval, Republican[1]

When Jaffré saw Laval in his cell that evening, the passion and the indignation had subsided. Laval was chatting with one of the guards. He was calm, relaxed, with a welcoming smile for Jaffré. He asked, as he always did, for news of his family, then took up his conversation with the guard. They were discussing the cultivation and care of fruit trees. Laval thrived on conversations like this, but the guard gracefully withdrew.

"I was just telling him," Laval said, "why I'm a republican."[2]

He paused to reflect. "M. Mornet had the kindness to accuse me, among other things, of wanting to overthrow the regime. Well to want to overthrow a regime you have to be hostile to it." The guard had heard about Mornet's accusations. "So he asked me whether or not I was a republican."

"I told him: what do you think I am? I said the same thing to the Comte de Paris."[3]

The Comte de Paris was the pretender to the throne of France. Laval recounted how he had met him in Paris. He was hardly, Laval said, a Henry IV or a Louis IX. And he probably thought Laval could help him. He had illusions. He was so sure of his chances, which to Laval seemed so slim.

But Laval agreed to meet him. His attitude was typical. "Even if you don't agree with someone," he said, "you can always learn something interesting from him." And so they had met, a curious pair, one of the bluest blood, the other proud to be of Auvergnat peasant stock. "*Entre la poire et la fromage*," between the pear and the cheese, the Comte had asked Laval's opinion of a monarchy. Laval had expressed the same republican sentiments to the Comte de Paris that he later told the Court and the prison guard.

"But," Jaffré asked, fascinated to be in an intimate conversation with a statesman of Laval's eminence, "was the Third Republic really your ideal?"[4]

Laval smiled. He lit another cigarette. "And you, did it represent your ideal?"

Jaffré was taken aback. "Oh, no," he replied. "My opinion hardly counts at all."

"I'm sure," Laval told him, "your opinion would be harsher than mine. First of all, because you're young, and the young are harsh judges. And then, you suffered from the Republic's faults. But I, I received so much in my youth, my education, later high posts and honors. I can't forget all that. I owe a debt of gratitude to a regime that made me, from time to time, minister, head of state. When I told the Comte de Paris I was a republican, it wasn't simply idle talk, I am a republican. But I'm not a demagogue."

"But you asked a precise question. Did the Third Republic represent my ideal? Well, aside from the demagoguery, it wasn't that far off. You could have had a more flexible constitution. You could have modernized it. It wasn't a problem but it needed attention one day or another. The Third Republic had its flaws; but it had in my eyes these essential virtues: a respect for the liberty of the individual and the chance for intelligent, hardworking young men to rise in the measure of their capacities. I would never have approved any restrictions on that."

"They were all wrong," he reflected, "when they called me a reactionary. I was never a reactionary." He had passed the social insurance law, and his decree laws of 1935 had arrested the fall of the franc and lowered prices, with fruitful consequences if only he had stayed in power.

"Let anyone show that I was the enemy of the Republic. I dared to confront the demagogues, the bureaucrats. I didn't think about privilege or party, only of the public interest. It was the demagogues, the real reactionaries who brought us so much trouble."[5]

"And the Parliament?" Jaffré suggested.

Laval was quick to reply. "Don't speak ill of Parliament. It was more complicated than you think. There was a lot of criticism of the members. But they weren't incompetent. They weren't thieves. Oh, there were some black sheep. But there were far more who took their responsibility seriously and the young put their hearts in it. They weren't all eagles. But even the less gifted were conscientious in representing their constituencies. I don't talk, of course, of the Communists. They had their own ideas. And the committees, they could have done good work if it hadn't been for party politics. They worked under the cloud of their parties. The parties, caused problems. They were responsible for so much demagoguery. They promised too much."[6]

He was thoughtful. "And I don't think it will be much better in the republic that awaits us."

"Me," he continued, "I always wanted to be independent. After my time on the extreme left, after I sowed my wild oats, I refused to join any party. Perhaps it was a matter of temperament. Perhaps I wasn't flexible enough to bend to imperatives. I always had in my blood the taste of independence. And I was the same when I stood up for my country under the German occupation. That said, let anyone show me you have to belong to a party to be a good republican."

Jaffré was silent, rapt. Laval went on: "Oh, I think the Third Republic, as it was when it produced statesman, empire builders, perfectly suited the French temperament, their love of liberty, their individualism, their spirit of initiative. We're not Tartars. We're not Prussians. Maybe the Tartars and the Prussians can accommodate to their regime. But we're French. We have our own habits, our tastes, our inspirations.

"I thought that before the war. I never stopped thinking that during the Occupation. And I'll tell you something. Even when the German victory seemed certain, and that was an eventuality we had to face, I had the ambition to make a peace that would be the least burdensome on France, to make a place for France in a more authoritarian Europe, a France as like as possible to the France before the war, a regime of individual liberty where the citizen would remain sovereign. I didn't know if it could be done. I worked with all my might to make it happen. I never hid that from the Germans, at least those who had some understanding of France."[7]

There were real collaborators, real pro-Nazis, the Ultras in Paris. Their press well knew and ridiculed his republican sentiments, Laval continued. "What I wanted was a Third Republic reinvigorated, reborn. Suppose I had had a weakness for authoritarianism. I would have been an idiot to believe that the French would bend to it."

"Believe me," he told Jaffré, "I know the French. I know their reactions. Don't think I didn't follow the shifts in public opinion as events developed under the Occupation. I guarantee that I did my best even if I wasn't always understood—I had no way to explain it clearly—by those I was trying to protect."[8]

He said it again. "I know the French. Maybe it's because I think of myself as one of them, with all the qualities and the faults of a peasant or an artisan. What folly to impose upon a people a regime they absolutely don't want. It would take main force. That's what a Stalin would do."

He was not complimentary to De Gaulle, who, he thought, was making things too comfortable for the Communists. "What stupidity! Like catching syphilis." In three months, the reddest of the reds would revolt against bolshevism in a way they hadn't against the Germans. It would be in the nature of things and that's what he had told Hitler at Montoire. France would revolt if pressed too hard. France was republican. But what was coming to France, the new regime, might be a caricature of the worst moments of the Third Republic. "There can be no republic without justice. And their justice," he hurled the words at the fascinated Jaffré, "is an imposture."[9]

Laval thought of the day's proceedings in Court. "Mornet has accused me of wanting to overthrow the regime. Well, let him prove it."

"I would love to know the reactions of M. Mornet to the situation of France in June and July, 1940. What were your own sentiments? Whatever Mornet may have thought then—and I have strong reason to think he would hardly have been a flaming resistant—I thought I should remain in France, to help it live in its sorrow. That's what I thought and that's what I did."[10]

He repeated what he had told President Lebrun—it had been his right and his duty—that he hadn't been responsible for the defeat nor for the Armistice. He hadn't been against it, but he would have negotiated it better. Pursuing the fight outside France might seem noble, and indeed profitable if Germany were vanquished. He hadn't rejected the idea without deep reflection. But France was defeated, Germany all powerful with Russia its accomplice, Britain without an army, America distant and unmoved.

That had been a situation for any French leader to ponder. Laval then made the essence of the case for his policy under the Occupation. Even supposing the Liberation would come, at some distant date, what would become of France in the meanwhile? Should forty million French be left at the sole pleasure of the conquerors? "With what we now know about the Nazis and their methods—and we didn't know it until the deportees started to return—we can imagine what the fate would have been of a France theoretically still at war, but in the hands of Hitler." He went on to sketch the outcomes, the mass deportations, the pillage of the factories and enterprises, the control of the food supply. Think, he said to Jaffré, what would have happened in France after 1940. It would have been like the last months of the Occupation, not one village burnt and its inhabitants massacred like Oradour, but hundreds. And Hitler would have moved into North Africa, and the whole war would have changed."[11]

"What I can't understand today," he reflected, "is that those who warned before the war of the havoc of a German victory today can't accept my reasoning. Now they say it would have been better to die than to negotiate."

"I always thought it would be better for a French government to exist, to act as a barrier between the people and the occupier. Hitler was capable of the worst of crimes. But he could also be generous if you knew how to deal with him. If Germany were to be the ultimate victor, there was no reason why France should be destroyed." The question was: Would France live—and how?[12]

The Armistice, Laval said, had been hard, with the diabolical line of demarcation and the attachment of the departments of the Nord to the German military command in Brussels. But, France still had its Empire, its fleet. The Germans were correct for a long time. There had been an unoccupied zone and a government. It was in Pierre Laval's nature to view issues from two sides. "It could have been worse," he said. "We lived badly. But we could try to live with hope for better days."

He lit another cigarette. He recalled Mornet's accusation. "He accuses me of a plot against the security of the state. I would be curious to know what Mornet would have done in 1940 if he had been a deputy. I think he would have voted Yes. After all, he served as a magistrate under Pétain."[13]

He thought again of 1940. No one should suppose, he said, that Parliament was absolutely free to do what it wished. It was tragic and the deputies and senators had understood perfectly. The country had placed its faith in Pétain, the savior of Verdun, whom Laval himself saw as the symbol of national unity and of the will of France to survive.

What happened at Vichy in July, 1940, he recounted, was the consequence of the defeat he had tried so hard to avoid. Pétain had tasked him to ask Parliament for full powers. And Laval had agreed. He had thought, under an Occupation, Parliamentary debate would be dangerous and the deputies and senators understood that too. It was a lie to say that they had acted under threats. "My colleagues of the Chamber and of the Senate, they had their faults, they had committed errors heavy with consequences. But they weren't careless, they weren't neglectful. What they did they did because at the moment there was nothing else to do and they did it to serve France.[14]

And what about those who voted Yes and are now making flamboyant declarations. Where were they then? I could respect those who voted No—nobody stopped them. They deserve our esteem today."

He could not refrain from comparing his fate to others, Jeanneney and Herriot. "They were full of praise for Pétain then. What a comedy!"[15]

He told Jaffré of an incident in the fall of 1943. The Ultras, the hard-core Paris supporters of Nazi Germany, Marcel Deat, and Joseph Darnand had sent him a twenty page proposal for a dictatorship. They would have thrown those who disagreed with them in prison and offer sinecures to the others. That would have been the overthrow of a regime. That is what he had never done.

He returned to his theme. "Even at Vichy the French wouldn't accept a regime that didn't respect the liberty of the citizen. France is the cradle of liberty. Parliament wasn't functioning but I always thought of it as the guardian of legality. I dreamed of reconvening Parliament. And I tried to do that when the Americans reached Paris, but the Germans wouldn't have it."[16]

Jaffré listened and thought, how quickly Laval passed, from irony to seriousness, from anger to objectivity.

"When I say I am a republican," Laval carried on, "I'm not talking lightly. I'm not lying to please the powers that be. But my idea of a republic isn't theirs. I have a higher ideal, that I share with the men who founded the Third Republic and made it a humane regime."

"But didn't," Jaffré asked, "the Vichy government have a certain personal character?"[17]

Laval's eyes lighted, a reply ready on his lips. "To answer that," he said, "you have to knock on another door. The personal power wasn't called Laval. It was called Pétain."

He told Jaffré that he had talked to Pétain little, had understood him less. He had never, by word or act, tried to diminish Pétain's stature. When he returned to power in 1942, he had accepted risks which the Marshal would have shared. But he wanted the Marshal's prestige to remain intact. What he had done, he did, not for Pétain but for France.

"The Marshal," he recounted, "was difficult to penetrate. He was a man of wood," he paused, "or marble if you prefer. But I never felt in him a real human warmth. I often asked myself, when he became chief of state, if he had not become Buddha personified. He called himself 'We.' He loved incense. When I saw that, I understood."[18]

No, Pétain's ideas had not been his, Laval said. Soldiers rarely had any political intelligence. Lagardelle once told Laval how he had had to explain to Pétain what a trade union was.

Laval had thought, he said, that what Pétain detested was the flaws of the Parliamentary regime. But, no, it was the Parliament itself. He didn't much like the Republic and his entourage supported him.

He was surrounded by a clerical-reactionary clique of singular ideas. They were no republicans. They burned incense under Pétain's nose, spinning glory out of icons and postage stamps.

"I don't say they were all idiots, or mal-intentioned, but they were apprentices, and I had to fix up their gaffes, their errors, which cost France dear."

"Well," he told Jaffré, "I tell you all this to show the climate I had to work in. Do you think it was fun? Between the types of Paris, who wanted the French to march in goose step and those at Vichy who ate Freemasons for lunch and dinner, removed mayors from their chairs, and suppressed the General Councils, who's the real republican? I ask you."

He then subsided. "When I see how history is written," he said, "it disgusts me."[19]

10

The Trial, October 5, 1945[1]

The trial of Pierre Laval would have in any case provided ample sensations. It was, after all, the trial of four years of history, among the darkest in the long history of France. It was the trial of a man who had held the highest offices in the state and was now on trial for his life. It was the trial of a man who had been fiercely independent, who had not courted popularity, and who had aroused strong passions.

All of this would have guaranteed an avid following of his trial by the curious, the concerned, and the genuinely involved in this judgment, it then seemed, of history.

This was magnified many times by the extraordinary events of the day before, the absence of the defense lawyers, the passionate declarations of Pierre Laval, and his violent clashes with the court, leading to his temporary removal and then to his expulsion from the hearing room. For the knowledgeable jurors, for the lawyers who were keenly aware of the drama being enacted in their accustomed halls, there was more to ponder: the manner in which the preliminary instruction had been curtailed and Pierre Laval had been cut off by the court, refused the opportunity to plead his case, and refused any extension of time to prepare for trial, and the unrestrained bias of the jurors, the presiding judge's protestations of virtue and concern for the rights of the defendant notwithstanding.

It was natural to speculate on the course of events. Would Laval return to the court? Would his lawyers make their appearance and would they plead their case?

At noon on October 5 these questions were, for the time answered. Laval took his place and the three defense counsel, Naud, Baraduc and Jaffré were seated at the defense bench.[2] They wore the attire of their order, black gowns and a white scarf that fell from the collar, a crisp accent to the somber robes.

Lawyers had not rushed forward to represent an unpopular defendant. Joseé Laval had counseled with the head of the Paris bar, the Batonnier Poignard who was punctilious in his duty despite a remarkable resemblance to Adolf Hitler. It was Poignard who recommended Baraduc. Second in his class of advocates, he was the son of a Chatelguyon doctor, known to be an admirer of Pierre Laval. Baraduc in turn nominated Naud, who had been first among his colleagues in the 1934-35 class of advocates. Active in the Resistance, he was a total stranger to Laval. Baraduc quickly became an intimate of the Laval family, the cherished friend of René de Chambrun. Naud always maintained a certain reserve, while Baraduc was more affected by the seductive powers of Pierre Laval.

These were brilliant lawyers. They were not the reigning stars of the Paris bar, nor were they experienced criminal defense lawyers. But neither their competence nor their devotion to their cause and their calling could be questioned.

They were a trio of contrasts. Naud was square faced, bespectacled, with a receding hair-line that added years to his age. Baraduc's dark hair, his aquiline nose, clean-cut features and his mobility of expression contrasted with Naud's stolidity. Jaffré's dark good looks commanded attention. His youthful inexperience was increasingly balanced by his total absorption in the proceedings and by his growing devotion to Pierre Laval.

The task of defense counsel would have been difficult in any case. It was complicated by the fact that their client was a brilliant lawyer with an intellect of the first order and an immense experience in the worlds of government and law, not to mention that he, of all people, possessed the most intimate knowledge of the facts of his case and the background against which those facts had played out.

He was, moreover, a man of immense self-confidence. In any discussion of the defense, his would be a commanding voice.

"I note with pleasure" the presiding judge said, opening the session at noon on October 5, "that the accused is here in the presence of his defense counsel. I have a few words for Pierre Laval. What I have to say is contrary to what I said yesterday. It is, and this is important, at the unanimous request of the jury and of the High Court. They wish to show their will to assure you a justice broad and free and in no way to limit the rights of the defense. So I have decided that you may attend this session, respond to my interrogation and furnish all the explanations you wish."[2]

These were eloquent words. Would Mongibeaux abide by them? His next statement offered cold comfort to the defendant.

"But I warn you for the last time. You don't have the right to make trouble. If you raise your voice, if you cause a demonstration like the regrettable incident of yesterday evening I will use all the powers of law at my command. And these means you all know. I can continue the hearing in your absence and pass judgment on you even if you're not here."[3]

"That said, what have you to say, Maitre Naud?"

"Your Honor, on the behalf of the defense, I have a declaration to make."

"Please proceed."

"We have been charged by M. le Batonnier with the defense of Pierre Laval. We feel it is both an honor and a responsibility. We thought it would be a long trial, a very great trial for you to judge. But inevitably, after your judgment, in the months, in the years to come, history will pass its own judgment."[4]

Counsel and the defendant were agreed on this point. But it was not without danger. France had passed through total military defeat, occupation, collaboration and had finally been redeemed, far more by the sacrifices and efforts of others than by its own, and whether in this moment France was ready to face the truth of its history of the war years or whether it preferred to adopt a more heroic version remained to be seen.

Naud related his first visit to Bouchardon who had presided over the Commission of Inquiry, and the assurances defense counsel had received that the procedure would be a long one, given its importance. They had been surprised, he told the court, by the abrupt termination of the preliminary examination. They understood clearly that it would be impossible for them to make out the defense that was required both by the honor of their profession and the importance of their case.

Naud continued in even tones. "There was no dossier. It was said yesterday—I have the transcript— that we had every opportunity to consult the files. With respect, this was less than exact." Baraduc would, he said, outline the other difficulties defense counsel faced; they had knowledge of only two of the ten charges in the indictment.[5]

"So we asked the Batonnier to discharge us from our duties." Naud's calm passed into eloquence:

"Certainly gentlemen, we knew better than anyone that you must never leave a defendant, whoever he may be, without a defense. We knew that. We had to, I cannot hide it from you, we had to protest publicly, so that the public would know that this trial did not meet the standard of true justice—lawyers without a dossier in a trial of this importance."[6]

The Batonnier had in fact discharged them. And yesterday, defense counsel had submitted their letter to the Court—Naud phrased all this with great deference—in which they stated, with infinite regret, that they could not take part in the trial. There was nothing in the letter, not a nuance, that involved any disrespect for the Court. It was nothing personal. But they had to say, and say it to the public, that it was a matter of conscience.

"They say Pierre Laval is a lawyer. But a lawyer and defendant may look at things very differently. He is subject to long interrogations and his material conditions are worse than those of a common criminal, a smaller cell, dark, a table as big as my briefcase. He has to sit on the floor to arrange his documents, in the obscurity of a cave."[7]

A juror interrupted: "We have known that, too."

Naud continued: "Under long interrogations, he is defending his honor, and, alas, his life, terribly depressed, and physically subjected to cruel strains."

"And us?" The juror replied.

"You are the judges," Laval calmly said.[8]

It was counsel's duty, Naud said, to be at the side of the defendant. He again expressed his respect for the Court. When the judge had yesterday ordered them to appear, they had not received the summons; they had only a letter from the Batonnier whose permission they asked to read it to the Court.

Mongibeaux stiffened. "Do you ask *me* for permission to read it?"

"We ask you, too," Naud answered. This was a petty matter of form, but Mongibeaux was clearly upset.

"You must," he sniffed, "have a certain respect for justice which I believe I represent here."

Naud was conciliatory. He had only wished, he said, to ask permission of the author of the letter to read it, and then immediately after that the authorization of the Court. Mongibeaux was not mollified. "I would rather see counsel's respect shown in acts, not words," he grumbled.

"I will authorize the reading of the letter," he said, "but only on the condition that you remember your advocate's oath and that you proceed with decency and moderation."

Naud was not in a mood to accept this implied reprimand. "I don't think I've ever lacked decency and moderation," he maintained.[9]

"That's for me to say, not for you," Mongibeaux retorted.

"Enough, Naud," Batonnier Poignard interjected. Naud obeyed. "I read the letter."[10]

Poignard's letter addressed to the defense counsel responded to their request to be relieved of their duties. The Batonnier recalled the promises of the preliminary examination, its abrupt termination when most of the charges and the indictment had never been the subjects of interrogation. Then there was the denial of documents and witnesses vital to the defense case. Poignard had himself addressed these concerns to the President of the Commission of Inquiry. The only result had been a supplemental inquiry which, however, had failed to relate to any of the principal accusations of the indictment. Nor had the hopes of counsel for a delay in the trial date been realized.

He lauded the scruples of defense counsel which were, the Batonnier wrote, in the highest traditions of the bar and their respect for the rights of the accused, whoever he might be. He then reminded defense counsel of the rule that required that a defense be provided to the accused. Having paid respect to the two opposing views of the duty of the defense, Poignard had declared that it was impossible to substitute new counsel and had admonished them to proceed, "with moderation but with firmness," on the course they judged best. In other words, he left defense counsel to their own devices.[11]

Naud now took the floor. "The indictment contains allegations of crimes committed many years before the 1939-1940 war. So a long preliminary examination was absolutely necessary. And Counselor Beteille promised us twenty-five sessions. Because the indictment has thirty-two separate charges.

"But the examination was abruptly cut off. The defendant is charged with a plot against the security of the state. But he has never been interrogated about the circumstances and conditions leading to the National Assembly vote of July 1940."

"My client is charged with intelligence with the enemy. But he has never been examined on his meeting with Hitler at Montoire or his negotiations with the Germans."

Naud did not hesitate to take risks. "What could explain the statements of the Presiding Judge that the case had to be finished before the elections? We read it in the papers, just as we read in the papers that the preliminary examination had been terminated."

Witnesses had been deposed of which defense counsel had neither notice nor knowledge. They had no copies of essential documents and there were others which had been locked in M. Beteille's cabinet while he was on vacation. They had been unable to draw up lists of witnesses.

This was Naud's opportunity to lay these matters out fully, not so much for the Court, as for the jury. Having laid a foundation, he now asked for a new and augmented preliminary examination and, and this was the point, a continuance of the case to a date which would allow defense counsel to make out their defense.

He closed with renewed assurances that the failure of counsel to appear the day before had not been out of disrespect— which he had never in his career shown to a Court— but out of dignity and a sense of duty.

"We have made a grave decision, not to be disobliging, not to be disrespectful to the court—that was never our intention. And it was certainly not with gaiety in our hearts that we have declined to appear at the bar."[12]

"For the first time in a career that has been without reproach, I do not appear at the bar. And I have a question to ask you. Don't you want the light, all the light to be shone on this trial? It's an exceptional case. I don't for the moment say whether Pierre Laval is right or wrong. Whether he is a traitor or whether he isn't. We are dealing with four years of history, of dramatic history, and it needs the light. Why not let the defendant explain his policies, his politics. We've only seen the most violent external mani- festations. If we look carefully, there may be surprises. Why not make this a truly great trial. Our country has recovered its equilibrium, its institutions, let it also recover its taste for liberty, the right to conduct a grand trial. I am proud of my country. Why should we take lessons from others in liberty and justice? I want the world to see true justice in the country I love."

"I want Pierre Laval to have the same rights of defense as the monsters of Belsen." Which could be accomplished, he said, "in a trial that is clear and luminous and shows France and the world what France has been for four years under the leadership of this man." He sat down.[13]

Baraduc then rose to second Naud's professions of respect for the Court and the jury.[14] He repeated the tale of the difficulties and deficien- cies with which defense counsel had faced. He renewed the appeal to history. Defense counsel were realists and realism required a delay in the proceedings.

Baraduc now ventured into more sensitive territory. They had been surprised by the press reports of Mongibeaux's statement about the tim- ing of the trial. Perhaps it was because Baraduc was younger than Naud, perhaps more impressionable that he dared more. They had wondered for a month he said, who had given the order that the trial be sabotaged.

He did not pause to take in the shock he had caused. He finished with a flourish: "Now we know. The trial has to be done before we vote." The implication was clear. The court was under orders and the orders came from De Gaulle.[15]

The presiding judge had opened the session with one retraction. Rather than anger, his response now was an effort to make a record more favorable to him. He was agile.

"I never spoke in the sense that defense counsel understood. I only thanked the jurors for their service. I knew they were very much concerned with the elections and active in their districts. All I meant to do, the case being ready for trial, was to balance the interest of the jurors as jurors and as electors and to let them know of my concern. And that's all I said.

Baraduc was unmoved. "So the press lied."

"The press didn't lie," Mongibeaux replied, "It's a matter of interpretation."

Baraduc stood his ground. "All we knew came from the papers, like the closing of the pretrial examination."

"Enough of these incidents," Mongibeaux declared, "It's irrelevant."

Baraduc was stubborn: "It isn't an incident, it's a fact."

Mongibeaux had had enough: "I have never taken orders."[16]

Mornet was not about to be outdone in virtue. "At my age, in retirement, I don't have to take orders from any minister. I'm here only because I was asked. Let no one suspect my independence for an instant."

Baraduc disclaimed any such suspicion. But in a high stakes political trial, he said, you had to read the papers and the press talked of orders.

"No one gave me orders," Mongibeaux insisted.[17]

"I never gave you orders," said, Laval, the sometime prime minister.[18]

"Except yesterday," Mongibeaux rejoined tartly.

This was a profitless colloquy insofar as any relief might be forthcoming from the Court. But if the appeal to fairness could touch some of the jurors or only a few...

The Court, Baraduc said, faced a grave decision. The election would determine the country's future. The Court's decision would also show the world what French justice was.

"Are they going to whitewash Laval after the election?" a juror speculated aloud.[19]

Mornet had had enough of this. He had a speech, he proclaimed, that he had long been awaited the opportunity to make. Those who looked in the trial for a search for the truth would have found only disappointment as Mornet spoke:

"The trial here is not simply the trial of a man, but of a policy, a policy—I don't hesitate to use the word—a criminal policy, a policy encapsulated in one man who is here before you.The defense has complained they lack the necessary files and documents. But it's six weeks since Pierre Laval returned to France and everything was open to his lawyers. If they had any problem, they had only to address the President of the Commission of Inquiry or one of the Attorneys General and everything would have been provided.[20]

"What are the essential documents. They are the radio speeches of Pierre Laval, his governmental acts, the laws he signed from July, 1940 until December, 1940 when he was vice president of the Council and since April, 1942 when he was President of the Council and head of government. All the evidence, all the documents are public. It is contemporary history and we are its victims. You have seen it all. The preliminary examination has been public, for all France and it has been going on for five years.

"The hour of justice has sounded for Petain two months after he set foot on French soil. It will sound for Pierre Laval."[21]

"Here is the real charge against Pierre Laval. His was a policy that not only oppressed France, but it made France the accomplice of the oppressor and dishonored France in the eyes of the world."

This went, of course, to the heart of the defense. What had been said in the speeches and in the circulars and under what circumstances, and to what end, and why should they be deemed criminal? Mornet claimed it was the words and the acts themselves that constituted the crime without consideration of intent, which is at the heart of criminal law, or the effect, which measures its consequences. To the contrary, it was the conviction of Pierre Laval and his defense that his acts had as their purpose to protect and defend France and the French from as much evil as could be, given the means were feeble and the occupier strong.

What was there to examine, Mornet asked? The words were there, they weren't contested. What remained was to debate them in open court. The examination had closed in fact in August, 1944, at the Liberation and judicially in October, 1945. To the jurors he addressed a simple word: "Jugez," Judge.[22]

Naud rose to reply. He covered familiar ground, the examination, the charges remaining in the indictment, and recounted those the court had dismissed. The attorney general had asked what need there was for witnesses, for documents, when everything was well known. "That was a little summary" Naud told Mornet. "You relied on what the lawyers knew of all these events. If the Court knows no more than the lawyers, then I tremble for justice."[23]

The Court retired to deliberate. It returned in forty-five minutes and issued its ruling. It found that the High Court was competent to hear the case, that the jury had been impaneled and that therefore the Court had no power to reopen the preliminary examination. The accused could make his explanations at trial. There would be no delay in the proceeding. The trial would continue.

The accused was ordered to rise to continue his interrogation. If he were fatigued, the Court added, he could remain seated.[24]

11

The Trial, October 5, 1945[1]

When the hearing resumed[2] Laval knew that relief must be found outside the Court in which he was being tried. He must look elsewhere, and he did. He had, he said, written to the Garde des Sceaux, the Keeper of the Seals, which is in France the title given to the Minister of Justice.[3] It was an office he had once held. He had pleaded the premature termination of his preliminary examination and the importance of his trial. The other audience who might bring influence to bear on his behalf was the public. He asked Mornet to ask the Garde des Sceaux, his superior, to publish the trial proceedings in the *Official Journal* (*Journal Officiel de la République Française*), as had been done for the trial of Marshal Petain. Otherwise the only people to know about the trial would be the spectators in the courtroom and those who might read articles in such papers as chose to print them.

"If I ask for the *Official Journal*," he told the Court, "it's because I don't fear the light. What I fear is the camouflage," -he chose his words carefully to avoid the sanctions that had been threatened—"camouflage that obscures the light. I fear the darkness. I want to present my case in the full light of day, before an informed public."[4]

He again reviewed the documents, the witnesses, the facilities he needed to defend himself. If the only examination were to be in the public hearing, as the presiding judge had suggested, then it was all the more important that those proceedings be made public in the *Official Journal*.

Mongibeaux's answer had not been reassuring. There were stenographers present; a record was being made. But for whom and how, Laval asked, could it compare to the circulation and the authority of the *Official Journal*?

Laval persisted in his plea. "What have you to fear from the truth? I said yesterday I would answer any questions, because I have nothing to hide, nothing to hide when I have served my country.[5]

The Presiding Judge cut Laval off. "I will continue the interrogation we started yesterday." He reviewed several issues: A speech Laval had made at Mayet-et-Montagne, the statements of one de Lapommeraye, a statement about initiating the "national revolution." He would then move on to the National Assembly proceedings of July 10, 1940 and how the constitutional acts had been drawn up, how they had been passed and what they contained.[6]

Laval did not accept Mongibeaux's resumé. "I never said what was attributed to me in the *Petit Parisien* at Mayet-et-Montagne." There had been reference the day before to the deposition of a M. Boivin-Champeaux. He had never seen it, nor had his lawyers. Could he see it? Could the presiding judge read it to him. He would pass it on to defense counsel, Mongibeaux said dismissively.[7]

Mornet now stepped in: "If you disagree about what you said at Mayet-et-Montagne," Mornet offered, "I won't use it. It's that simple." "But you already have," Baraduc replied. "I won't use it," Mornet persisted. "I have lots of others." "I don't want to answer it," Laval said grimly. "I want to destroy it."[8]

Mornet moved on: "Then commenced the swindle of the Releve." This was a program for the release of French prisoners of war in exchange for French workers for German factories. It was a swindle because two months later at Compiegne, the same Laval, after insisting on Germany's need for manpower, had added "As to the liberation of the prisoners, their hour will sound in the day of the German victory."[9]

Laval insisted that he had told Bouchardon that the phrase was false. He had never said it. Here, printed, was what he had truly said that day:

> I wanted to give words of hope to those in the prisoner or war camps. There are yet 1,200,000 and France awaits them with a natural impatience. Their presence is indispensable because they represent a vital force in our country. There were nearly 2,000,000 in the camps at the time of the Armistice. Many thousands had been released. But there are laws of war that have unhappy consequences and the captivity of the prisoners until the signature of a peace treaty is one of them.

"Where is the analogy," he asked, "between those words and the phrase of which I am accused? All I said was what was plainly a part of the Armistice itself."

Three important accusations had been made, Laval said, in a single session: the testimony of Boivin-Champeaux, which he had never seen; a phrase at Compiegne which he had never uttered, and a phrase at Mayet-et-Montagne which he had most certainly never pronounced.

"I'm absolutely bewildered," he told the Court, "by the frivolity of these proceedings. I don't want to use any other term—because I remember vividly your amiable words at the beginning." This was a reference to the Court's threats of sanctions. "I'm talking, you may be sure, with decency, and if my speech is sometimes a trifle lively, permit me to say"—here he paused- "that I have reasons to be deeply affected by the way this trial is proceeding."[10]

He now drew the Court's attention to a distinction that was at the heart of his defense. What was the borderline between an act and a crime? He was accused of a circular of July 12, 1943. It contained penalties against doctors who gave false certificates to workers who had been drafted for labor in German factories. The penalty was severe—the right to practice medicine. There were penalties for parents, too.

This introduced the whole issue of Laval's part in the program of furnishing French labor to Germany. Had he signed the circular? "If it shows my signature," Laval replied, "then I signed it. But that isn't the question you ought to ask. Why did I sign it? I can understand that question. That's what a preliminary examination is for. But no one ever asked me that."

He had little hope in the Presiding Judge, none in the Attorney General. He still nourished shreds of hope in the jury to whom he now turned his attention. Could he revive the ingratiating, the seductive spell he had so often before cast?

"Yesterday I heard words from jurors which hurt me deeply. But I didn't object. They spoke in good faith. If a juror said it, it was because he believed it."

"All I ask is that you reserve your judgment until you have heard the case. I have recused no one. I have been warned there would be jurors who were stirred by passion. That's only human. I accepted the strange decision to proceed with such haste." He again reviewed the difficulties, the obstacles that had been placed in his way. He would do his best to help them to understand his case. "I hope," he finished, "you will have a different opinion than when you first came here."[11]

Pierre Laval had made his appeal to the jury. He had raised a critical issue. He now responded to the statement of the presiding judge about the issues surrounding the meeting of the National Assembly of July 10, 1940 which had transferred the powers of the Third Republic to the new regime of Marshal Pétain and his part in them.[12]

It will be useful to the reader, at this point in this account of the trial, once again to review briefly how the transition from the Third Republic to the Vichy regime of Marshal Pétain came about.

The Armistice had been signed in June 1940 by the fast-fading government of the Third Republic. Both houses of Parliament, the Chamber of Deputies and the Senate, had been convened on July 9, 1940. Parliament possessed the sole constitutional power to convene a joint National Assembly which alone could change or abrogate the 1875 Constitution of the Third Republic. Whether and how that might be done had obviously been the urgent subject of continuing discussions among the members of Parliament now established in Vichy. The issue, then, was what kind of a government a defeated and conquered France should have under the German domination.

The two chambers of Parliament had voted on July 9, by overwhelming majorities, to convene the National Assembly. It had, in turn, on July 10, adopted the acts by which the Third Republic transferred its powers to the new regime of Marshal Pétain.

What part had Laval played in all of this? He had certainly been a leader of those who called for a National Assembly. More than that, he had been Pétain's delegate to the National Assembly who made a brilliant and comprehensive presentation in favor of Pétain and his regime. He had appealed to the members on the issues dearest to them and the emotions deepest within their hearts. He had made an appeal to every party and to every interest. For the nation, to mollify the consequences of the disaster, to spur the determination to see it through, he had resorted to the appeal to national pride.

For the right, he had spoken of the perfidy of Britain and the need to restore patriotism to its rightful place. The proposed new constitution, he had said, might be authoritarian, but from the social point of view it was humane and generous while not permitting the authority of the state to be mocked.

For the liberals and the left, he had given assurances that the new constitution would not be reactionary. Labor would be given its rights, its real rights under the impartial control of the state.

He had then struck the note that resonated so deeply across the stricken France of 1940-reverence for Marshal Pétain. France, he said, had the good fortune, indeed the happiness, to have at its head a victorious soldier of the First World War, the hero of Verdun, a Marshal of France behind whom they could join to assure the well-being of the country.

All of this had been met by prolonged applause and an affirmative vote for the new regime of 569 to 80 including a majority of Laval's political opponents of the Socialist and Radical Socialist parties.

Given the profound respect amounting to reverence in which Pétain was almost universally held, Laval's most effective weapon had been a letter from the Marshal delegating to him the task of passing the new arrangements which had already been approved by Pétain's Council of Ministers.

The National Assembly had then voted to entrust to Pétain the promulgation of a new constitution in these terms:

> The National Assembly grants all the powers of the government of the Republic, under the authority and signature of Marshal Pétain, to promulgate by one or more acts a new constitution of the French state.

> The Constitution shall guarantee the rights of work, of the family and of the country. It will be ratified by the assemblies it creates.

This was accomplished the next day by the Cabinet which adopted three constitutional acts. The first appointed Pétain head of state in the place of the resigned President Lebrun. The second granted Petain full legislative and executive powers until a new Constitution should be adopted. But he could not declare war without the assent of both houses of Parliament and this was critical to France's relationship, both with Germany and with Britain. The third constitutional act provided that the Senate and the Chamber would remain in being until the assemblies of a new constitution should be established, upon which they would be adjourned until further notice.

The Parliament of the Third Republic lived, but in a state of suspended animation. The new constitution could only be promulgated based on a popular vote and ratified by the new assemblies.

The final step in the process was the fourth constitutional act adopted July 12, 1940. It appointed Laval the Marshal's successor. This, then, was the train of events that now occupied the attention of the Court.

Laval recounted the letter of authorization from the Marshal. He wanted it, he told the Court, to make clear that the text of the acts submitted to the National Assembly was the Marshal's, not his. This was disingenuous. The text surely bore the marks of Laval's head and practiced hand.[13]

But why, he then asked, had the National Assembly been convened? The old constitution had served France well. Why had those who had earlier been so eloquent in its defense been so silent in July, 1940?[14] He himself had prepared no response to the defenders of the Republic who might render it a final salute. But he didn't need to. He recalled two comparable events. Extraordinary powers had been granted to Prime Minister Daladier on the declaration of war in 1939. And he added this: "If the Constitution of 1875, that you accuse me of destroying, was so sacrosanct, then how can it be that on October 21 and October 22 next the exact question will be posed to the voters whether, under what form and by what means the Constitution should be modified."[15]

They might ask him: why had it all been done so quickly, perhaps too quickly, in 1940. To that he had replied that the circumstances were extraordinary. They were at Vichy, not Paris. The members of Parliament were in almost continuous session. They had assembled in ample numbers; there was no issue of a quorum.[16]

And the votes had been overwhelming. In the Chamber on July 9 the vote had been 395 to 3 and at least two of them were on the jury. In the Senate the vote was 229 to 1 and the only adverse vote was cast by the Marquis de Chambrun. He was, Laval said, genuinely baffled by this accusation of the court. His bafflement gave rise to new heights of indignation. His eyes flashed; he raised his arms up to the heavens. The members of Parliament had all voted for the convening of the National Assembly the next day. They all knew the constitutional acts would be submitted to it. Those acts had been widely discussed. The members were well informed. It was said they had voted out of fear; but they hadn't feared to vote. Six hundred and twenty-four in all, they had voted to convene the National Assembly and only four against, and he alone of all of them was charged with treason under the death penalty.[17]

The presiding judge now made another major concession. He had earlier pronounced the exclusion from the charges of all matters preceding the 1939 war. He had excluded the matter of the Armistice in which Laval had no part. He now said: "I don't charge you with the vote on the constitutional law. I only charge you with the abuse of it."[18]

With exaggerated courtesy Laval replied, "You are becoming kinder and kinder. I thank you. I'm glad to exchange explanations with you. You tell me that you don't charge me with the vote on the constitutional law. Let's put that in the record, because up till now it hasn't been. The indictment still talks about intrigues, menaces, maneuvers, and promises."[19]

"I'll tell you exactly what the charge is," Mornet stepped in. "It's about what you have properly termed the hijacking of the law voted on July 10. You were part of the hijacking as vice president of the Council."

Laval knew an opening when he saw one.

"Ooh la la, gentlemen," he told them. "I'm winning on the first question but you don't want my defense to succeed, so you're trying to hook me on something else. But you'll see M. Attorney General, that we're in agreement there too."[20]

A juror had a question, all the more interesting because the juror had been a member of the National Assembly. The question was whether in meetings at the Petit Casino before the vote of the National Assembly, Laval had promised members of Parliament government jobs or membership on certain Parliamentary committees if they voted for the government's bill. Indeed, hadn't he said that there were able members of Parliament who would make excellent prefects in the place of mediocre officeholders.[21]

Laval fielded this question with ease. He was not in the least embarrassed by it. He had said that members of Parliament could be called on for advice, and if some of them had no further work in government, other work could be found for them. To a veteran politician, that hardly seemed shocking and he described at length the system of pay and allowances for members of Parliament. He had wanted to carry on those payments under the new regime.

He said he regretted that Pétain hadn't taken his advice about the abilities of the members of Parliament. There were members who had been appointed prefects or regional prefects, or ambassadors, and they had all done well. So he could answer: there was nothing shocking about that and he was only sorry that more of these men, men of ability and experience hadn't been used.

Laval was happy to discuss the mechanics of the new government. "Pétain had received a mandate to frame a new constitution. Nobody thought then that the Occupation would last four years. I thought Pétain would promptly tackle his constitutional task, appointing committees to prepare a draft for the Cabinet. And there was such a committee, eighty members strong, headed by M. de Courtois with Boivin-Champeaux as reporter. I appeared before it and I told them that the new constitution ought to be written in the accustomed spirit of France's constitutional laws and that there ought to be strict control of public spending."[22]

He had no problem in answering the juror. In fact, he had explained to the Marshal how important it was to carry out the engagements made in his name—and made with his full knowledge.

He was baffled, he told the Court, once more, that he was being charged as much for trying to fulfill the engagements he had made to his colleagues, the senators and deputies, at the National Assembly, among them never to adopt a constitution outside the spirit of the law, as for trying to protect his country against German oppression.

He returned to his principal theme. The two chambers had been regularly convened and had voted. The National Assembly was convoked in accordance with the law. There could be no question of that and no question or protest was ever raised.

But there had been demonstrations in the gallery of the National Assembly, the juror Biondi insisted. He had been there. He wouldn't say, Laval replied, that it hadn't been an emotional scene, that the atmosphere wasn't feverish. That wasn't his fault. What was incontestable was that the proceedings were regular and only eighty members of Parliament had voted against the constitutional law, 569 for.[23]

And was there anyone, he asked, who thought that by their vote they were about to suppress the very idea of a republic? "If that had been true," Laval thundered, "I would never have gone before the Assembly as the Marshal's spokesman."[24]

He paid his respects to the Resistance: "Everybody knows that the Resistance started up almost at once. There were those who got to London by whatever means."

"But I speak of those who remained in France. Nobody, Your Honor, nobody made any protest against the Armistice. They deplored the tragedy it had brought France; they deplored the harshness of the terms. I said yesterday that ninety percent of the French supported the Armistice. But I've seen in the papers..." He paused here for a brief digression. His trial, he said, was a trial of public opinion. He had to know how he was being depicted in the press. Yet he was permitted only two newspapers a day and forbidden to keep them.[25]

He had seen it said in the papers permitted to him that 99 percent of the French had supported the Armistice. "Were they competent? Competent enough to say the military leaders were competent enough to decide."

The presiding judge once again tried to stem the flood of Laval's oratory. "You realize that I've let you explain as long as you like."

"I was talking of the Armistice because it's in the indictment. No one is doing me any favors." The prosecution might formally have dropped the charge, but what did the jury think?

Laval again insisted that no one at the National Assembly had charged him with the responsibility for the Armistice. How could they lay on his shoulders a decision that had been taken by others. If he had been chief of state and had believed the Armistice necessary, no force would have stopped him from making that decision. It would simply have been his duty. He essayed a flight of eloquence. In the country of Descartes, he declared, reason and truth ought to be upheld.[26]

"And the truth," he said, "is simple. To blame me for the Armistice is not simply an injustice, it is worse than an injustice. It is an offense against the truth."[27]

And why blame him for the convening of the National Assembly. Why not blame Pétain; why not blame the members of Parliament who had sat there?

He said he would talk later about the abuses of the new regime. But he wanted to make this clear. The idea of the National Assembly hadn't necessarily been his. It had been discussed in the cabinet. Even the Socialists had taken part in the discussion. "It wasn't a bill that we wrote on the corner of a table that I had in my pocket, and that I brought secretly to the National Assembly."[28]

He couldn't seem to say it often enough. "I had no means of pressure, of seduction, to exert on the members of Parliament. If they voted in response to my bill, it was because they didn't think they could do otherwise. They acted out of high patriotic sentiments. They never thought to put an end to the Republic but they thought in that dramatic moment of the history of France, not of themselves, but of France."

"They thought their vote would facilitate the negotiation with the Germans, lighten the burdens of the Occupation. These were noble sentiments. Maybe the eighty who voted No foresaw the abuse of the constitutional laws. But nobody thought they voted to overthrow the Republic. That remained to the imagination of M. de Lapommeraye."

He now uttered a profound comment on history, as it is written, as it is read. "The attitudes of men today, in 1945, are very different from what they were under the Occupation. It's a little lesson in psychology—a bit late, but"—and one can imagine the irony he felt when he spoke—"singularly instructive."[29]

The juror Chaussy had another question. Hadn't Laval heard it said that the eighty who voted against the government bill wouldn't sleep in their beds that night. No, Laval replied, he'd never heard that at Vichy. What they did say was that there was a French division at Clermont-Ferrand that threatened a putsch. And what had he done and said? He had taken the floor to say he would defend the civil power, all to the immense acclaim of the members.[30]

He thanked M. Chaussy for his question, always a good forensic move. Another juror, Bedin rejoined: "But the evil was done." "And you were the head of government," the Presiding Judge added, "You were a Minister of State."

Laval's patience snapped: "Listen to me, M. Presiding Judge. It's better for me to tell you the facts. Because I was there."[31]

He went on to explain. In the new regime there were two vice presidents of the Council and the other was Camille Chautemps. Yes, Laval had been a minister of state but without portfolio. That is to say, he had no department under his direction. "You could ask Herriot. You could ask Tardieu. They were ministers of state and what did they call the post? They called it a decorative vase." He had no function and only such influence as he could bring to bear on Pétain. Pétain, he claimed, had rarely consulted him. He had his own circle. Laval named them. They were always there. They were the ones who had influence. And if he offered his advice in council, it was often rejected and an opposite course taken.

He now leveled his best argument: "If I had so much influence on Pétain, why was I so rudely dismissed from his government on December 13, 1940?"[32]

12

The Trial, October 5, 1945[1]

Pierre Laval acknowledged that he had made broad claims in court that he lacked influence or standing in the Pétain regime. It was natural for the Attorney General to view such claims with suspicion. How, he asked, did it happen that the day after the adoption of the constitutional acts, Laval had been named Pétain's successor or, as he put it more elegantly, his heir presumptive.[2]

Laval was glad to tell his story. Pétain at the time had been eighty-four or eighty-five. He could die or be incapacitated. There had to be some recognition of this in the constitutional acts and, Laval maintained, had he written into these laws that in the case of Pétain's death or disability, he, Laval, would succeed him, he was certain that Parliament would have agreed. But no such language had been proposed and no question had been raised in Parliament. He had presented the constitutional acts to Parliament as Pétain's spokesman.[3]

"And you're astonished that I was designated in the acts," he challenged Mornet. "Do I lack modesty? Maybe. But at that moment no other name was raised. And if the Marshal died, everything would have to be reconsidered, all the more so under the problems of the Occupation."[4]

They could believe it or not. What he had offered in the constitutional debates was not promises, but in essence opinions. He had, after all, been in Parliament for thirty years. He knew the game. He knew the players, and if he had been called upon to succeed the Marshal, he would have enjoyed the solid support of Parliament.

From time to time Laval's patience exploded into a surge of indignation, not without a certain tinge of self-pity.

"Why do you reproach me?" he asked. "Because there was the Occupation, because I'm in a tight spot, because today somebody has to shoulder the responsibility for our misfortunes. I'm accused of things I ought not to be. What I invoke as my defense is used against me. But my attitude at the National Assembly was perfectly correct. My attitude when the Marshal signed his constitutional acts was perfectly correct. And I didn't do it to become the successor."[5]

"You were not only the successor," Mongibeaux said, "but the vice president." That meant nothing, Laval insisted. Either you were prime minister or you weren't. A prime minister, was somebody. A minister without portfolio was nobody.

"But," Mongibeaux insisted, "you were the beneficiary of the whole operation. On the surface it was Marshal Pétain, but you were the artisan of it all."[6]

"The beneficiary," Laval exploded, "The beneficiary of what? The beneficiary of unhappiness, the beneficiary of disaster?"

"The beneficiary of power," Mongibeaux said simply.

"The beneficiary of power?" Why, Laval asked, hadn't those who were responsible for the defeat taken on the delicate task of representing France in the face of the Occupant? "No, all I did was to try in good faith to help my country and in circumstances and for reasons I'd be glad to explain."

"You had a policy of entente with Germany," Mongibeaux insisted. "You returned to power to carry out that policy and you did it under German control."[6]

"That's the accusation," Laval replied. "But it's not what I thought."

"There were things," Laval said, "that I never accepted. I'm too proud of being French to accept the supremacy of any other country over mine. I accept only that my country should be on an equal footing with any others. France is unhappy today, but it will recover. It has known many hard periods—everyone knows the history of France—but to imagine that it was my idea to put France in the tow of Germany, to lay down its arms, the hegemony of Germany—I know its inferiority complex and I know the prestige of France. I know the condition of Europe today. We have a long way to go to put France back on its feet. But I never conceived the idea that Germany would be the mistress of my country and that we would be at its disposal."[7]

The Presiding Judge had a line he wished to pursue. Hadn't the accused said in his deposition that in 1940 no man of good sense could doubt the definitive victory of Germany?

The shaft struck home. But Laval was resourceful in deflecting it. "You want to charge me with everything at the same time. What I was discussing was the National Assembly."[8]

Mongibeaux accepted Laval's plea and returned to the use that had been made of the constitutional acts. How could anyone believe, Laval insisted, that he would accept Germany hegemony. There should never be, he said, any one country in Europe that could dominate all of the others. Any great country had a part to play and France could play its part in an entente to limit German power.

Laval turned to the jurors. Did they, he asked, wish a recess?[9]

Mongibeaux was clearly offended. He repeated Laval's question and immediately answered that the session would continue until five P.M.

He now turned to Laval whose appeal to the jury had irritated him. "I won't go so far as sanctions," he said, "but try to keep a tone in this hearing without that allure, without that intimacy, that *plaisanterie*, that bantering tone for which there is no place in this hall of justice."[10]

"I'll try to follow your counsel," Laval smiled, "But there are certain facts I can't tell without putting them in the right light."

"I see," Mongibeaux replied, "You can strike a picturesque note from time to time, but, as much as possible, not in that tone of familiarity, of mockery" adding sternly, "We're now at the constitutional acts."

What, precisely, were the charges? It was the second day of the trial and so far the only crime charged was the act of succession.

"That's not the only charge," Mornet said, "There are lots of others."[11]

Laval again raised the plea of proper procedure. He couldn't answer to everything at the same time. The only question then before the Court, was the constitutional acts and the use the Marshal had made of them.

Laval again summed up his position: "I've already explained. There was no surprise. Those acts passed without protest. There were members of Parliament who feared a putsch by General Weygand and the act of succession was designed to reassure them."

But, Laval added, the acts had been ill-used. The law passed by the National Assembly had charged the new government with promulgating in one or more acts, a new constitution of the French state under the signature and authority of the Marshal.

The Marshal had published his acts. "The first phrase," Laval declared "bowled me over: 'We, Phillipe Pétain.' Suddenly I saw that Pétain had abandoned the assurances I had given to the National Assembly. This was the formula for a monarchy and it was far from the spirit in which I had asked the members of the Assembly to vote."[12]

"The Attorney General might ask why I hadn't then and there protested. My honest answer is to go back to that time and place and recall the extent of the Marshal's authority. He was more than a king, more than an emperor. He symbolized France. He was France incarnate. Beside him there was nothing. And if I had made the least protest, it would have blown up not only in the face of the Marshal but in the face of the government. It could only have made matters worse."

"I knew there and then that my Parliamentary colleagues had been fooled. I never saw the acts before they were published, but Pétain had taken all of the powers unto himself."[13]

"Except that he made you vice president," Mornet was quick to add.

"I've already told you," Laval shot back, "The vice president was nothing. Even less than an Attorney General." The proceedings were drowned out in laughter.

Laval once more explained the role of the vice president and of a minister without portfolio as he saw it. He presided over the Cabinet when the prime minister could not. That was all. He had nothing to do. He was a coadjutor. "The coadjutor of an aged bishop," Mornet remarked.

"Yes, a coadjutor," Laval agreed.[14]

But, Mongibeaux insisted, "You were chief of government." Again and again Laval denied it: "I was fifty percent of vice chief of government. There were two vice presidents." The other one, Mornet said, had resigned shortly thereafter.

But, Laval replied, he had never advised the Marshal on the constitutional acts. That had been the work of Pétain's inner circle, notably Rafael Alibert and his Cabinet director, Henri Du Moulin de la Barthete and Alibert wasn't even a political person.

"You never saw the act that named you successor?" the juror Biondi asked. "Yes," Laval said. "They showed me that out of courtesy." But, he said, he would now put this whole succession question to rest.[15]

After he had been dismissed in December, 1940, he said, Admiral Darlan had been named Pétain's successor. When Laval returned to the government in 1942, he claimed he had charge of civil affairs only, one half the responsibility for government and Darlan had the other half as chief of the armed forces. Had he been so infatuated with the title of successor, he could have made it a condition of his return. Instead he had told Darlan not to worry, he had no such pretensions, he had no interest in the succession. The reason was, it was risky. It had probably contributed to his dismissal in 1940.

Then, in 1942 Darlan had gone to North Africa, never to return. So there was a new constitutional act. This time, Laval said, he had been in charge; he wrote out his own concept. Yes, he had been named successor—but only for a period of one month. And more to the point, it was the Cabinet who would choose Pétain's successor, and fix the terms and the prerogatives of the office.

Mornet had heard enough about 1942. He wanted to return to 1940. It will be remembered that he no longer charged Laval with any acts before the war, with any complicity in the Armistice, nor with any responsibility for the action of the National Assembly. The only charge he now leveled was, that Laval had accepted the post of vice president in a regime that abused and traduced the Republic and that he had continued to support constitutional acts in derogation of the legal government. That was the charge he addressed to Laval.

Laval was, as always, voluble in his reply: "I don't understand how by my presence alone in the government I should be held responsible for all of the irregularities committed by the new regime. What would the Senators, what would the Deputies have said if twenty-four or forty-eight hours after the vote of the National Assembly they had been told that the man who had taken responsibility for the vote was leaving because he disagreed with the Marshal?"[16]

"And I had another responsibility. The Marshal was a man wholly without political experience. But he had a taste for power, an immoderate taste for power. I learned that too late. I thought it was my duty as best I could to stop certain acts from happening."[17]

"What a scandal it would have been the next day to say: 'Marshal I don't accept that you begin your acts with "We, Philippe Pétain." I don't accept that you sign constitutional acts without submitting them to the Cabinet. I told Alibert that they should be submitted to the Cabinet, which would have refused the Marshal nothing. But Alibert said no, it was better his way."

Laval had an anecdote to offer. He loved anecdotes. He slipped into that intimate, bantering mode that had upset the Court earlier. "One day I said to Pétain: 'Do you know, M. le Marechal, the extent of your powers?' He said, 'No.' I said, 'They're greater than those of Louis XIV because Louis XIV had to submit his edicts to Parliament and you don't have to submit your constitutional acts to Parliament.' He said to me, 'It's true.'[18]

"The next day I saw the Marshal. He said to me: 'Do you know the extent of my powers?' And he repeated just what I had told him the day before. Yes, he had a taste for power and I wasn't strong enough, I recognize it now, to stop him from exercising it."

When he first saw the Marshal's constitutional acts, he had known they would never be acceptable. "I can't conceive of a reactionary constitution," he said. "France doesn't want it. France won't go back to it."

He had, he said, something even more to the point. He searched his briefcase. The jurors followed the search. He played to them cannily. It became apparent that he wouldn't find the document. He smiled, he shrugged his shoulders, and said that if he had he found it, it would have been magnificent. And again he wheedled appreciative laughter from the sullen jury.

He repeated in a summary way his activities at the National Assembly, how he had said the new constitution must not be reactionary, protecting liberties, protecting labor. But what had hurt him most were not the constitutional acts. He had some little experience with politics and he knew they would not survive long in a free France that would never ratify them.

What was more important was breaking the engagements he had surely given the General Councils. These were important regional governing bodies. The new regime had dismissed the General Councils.

"But you remained in the government," Mornet reminded Laval.

"Yes," Laval replied, "And you know that it was a moment when all of the French administration remained at their posts. Should I, because of the mistakes of others, abandon my duties and flee? No, I thought it my duty to oppose the measure by what feeble means I possessed. And I did protest."

When Mornet posed a question about Montoire, Laval reacted angrily: "I was talking about the National Assembly. The Attorney General is provoking me." "I provoke no one," Mornet replied, equally angry. The Court declared a recess.[19]

When the Court resumed, Laval must have doubted he had made himself clear. He repeated how, when he had returned to government in 1942, Darlan had offered him the succession and he had declined it. He never wished to be the Dauphin. And when Darlan had departed for North Africa, and some provision had to be made for succession in view of the Marshal's advanced age, he had been named successor for an interim period of one month, while the power of permanent appointment lay with the Cabinet. His reasoning was that he did not think the chief of government and the head of state should be the same person. He had seen the abuses when Pétain had exercised both.

But there were, Laval told the jury, other abuses. After December 13, 1940, Pétain had created a National Council, a sort of Parliament. Laval had never agreed to that and when he returned to government he had suppressed the National Council, saying he would create another. But he never did and that was deliberate. Even so the Marshal hadn't conferred absolute power on the National Council. That he always reserved for himself.

When he returned to government in 1942, Laval said, had he desired personal power, he would have never have suppressed the National Council which was a support organ for Pétain's personal power. He could have packed it with his friends and supporters. But he didn't. He believed in the long established General Councils. He was, Laval said, a man of the Third Republic. It had honored and conferred power and offices upon him and he was sturdily loyal to its institutions.

"I advised the Marshal: don't touch the General Councils. But Pétain only shrugged his shoulders and smiled. The trouble," Laval said, "was that I was a parliamentarian, and in Pétain's eyes, that was a fault."[20]

M. Biondi was informed and alert. Had Laval been in government, the juror asked, when the Municipal Counselors were dismissed. Indeed he had been, Laval replied. And had not the General Councils, instead of being suppressed, been superseded by the Departmental Councils?[21]

Laval conceded that he was right. The General Councils hadn't been abolished. But they had withered on the vine with nothing left to do. So when he had returned to government, he had used the Departmental Councils to duplicate the General Councils and he had appointed officials, prefects, good republicans all, to the councils.

The point of all of this was that Laval had always thrived in the rough and tumble of elective politics. Only once in thirty years had he been rejected at the polls, in 1919, in the aftermath of the First World War. He had great regard for the voters and great rapport with them and a corresponding suspicion of those who, in Lyndon B. Johnson's lapidary phrase, had never been elected dogcatcher. These were the Marshal's men, inexperienced in politics with a predilection for personal power.

And then there was the Legion, the Marshal's all-encompassing veteran's organization. It became the Marshal's organ of propaganda and played a great role in public life under Vichy. But he, Laval, had nothing to do with the Legion.[22]

"After all you have said," Mongibeaux inquired, "wasn't the Legion a single party like Germany?"

"It might have been a single party for France," Laval replied, "but it was nothing like the single party in Germany."

Mongibeaux had a point to press: "Didn't you say to de Lapommeraye that France should adapt its institutions as much as possible to those of Germany, and the single party..."

Laval interrupted ferociously: "de Lapommeraye's dreaming. The Marshal might want a single party, but he could never do it. Never in the image of National Socialism. Oh, the Legion had its faults, but they were brave chaps, good men." He was being sincere. The veterans of the Legion were his people, common people, like his blue-collar supporters in Aubervilliers.[23]

He clearly enjoyed talking shop about government and its works. Yes, the Marshal wanted one party, the Marshal's party. Laval himself had tried to use the Departmental Councils in effect to replace the General Councils. But he had to get the approval of the Legion. That was his bargain with Pétain, so there were many things he wanted to do that he could not.

And he told all of this to show that far from abusing the spirit of the law of July 10, 1940 he had labored unceasingly to preserve republican institutions against personal power. All this was talk of politics, much of it local politics, in a death penalty treason trial. The reason, of course was that it was in fact a political trial, a trial of political decisions, political programs, and political men. Laval relished the anecdote of M. Maroux. He was eighty, perhaps eighty-two, senator from Puy-de-Dome, long- time mayor of the little village of Ceyrat. He loved being mayor. Everybody knew that. "He came to see me in Clermont. He looked bothered and upset." Laval brushed aside Maroux's denial that he was upset. What was it? Laval asked. They had dismissed him as mayor, Maroux replied. It was because he was a Freemason, a bête noire of the Marshal and his party.

"Ridiculous, odious," Laval stormed, "they punished a man who didn't deserve it. He had rendered service to his community. I never approved such acts. I fought against them to the best of my ability."[24]

This, then, was what he had to say about the National Assembly: "I voted for the law. That's certain. I contributed to it. That is incontestable. But I wasn't the only one."

"But that dictatorship against which you rail," Mongibeaux charged, "you hoped to put it in place and there are witnesses, especially de Lapommeraye."

"Don't talk to me about de Lapommeraye," Laval retorted, "I'll bring in witnesses who will impeach him."[25]

"And in the same period," Mongibeaux continued, "you prepared the meeting at Montoire and at the same time you said that no one of good sense could doubt the finality of the German victory." "It was a pleasantry," Laval replied.

"You were marching in the ranks of the victorious power," Mongibeaux said and proceeded to a new set of charges: Laval had made important concessions to the Germans. He had let Germany annex Alsace-Lorraine. He had initiated a racial policy in Germany's image.

"You've read my preliminary examination," Laval ironized, "but not in a sense particularly favorable to me." How could the Court accept that everything to which he had so fully testified should be destroyed by the sole affirmation of de Lapommeraye that he was hostile to the Republic?

Laval was passionate. "I owe everything to the Republic. I don't know if it was you who said it in tracing my career, but it pleased me greatly: I came from nothing, and for me, nothing, that's the greatest title of nobility. I've climbed up through all the echelons to mount to the Senate. I owe everything to the Republic. I was nothing, and by my own labors, with a little intelligence, I pulled myself up. And you believe I was against the Republic."[26]

He turned to the matter of de Lapommeraye, coming out of retirement to retail gossip. His acts, he said, spoke better than de Lapommeraye's words. He would show by a witness that de Lapommeraye had not always had this attitude toward him.

Naud was present at all this. "Two witnesses," he spoke up.[27] When de Lapommeraye came to testify, Laval added, he would answer his allegations forcefully.

"I have too much respect for the jury," he told them, " to believe that on the testimony of de Lapommeraye you would condemn a man who has occupied such high places over so many years." He added a stinging comment: "I don't need to take lessons in republicanism from the likes of him."

"You can say that to M. de Lapommeraye when he gets here," Mornet said.

Laval now appealed out of humanity he said for a recess. It was 6:15. He had testified since 1:00.

"I've already said it," Mongibeaux replied. "You will always find me on the side of humanity."[28]

He adjourned the hearing until 1:00 the next day.

The drum beat of *L'Humanité* persisted in its issue of October 6, 1945. The banner headline read:

LAVAL SEEKS TO GAIN TIME
WE MUST FINISH THIS DILATORY CONDUCT AND HAVE
DONE WITH THE INSOLENCE OF THE TRAITOR.

The story began by characterizing the proceedings as a "sinister comedy." But the paper paid a left-handed compliment to Laval:

It was Laval who conducted the proceedings. It was he who set forth the plan of work. It was he who decided on the suspensions of the sitting.

If President Mongibeaux persists in the way he is letting things go, it will only be a few days before Laval occupies the seat of the President. It's time to put an end to such insolence.[29]

La Croix's story soberly depicted the proceedings in the court much as they had taken place there. The same was true of *Combat. Figaro* paid tribute to Laval's powers of oratory with this headline:

IN AN ALMOST UNINTERRUPTED MONOLOGUE THE AC-
CUSED TRIED TO
DIMINISH HIS RESPONSIBILITIES.

Figaro offered this vivid portrait of the defendant:

Laval seemed to be not the accused but a Prime Minister, who, questioned by his colleagues, rises from his seat, responds without haste, master of the event, marching about, a hand in his pocket, or sitting on the arm of his chair, facing up to questions whether from the right or from the left, speaking familiarly as to an old friend-one of the parliamentary jurors- and proposing a suspension of the session.[30]

This portrait accorded well with Laval as sketched in *Combat* the day before:

Laval, very much at ease, passed before his table and spoke in the middle of the courtroom. He turned sometimes to the parliamentary jurors, sometimes toward the Resistant jurors, sometimes toward the magistrates, modulating his voice and offering anecdotes to the newspapermen. Save in those moments of great eloquence when he raised his two hands before him, he spoke, the left hand in his pocket and with his right hand pleaded and monstrated.[31]

13

Pierre Laval, Collaborator 1

There are epithets which history imprints on certain of its actors. For Pierre Laval, that epithet is "collaborator." Indeed, he is remembered today as the leading champion of "collaboration" between Vichy France and Nazi Germany.

Yet Laval did not coin the term as it was used in German-occupied France. The word appeared in the Armistice, signed June 22, 1940. All French authorities and services in the occupied territories, stated Article 3, were "to conform to the regulation of the German military authorities and to collaborate with the latter in a correct manner."[1] Laval took no part in the Armistice.

Nor did Laval have a hand in Marshal Pétain's radio address to the French people on October 11, 1940. "France is ready to seek this collaboration in all fields and with all of her neighbors..." Pétain announced. "No doubt Germany can choose, on the morrow of her victory over our arms, between a traditional peace of oppression and an entirely new peace of collaboration."[2]

A fortnight later, Pétain and Laval traveled to the remote French village of Montoire to meet Hitler in his railway car. Hitler wanted French backing in his continuing war with Great Britain and its empire; the French sought amelioration of the harsh terms of the Armistice. The two sides came to no agreement.

Upon his return, Pétain reported on the meeting to the citizens of France. "I responded freely to the Fuhrer's invitation," he said. "I underwent no diktat, no pressure from him. A collaboration was envisioned between our two countries. I accepted the principle. The details will be discussed later.[3]

By entering upon the path of collaboration, the Marshal continued, France could hope for a lessening of its suffering. He named the goals that Vichy would pursue – and, in fact, did, up to the day of Liberation: the return home of the prisoners of war, reduction of the occupation costs, more flexibility in the demarcation line, and, above all, the supply and feeding of the French people. "This collaboration," Pétain told his countrymen, "must be sincere. It must exclude any thoughts of aggression and must involve a patient and confident effort."

Pétain was explicit in his conclusion: "The members of the government are responsible only to me. It is I alone whom history will judge."[4]

In this last, Pétain has been proved wrong. It is also Pierre Laval, not Pétain alone, whom history has judged.

Collaboration was hardly thrust upon a recalcitrant and unwilling public by Pétain and Laval. Not a single public figure spoke up to condemn the Armistice over which Pétain presided and in which Laval had no part.[5] In the shock of the debacle of 1940, the French people were very much of a mind: They sought refuge under the comforting image of the Marshal, under his reputation, and under the comforting aura that seemed to emanate from him.

France was unique among the nations occupied by Germany in 1939-1940. When Poland, Norway, Belgium, and the Netherlands were overrun by the Wehrmacht, their governments relocated to London, where their flags flew as emblems of sovereignty and defiance. But, the claims of General de Gaulle and the Free French to the contrary, Pétain's Vichy regime was widely recognized as the legitimate and lawful government of France, the successor, by constitutional processes, to a defunct Third Republic. Many countries maintained full diplomatic relations with Vichy, recognizing it as sovereign in its homeland and in its territories abroad. The United States did not close its embassy, or withdraw its ambassador, Admiral William D. Leahy, until November 1942, when its troops landed on French colonial soil in North Africa.

And so, while the Third Republic perished in July of 1940, the government of France carried on, in changing times and circumstances, until the Liberation of 1944.

The transition took place at all levels of the French bureaucracy. The prefects, the administrators, the mayors – officials high and low who operated the system – migrated smoothly into the new Vichy government without revolt and almost wholly without defections.[6] The multi-layered, highly centralized bureaucracy of the French state remained at their posts even after the November, 1942 allied landing in North Africa when America finally severed its diplomatic ties with Vichy.[7] Not only did the French bureaucracy remain at their posts, but they continued to operate efficiently and effectively.[8]

What was true of the administrative bureaucracy was true of the judicial apparatus as well, where no purges were needed to assure loyalty to the regime. As Laval angrily insisted at his trial – "You were all working for the government then" – Mongibeaux and Mornet seamlessly carried on their duties under the Vichy government they now attacked as illegal. More to the point, Mornet had served as vice president of a denaturalization commission that reviewed 16,508 dossiers: 6,708 of them Jews, the rest from a mélange of countries of origin – Spain, Italy, Czechoslovakia. All such persons, under Vichy rules, were candidates for deportation, which in most cases meant the death camps.[9]

No institution was more deeply immersed in collaboration than the police, and no institution better showed the conflicted intentions involved in collaboration. What Vichy always feared was the erosion of its sovereignty by German direction or control of the French police.

It is easy today to look back and ask why these men loyally served Vichy. The answer, writes Julian Jackson, is that, in almost all cases, they thought it was their duty. "At bottom…the decisive reason holding men to the Vichy solution was an instinctual commitment to public order as the highest good."[10] Remaining by their posts, these Frenchmen sought to spare their country from the worst of the German onslaught of deprivation, terror, and death.

These are thoughts that Laval expressed to young Jaffré during one of their prison talks.

"The indictment," said Laval, "absolutely ignores everything positive that I did. Others may dream of grand politics. I wanted, and I've said it a hundred times, for France to suffer as little as possible."[11]

The vast majority of French under Vichy agreed with these sentiments. And among the minority who disagreed, only a relative handful – by scholarly analysis perhaps two percent of the population – joined the Resistance.[12]

Andre Gide was an eyewitness to Vichy. He passed the judgment on his fellow citizens: "If German occupation were to secure for us affluence, nine out of ten French people would accept it, three or four of them most cheerfully."[13]

Another observer was the preeminent Catholic theologian and philosopher Jacques Maritain. Writing from New York City in 1941, after a year of Vichy and before America's entry into the war, he pondered the duty of the French and of their leaders under the Nazi occupation.

All it [Vichy] can do is try its best to save the shreds of independence left, and to fight day by day against the dreadful evils which are crushing the country. The Vichy government has been very zealous in such a kind of social service work. This work, which concerns the elementary conditions of physical existence and which must needs be undertaken under similar circumstances by any government whatever, cannot atone for the faults committed in the political domain, but it is pressingly urgent, and although not, speaking absolutely, the most important, remains at this moment the most needed.

He added:

Given an existing situation and circumstances as tragic as those that reign in France today, it is sound doctrine that duty toward the common weal and a desire not to aggravate the common misfortune require legal respect for a government *de facto* (however severely it may be judged) except in such things as forbidden by conscience.[14]

But how to determine those things that are forbidden by conscience? This was a question for all the French – and especially for their leaders – to ponder each day of the German Occupation.

Pierre Laval joined the Pétain government in June 1940 as one of two Vice Premiers and as Pétain's designated successor. He served until December 13, 1940, when he was abruptly dismissed. His replacement as Pétain's Dauphin was Admiral Francois Darlan. Collaboration reached its peak under Darlan. Robert O. Paxton, a preeminent authority on Vichy France, writes of Darlan: "...the metamorphosis of 1940 carried him further into bold initiatives than even Laval. Whereas it is usually Laval who is treated as a turncoat and opportunist, it was Darlan who was actually to move France closest to actual military collaboration with Germany in 1941..."[15] Laval returned to the Vichy government in April 1942, having had no part in the development of collaboration in the interim. Paradoxically, Darlan, the ur-collaborator, ended up on the side of the angels. At the bedside of his gravely ill son in Algiers when the Anglo-American invasion of North America commenced in November 1942, he switched sides as the Allies advanced. His reversal of allegiance did him no good, however – shortly after, he was assassinated in Algiers by Ferdinand Bonnier de la Chapelle, a twenty-two-year old royalist. Who ordered the killing has ever since been a matter of conjecture.

Laval's collaboration with the German occupiers and his relationship with Pétain were often mentioned in court – Mongibeaux referred to these subjects in his rambling discourses – but Mornet made no effort to lay out a considered case of crime based upon them. Laval discussed collaboration in greater detail during his jailhouse conversations with Jaffré. If the younger man felt awkward and naïve at times, Laval always put him at his ease and never tried to evade what Jaffré thought were difficult questions.

Otto Abetz was the German representative in France. "They make a big thing out of my relationship with Abetz," Laval said. "They think I spent all my time in Paris with him. That I went on a honeymoon with him. What stupidity!"

"I only had those conversations with Abetz that my duties required and they were always in defense of the interests of France. We didn't meet to amuse ourselves." No more than with any other German was their relationship one of pleasure. Their talks were always difficult, harsh. But somebody had to have these conversations. "If there hadn't been someone to lighten their perpetual demands, the Germans would have helped themselves, and I guarantee you they wouldn't have used the back of the spoon."[16]

Laval made a critical distinction. "When they talk about the Germans, they say 'the Germans' as if they were all the same. They say 'the Germans did this or the Germans did that, the Germans demanded this or the Germans demanded that, the Germans took this or the Germans took that." But things weren't always that simple. "It wasn't 'the Germans', it was some Germans. I never met a species of homo sapiens they called Germans. I only dealt with real human beings."[17]

This was vintage Laval, the parliamentarian who worked most effectively one-on-one in the corridors and cloakrooms rather than at the rostrum, the minister who resolved issues by compromise based on an insight into the interests of the parties, the diplomat who preferred tête-a-tête, head-to-head talks among principals to diplomatic protocols and evasions. To deal with issues, yes, but always to deal with men.

"I would have been an idiot," he told Jaffré, "if right at the start it hadn't been my first step to locate, among all those I had on my back, those who were the most approachable, the most open, the most inclined to treat France generously, to help in dealing with the others."

He inclined his head toward Jaffré with a knowing smile. "It isn't a new method. But it's useful in all negotiations. Only a blockhead wouldn't do it. And it was necessary because the means I had at my disposal were meager indeed."[18]

"If Abetz had been a brute, closed-minded, I wouldn't have had a relationship with him. I would have looked for someone else. But I did have good relations with Abetz, better than with anybody else. Not for his own sake but for France, and it paid off." "It's a funny thing," he reflected. "I never met Abetz before the war. That's not what people thought."[19]

Jaffré seemed surprised. But Laval continued. Abetz had been well known in Paris before the war, in political circles, in the press. Laval had never had any private contacts with any Germans, only official.

At the time of the Armistice, Laval said, he knew none of the leading personalities of the Third Reich, save Goering, whom he had met in Cracow in 1935 while prime minister. During the four years of the Occupation, he had met Hitler three times. The first time was at Montoire, and that had been, he said, a thankless task but one that could have brought advantages to France, had it not been for his dismissal on December 13, 1940. He didn't see Germans every morning. He didn't see Goering or Ribbentrop any more often than he saw Hitler. He really only had repeated contacts with the German services in France and they were underlings who took orders and wrote reports. That wasn't to say that they were unimportant. They had, at least in current affairs, often of great interest to France, some margin for initiative. And he quickly saw that there were differences among them.

"As much as they said?" Jaffré asked. "More than you think," Laval replied. "There were things I couldn't do except in the most difficult moments. It makes me laugh when they talk of a monolithic state... I guarantee you, the Germans swore by the Fuhrer, but they weren't all pulling the same wagon."[20]

"But getting back to Abetz. I don't know if at heart he was a Nazi. That's a question you didn't ask the Germans. I think that Abetz was loyal to his chiefs and his country. If he was a Nazi by conviction, and I have reason to doubt it, he certainly wasn't by temperament. Oh, I've met some hundred percent Nazis in negotiations."

He described some of the hardest cases. He called them dingos. "I remember one. He foamed at the mouth, his eyes popped out of his head when he spoke of the Jews. I refused to do business with him. I demanded another intermediary. And that one frothed at the mouth less but wasn't much better. "*Voyez vous avec quels cocos j'avais parfois affaire.* Look at all the nuts I had to deal with."[21]

"But Abetz wasn't like that. If they had all been, I would have quit. Abetz wasn't a brute, he wasn't an idiot, he knew France and that made him more amiable than the others. Don't think it was easy." He had, Laval said, to work hard to put across his point of view and then that wasn't always the end of it. "Abetz had to deal with his bosses. I couldn't always get what I wanted. He often made suggestions I hadn't anticipated, not what I had asked. But it was progress. I had to start over, on another tack to reach the goal. But that," he knowingly told Jaffré, "that's negotiating.

It's never been any different. And I wasn't wasting my time when I could safeguard French interests, save French lives.[22]

He had spent profitable time with Abetz. What a joke to criticize that relationship. He could have had good relations too with Sauckel, the German labor boss, if Sauckel had been a gentlemen who said "You're right. Protect your workers."

"I never got anything from the Germans except after tough dealing. Maybe the results weren't so good. But small as they might have been, I didn't think I was wasting my time. That's the big picture. You must always have an overall goal, think in big terms. But politics is also the details. And when a country is unhappy, it's often the immediate realities that the chiefs have to face. They have to weigh immediate needs against daily risks."

"Well, that's what I did, day after day. When you're in s____ up to your neck, before dreaming of building a palace, you have to think about breathing."[23]

"The old Marshal," he went on, "dreamed of glory and his dreams resulted in lots of foolishness. When I had contact with the German Embassy, it was often on matters with which the Marshal and his people disdained to bother themselves. But I didn't stand on rank. If I thought one of Abetz' subordinates could arrange something, that's the person I went to. There was a better spirit in the Embassy than any place else. Was it because of Abetz? Was it that they were diplomats, not soldiers or S.S.? There were men there who knew French culture who spoke French like you and me, who sincerely wanted a rapprochement between their two countries, who didn't want to injure France and they were far from negligible elements in the game."

But what had impressed the Embassy did no good with the other German services, a Sauckel, an Oberg. That was stickier work.

But Abetz had been helpful in important matters, especially in Laval's dealings with the labor boss Sauckel. "In doing that," and here Laval paused thoughtfully and significantly, "he no more betrayed his country than I betrayed mine. He was simply more human and more intelligent than the other German chiefs who operated in France."[24]

Jaffré asked about the soldiers. The response was what he might have expected from a veteran of the political wars. "The soldiers!" Laval smiled. He told Jaffré what he thought of soldiers in general. "Hitler's were no different than ours, except that they had more initiative. Pétain told me one day that I wasn't competent in the military area and had no right to contradict him. But among the Germans there were two kinds of soldiers. There were the regulars, the Wehrmacht and they weren't necessarily fools."[25]

Bitterness sometimes crept in. "Paris wasn't burned," he observed, "as the Communists and some glorious loudmouths would have liked, thanks to a general of the Wehrmacht. Then there was the S.S. That was a different story. They were ferocious, impenetrable. They understood nothing and didn't want to understand. And they didn't have the least idea what France was." "You can see," he told Jaffré, "what a task it was to deal with them. Talking to Oberg was like talking to a millstone. But even with 'cocos' like that, I didn't quit; and when I think about what I got from them, it's amazing."[26]

"And do you think for a moment," he declaimed passionately, "that after seeing types like that that I would have been converted to Nazism, that I'd want my country to be run by citizens of that stripe? Even if I'd been ideologically attracted to Nazism, seeing those types in action for five minutes disgusted me. I've told you before what I think about ideologies. That's where all the partisan ideologies will get you."[27]

"What about Sauckel?" Jaffré asked. Laval had vivid powers of description. "He was a squat little man with a close cropped head. He looked" Laval searched for the right words "like a worker dressed up in his Sunday best. A schoolteacher, a Prussian adjutant. He was an old-time worker, who might have been a communist in his youth. He was a militant ideologue who had gone far in the party. I saw the same types in Moscow, probably with the same spirit."

"Sauckel wasn't very bright. A Nazi through and through. His aim was to empty territories of manpower. That was his fixed idea. He acted like a maniac. So," Laval said, "I had to have a ideé fixe, too,only," he smiled, "with a lot more flexibility. Because Sauckel had all of the advantages; he had time on his side. And I didn't have anything but saliva."[28]

Jaffré couldn't resist. "What about Hitler?" he asked.

"Hitler," Laval reflected, "was a little more complicated. I've seen lots of men in my career, men who made a great noise in the world. Stalin was the one that had impressed me most. He was the strongest. He had total self-control. He never yielded to an impulse.

"Hitler was different. He and Stalin had certain things in common— their ascendance over their entourages. But Hitler wasn't as balanced as Stalin. He was a fanatic and I don't like fanatics. He was capable of the worst, bizarre impulses. He was a romantic, a Wagnerian. He played music at night to inspire him." Jaffré spied in Laval an ironic smile. The thought of a statesman who needed musical inspiration amused him. He told Jaffré of his intimate one-on-one talks with Stalin in Moscow. "That's always the best way to judge a man." If Stalin was a fanatic—and Laval had reason to doubt that—he was at least a lucid fanatic whereas there was a good deal of Valhalla in Hitler's fanaticism.[29]

Ribbentrop was colder, more reflective, more methodical. He gave himself airs. He was a lot less clever than he thought. "He detested me." Goering was a kind of a force of nature. But he had the power of life and death over the others. Before him, Ribbentrop acted like a little boy.

"At the bottom of it all," Laval summarized, "Hitler was an incomplete statesman. He never had a coherent policy. He was too stubborn. The idea never to surrender was pure madness. He covered his country with ruins and cadavers." Laval paused again. "That's what would have happened to us, if we hadn't signed the Armistice. And if we had tried to defend Paris, Paris would be in ruins."[30]

Laval hated war. "But there are things more important than war for a statesman worthy of the name—cities, homes, monuments, the human lives of generations which must be preserved for the future. Wars don't last forever, the fortunes of war change. But the destruction of a city like Paris..."[31]

"Hitler knew the Germans. He knew the right words, the right formulas. And they followed him. Hitler could have led Germany to reasonable goals. But he went off on adventures. If Hitler knew the Germans, he was ignorant of other countries. He never left Germany and he took himself for the Messiah. Stalin was stronger, cleverer, but in the end I wouldn't be surprised if that didn't play him false. But, he's on our doorstep now. The English and the Americans, that's what they've done."[32]

Jaffré listened intently. He knew Laval was open, unresentful of probing inquiries. He launched one.

"Were you a convinced partisan of collaboration?" he asked.

Laval smiled a sibylline smile and dragged on his eternal cigarette.

"I'm always, and in all cases a convinced partisan of collaboration."[33]

When Jaffré seemed surprised, Laval continued.

"The minute you start to talk about interests with someone, you start to collaborate. I've always thought it's a good thing, to make contact, to explain when you have business or when you're in the position of petitioner. In the past, when I was in power, I was always ready to collaborate with everyone, to work for peace with everyone. That's what I told the English, the Italians, the Germans, the Russians. No one was more convinced of the need for formulas for collaboration and for collective security. I was never an isolationist. I never thought France could live in an ivory tower. Slogans like Maurras' 'France Alone,' whether before the war or during the war, were pure stupidity to me. The United States, Russia, they can live alone. But not France, not for a long time.[34]

"The war came, then the debacle. We signed the Armistice. The Germans occupied our country. Should we collaborate—or not?"

"Your question is interesting," he told Jaffré. "You asked if I were a convinced partisan of negotiation." Laval insisted on the word "convinced."[35]

"There are things," Laval said, "of which I'm convinced. That peace is the greatest good man could aspire to. That demagoguery is evil and ideologies dangerous. That in the governance of the nation there are certain rules that must be observed. That the prime duty of the state is to serve its people and you can only do that by observing the rules."[36]

"The Germans were on our soil," he told Jaffré, "And evidently for a long time. They could well win the war."[18] So, Laval said, he hadn't immediately rejected the policy of collaboration if it could be fruitful for France. "To collaborate to me meant to negotiate. Negotiate to find out the intention of the occupant. Negotiate to obtain a softening of the terms they had imposed. Negotiate, sometimes to gain time."[37]

"The Germans weren't naive. I never expected to get everything I asked for, that they would yield without taking into consideration their own needs or interests. Well," he told Jaffré, "that's how the game is played."

"My ambition was always to get the maximum and give the minimum." He reminded Jaffré that the terms of the Armistice required France to collaborate. That was a useful clause. So the answer was he was a convinced partisan of collaboration because he was convinced of its necessity.[38]

And he stated the limits. He would collaborate only so long as it was in the best interests of France. That would always exclude military collaboration, entering the war on the side of Germany. He would never consider that. And when Hitler, in November 1942, face to face, had demanded a military alliance, he had, he told Jaffré, refused, whatever the risks to his country-or to himself.[39]

The Vichy government was, after all, the legal government of France. "What should I do? See more Frenchmen killed, see bombs raining down on the country, multiply the ruination of its people? Anyone who knew me knew I wouldn't want that. But there was a cruel necessity. I didn't create it but I couldn't escape it. I had to safeguard the essentials. And that was called collaboration. That's all. And if you carefully examine my acts, you would see that what I did was more to negotiate, to discuss, to quibble, to temporize, than to collaborate."[40]

Laval leaned against the wall as was his custom. He dragged on his cigarette. Jaffré had another question. Weren't there variations in the mode of collaboration, he asked. Of course, Laval replied. When, using his favorite phrase, the Germans were on his back, he spoke the language of collaboration. He had to. But it was his acts that counted. You had to judge a man by his acts.[41]

"I would have been lame-brained if my actions in 1942 had been the same as in 1940, or in 1943 and 1944 the same as 1942. In 1940, Germany had triumphed. Neither America nor Russia was in the war. What I tried to do at Montoire in 1940 was to give France some breathing space. In 1942 it was different. Germany was resolved to crack down on France. I used the same language, but I maneuvered so that France would suffer as little as possible. If you looked at the period carefully, you would see how much I negotiated, how little I collaborated."[42]

"Me," he said, "I tried to practice a flexible policy, always driven by the necessity of the moment, and amid the fluctuations, always closest to the true aspirations and real needs of our people and nothing else."[43]

"I didn't think of Germany, or England, or Russia, or America. I thought of my country. I negotiated. I temporized. I collaborated. And I resisted, yes, I resisted, often all at the same time. Because it was in the interests of France. Words are such poor things. It's the realities that count. But words can be useful. Remember what I said: you can't make foreign policy without a certain number of ruses. The word doesn't shock me. Not if it's for my country."[44]

"Collaborate. I didn't collaborate in the same way with Abetz and Sauckel. When the facts are all known, you'll see how I collaborated. I didn't collaborate with Oberg the same as with Hemmen of the Armistice Commission. You'll see what I extracted from them, French lives, money. That was my task. All I ask is a fair trial and that the light be shown on all of this."[45]

Jaffré believed what Laval told him. He had always been direct, clear, precise but passionate for his truth. How could they condemn him? He remembered what Laval had said to him again and again: "Take any hundred people in France, totally by chance, from the streets, in the factories, in the fields, and let them be my judges."[46]

Jaffré was especially interested in the events of December 13, 1940 when Laval had been dismissed from his office as vice president and minister of state.

Pétain and Laval had talked amiably enough that December day. They had talked about the proposal to bring the ashes of L'Aiglon, Napoleon's son to Paris. "Oh, I knew that there were those who didn't like me, but that didn't bother me. But what happened to me on December 13 was entirely outside my political experience. If the Marshal didn't want me, he could have found a better way. He didn't need a state of emergency, transforming the Hotel de Paris into Ali Baba's cave where the henchmen of the Cagoule reigned. So I was arrested and held at Chateldon under guard. I'm sure that those who pulled it off were practicing for some future action against others. But the Marshal hadn't the wits to see this or to reject it."[47]

"The Marshal was pulled one way and then another"—Laval's language never lacked color—"by the zebras who were as adept at politics as I would be as personnel director of the Barnum & Bailey's Circus. The Marshal had got it into his head that I would entice him to Paris and kidnap him. You had to be a soldier to think like that. It was fantastic. What possible interest could I have had in removing Pétain? Wouldn't all France know in the twinkling of an eye who did it? What would it have done to me? No, I needed the Marshal and the Marshal needed me. We could have, if he had understood and if he had wanted, complemented each other admirably and for the country's good. France needed Pétain and I knew it."[48]

At the heart of the affair had been the Marshal's cult of personal power. Laval smiled ruefully. "His civil and military establishments had all the caprice of the court of an African king. When the scent of incense wafted up to his nostrils, Pétain loved it. It was, to be more exact, the court of a petty principality. Sunday there were fanfares under the windows of the Hotel du Parc. Pétain took the salute. The soldiers, the same ones who were responsible for the debacle, decorated and congratulated each other. It was all so ridiculous. More than ridiculous. France deserved better. France, even France defeated, deserved better than these grotesque parades. It would have been more dignified to live in silence, to work in silence."[49]

"Amid all those types, the kepis and the oak leaves, apparently I seemed like an angry bear who didn't show enough veneration for the Marshal. If I had prostrated myself before Pétain, there never would have been a December 13. But I never did. And I never asked anyone to prostrate himself before me. I had better things to do. I always thought that with Pétain, even taking into consideration the position he held, protocol was more important than France."[50]

"They say he complained that I blew smoke up his nose. What a joke! I never blew smoke in his nose. I smoked in his presence, sure, but if it bothered him, he had only to say so. You know, if it had really given him pleasure, I would have taken off my shoes before going into his office, like going into a mosque. What a farce! But I have to ask myself if details like that weren't part of December 13."[51]

Pétain had complained that Laval didn't give written reports. That wasn't Laval's style. He liked to talk to a man, ask questions, sharpen important points, assess sincerity. No he had never refused to talk to Pétain and to keep him informed.[52]

"If," Laval continued, "Pétain had had a policy opposite to mine, then to dismiss me would have made some sense. But the people who came after me went to the Germans to say collaboration would continue, even be reinforced, and the new team took measures that I would never have. And without the results I would have gotten. And the Germans only became more exigent."[53]

"Do you know why they really wanted to get rid of me?" he asked Jaffré. "Because I didn't want to 'Marshalize,' Because I didn't hide my opinion that the National Revolution was stupid. Because I was against the personal power which Pétain was using in ways far from the customs of France. And above all I seemed to the oak leaves to be too parliamentarian, too democratic. I was always an obstacle to them, all the more so as I seemed to succeed."[54]

Laval reviewed those who engaged in the struggle for power at Vichy, their appetites and their ambitions. It was he said, a basket of crabs. But there were imbeciles who seriously thought that he had sold out to Germany.[55]

"Sold out to Germany? When I was about to obtain the release of 500,000 prisoners, a substantial reduction in the Occupation costs, a flexing of the line of demarcation?"[56]

"What I couldn't forgive was that they gave up all that. My personal case didn't count. It was France that counted. They acted like children with their little games at Vichy without the least idea of the consequences. You had to think of how it affected the Germans. They knew where I stood. With what frivolity I was tossed out you can hardly imagine. The plotters of December 13 were like children who played with glass until it shattered and then tried to put the pieces back together. And it was France that paid. Pétain could have done it another way. I wasn't hooked on power. I didn't have the taste for it, nor the means."[57]

He had tried to be, he told Jaffré, objective and without passion. They had let him go without garnering the benefits of the meeting with Hitler at Montoire. "That," said Laval, "will give you an idea of the political capacity of those who pulled off the job of December 13."[58]

14

The Trial, October 6, 1945[1]

When the Court re-opened on October 6, the presiding judge had a question for Pierre Laval. "You said, and you have said it repeatedly, that you had no understanding with the Marshal, that you had many difficulties with him. You said that he was more powerful than Louis XIV."

He brushed aside Laval's attempt to speak. "There's a little problem of psychology, which perhaps you can help us solve. How can it be that if he was more powerful than Louis XIV, and couldn't get along with his prime minister, that he would have kept you on for three years. What's the explanation? You said you had no understanding with him, but you stayed with him. Why did you stay?"[2]

"That's easy enough to explain," Laval replied. But first, he wanted to read the document he had been unable to find yesterday. It was the letter he had sent to the Garde des Sceaux on September 22. He had as yet no reply.

He put on his eyeglasses and tested the proper length at which to hold the letter and at the same time fix his eye from time to time on the jury and on the audience. The moment was critical. This was an opportunity to tell the jury, the audience, the press, and he must have hoped, the public, how justice had been denied to him. He began to read.

Monsieur le Garde des Sceaux

"I have the honor to call to your attention the abnormal conditions under which the pretrial examination of my case has been carried out."

"I am accused of a plot against the security of the state and of treason, the gravest and most abominable crimes that can be charged."

"The indictment refers to acts I committed before the war and during the Occupation."

"I have no doubts of a justice founded on truth. But it seems to me the examining magistrates were hardly searching for the truth."

He explained how his examination had been cut short because the trial date had been set.

"That is why I appeal to you not to be deprived of the right to defend myself."

"I have exercised the highest functions, I have been involved in the direction of the country's policies for many years. My trial is about governmental activity during almost all of the Occupation, that period when France suffered so cruelly."

"How could one imagine a trial, which concerns not only a man but a policy, that wasn't preceded by a complete investigation?"

"I can make important declarations to show them I had no responsibility for the misfortunes that beset our unhappy country."

"If you will not listen to me today, how will history tomorrow discover the truth?"

He now catalogued all those critical issues, issues which in many cases formed the basis of the charges against him and on which he had never been examined. These included his negotiations with the German government, his meeting with Hitler at Montoire, the German requisitions of French manpower and food, the Milice, his forced departure from Paris on August 17, 1944, and his captivity in Germany. Nor had there been any preliminary inquiry into his role in the National Assembly of July, 1940, nor his effort with Herriot in Paris in August 1944 to reconvene the National Assembly. No more had there been, despite the charges of the indictment, any inquiry into his personal fortune, nor his policy and politics before the war. Instead he had often been examined as a witness in other cases. He had, he complained, been examined on scattered and isolated matters which, for any equitable judgment, had to be placed in a larger context.

"I am ready to show that if I accepted to serve during the Occupation, it wasn't to betray my country but to protect it. I reject the word treason as in outrage. It hurts more than the confinement to which I am subjected, more than the other charges of the indictment that weigh upon me. How can you prevent me from defending my honor which I hold more precious than life itself?

"The passions which accompanied the grave misfortunes of our country cannot be a pretext to obscure the respect for justice which ought to remain one of France's most precious virtues. France is no longer bound by the Occupier. It has recovered its liberty. It ought now to show its true visage of calm and of a justice that is serene.[3]

This man who had eschewed eloquence in favor of the common parlance of common men now said:

Out of respect for the functions which I have occupied for twenty years, the history of which must be written with impartial justice, it is to you, M. Le Garde des Sceaux, the repository of our highest judicial traditions, that I ask your tutelary protection.[4]

He sought, he read, neither obfuscation nor delay, but only that the light be shown on his person, his policy, and his deeds. They would show whether his actions had been fatal or profitable to his country. He again asked for a full preliminary examination and for the publication of the proceedings in the *Official Journal* so that France might know the truth.

"For four years I helped our unhappy country under the Occupation while others fought courageously for the Liberation. I saved it by exposing myself from dangers worse than those it knew. I saved the lives and liberty of thousands and thousands. No one, when they knew the facts, would question either my patriotism or my courage.[5]

Once more he made his persistent demand for a full pretrial examination and at the same time a fair hearing in another case pending in Marseilles. That case was another accusation of intelligence with the enemy of the same kind that had brought him before the High Court.

He wrote, in closing, that his lawyers had also written to the chairman of the Commission of Inquiry to object to the termination of the preliminary examination.

"I am paying," Laval concluded, "with my liberty and suffering because I loved my country too much. But I await your decision with confidence."

"And now," said Pierre Laval, "we come to your question."[6]

But Mornet wished to be heard. Laval's letter was nothing, he said, but another example of Laval's efforts to delay the trial indefinitely.

"Until the light is shone," Laval shot back.[7]

As to the proceeding in Marseilles, Mornet said, he had nothing to add to the judgment of the Military Court there. That was another case. It concerned the sale of a local newspaper to the Germans and allegations of the role Laval had played in the sale. It had nothing to do, Mornet said, with the present case and was no pretext, therefore, for any delay.

What was before the Court, Mornet said, was the policy Laval had followed for four years, and he did not hesitate to label it criminal. What was not before the Court was a newspaper affair in which Laval had served as an arbiter among a group of German buyers.

"But look at the file," Laval cried out. "I never served as an arbiter for a German group."[8]

"I didn't interrupt you," Mornet snapped.

"You not only interrupt me, you outrage me," Laval replied with equal fervor.

That affair in Marseilles had nothing to do with the indictment, Mornet maintained. What the indictment charged was treason of honor and country.

The Attorney General now took the floor. Again, he asked the question the accused had not answered. "How could you claim to be the adversary of Pétain's abuse of power when you remained vice president and associated yourself with the policies you decried?"

"How could you, after the defeat, to the detriment of France's ally and against the laws of loyalty and honor, allow the re-annexation of Alsace-Lorraine? Why did you return to office in 1942 with an openly pro German policy? Those are the charges, not your pre-war policies, nor those that constituted the coup d'état of July 1940. It was from that very moment that the charges lay to which you are called upon to respond."[9]

"There were acts we all remembered, the laws, the circulars you signed..."

The bitterness of Pierre Laval now reached its climax.

"And which you applied" he said grimly. Everyone in the Court knew what Laval meant—Mornet's service under the Vichy government, on a commission charged with the registration and sequestration of Jewish-owned property.[10]

"I never applied them," Mornet insisted, "but you signed them."

Laval had struck home. The Presiding Judge rushed to Mornet's rescue. He warned Laval of the power of contempt which he held ready to hand.

"It's only because I talk that you say I'm insolent," Laval replied.

"You're out of order," the presiding judge told Laval. "And if you cause any more trouble, I won't tolerate it."

Mornet again summed up the charges. They did not rest on the testimony of witnesses, nor on the preliminary examination—he made a curious concession—"exactes ou inexactes," about Laval's pre-war policy. No, the charges rested on the documents, the laws he had signed. He might deny drafting them, but he signed them as chief of government. And there were his radio speeches and "Those abominable words against which our consciences protested."[11]

It is worthwhile to ask at this junction: what circulars, what documents, what speeches were being referred to? For it is not in generalities, but in the particulars of an action, strictly defined and strictly construed, that criminal charges must lie. Had there been any attempt to define and enter evidence as to these particulars? And if such had been done, was it not the right of defendant to put in his defense, to answer what the circumstances may have been under which the documents and the circulars and the speeches were drafted and delivered? And was it not open to the defendant to show with what intent, and whether or not, or to what degree such criminal intent may or may not have existed? And in the end was it not vital to ask, what was the effect of the alleged statements and acts, especially when it was the fundamental claim of the defendant that the very acts had not only been intended to benefit but had indeed redounded to the benefit, the safety, and often the lives of the French and of France?

All these procedural and evidentiary deficiencies the Attorney General conceded with his next declaration. It measured and defined the character of the entire trial and surely in any developed system of justice, would call for the severest reproach, if not for a new trial.

"There lies the accusation against you, Pierre Laval," Mornet continued. "And the truth is that on the day of the Liberation in August or September of 1944, had Pierre Laval been arrested and brought before a trial, without all of the procedures of which you are now the beneficiary, your condemnation, followed by you know what, wouldn't have been a judicial error."[12]

Pierre Laval smiled a grim smile. "That would have deprived me of the pleasure of hearing you."

"And that result would have given satisfaction to every Frenchman," Mornet continued. "Today we have the duty to judge you in all the forms of justice. All the documents were at your disposal."

It may have been forgotten that Baraduc and Naud, if they had not participated in the trial, were still in the courtroom. "No, no, no," cried out Baraduc.

"It's not true," Laval added.

"Decency and moderation," Mongibeaux commanded.

"It is moderation," said Baraduc. "We didn't have the documents."[13]

Mongibeaux insisted that they had.

"No, no," cried Naud, "on my honor."

Against Mornet's insistence, Laval, Baraduc, and Naud once more joined in denial.

"But everything was in the indictment," Mornet said.

"Ah," breathed Baraduc as if in that moment he had finally grasped the mentality of his adversary.

Mornet stubbornly maintained his assertion. Had the documents not been available, the defense needed only to ask for them and they would have been made available the next day. Having uttered this palpable untruth-the truth had been for some time under lock and key in Beteille's cabinet—Mornet went on to repeat his incendiary appeal.

"I'll say it again. If the accused had faced summary judgment a year ago, he would have been judged, documents or no documents, and in a way that would have satisfied the conscience of France."[14]

The defense could make its explanations in Court. But Mornet asked, in the interest of truth, of light and of conscience, that the proceedings not be drowned out in "useless discussions."

Naud asked to be heard. "After me," said Laval. "I didn't want," he said, "to provoke a scene. I only wanted to read my letter to the Garde de Sceaux."

"You've read it," said Mongibeaux.

"Enough," cried the juror Bedin.

"You haven't answered the question," said the juror Biondi.

The presiding judge took his cue. "I asked you why you remained at Petain's side in the hostile atmosphere that reigned in Vichy." It wasn't difficult to know. It was, he said, the same forces that had compelled his return to Vichy government in April, 1942, after a year and a half."

"It was the Germans."

"No," Laval objected.

"It was Abetz," Mongibeaux declared.

Naud asked once more to be heard. But Laval preempted him. "I have nothing to reply."[15]

"Then don't reply," said Mongibeaux.

Laval came back fighting. "I have a right to answer the Attorney General. I never took part in any newspaper deal in Marseilles. If the Attorney General has the file, I've never seen it." He had only learned the day before that he had been condemned to death in Marseilles. He didn't even know by what court. The trial record throws no light on this extraordinary issue and raises the question of how Laval could have been the defendant in and condemned to death in a proceeding of which he had no knowledge and in which he had never participated.

"This isn't about the trial in Marseilles," Mornet said.

"But you just talked about it," replied an exasperated Laval.

"You're the one who talked about it," the juror Bedin cried.

"Even if he did," said Mongibeaux, "that's not what's before us."

"But I only wanted to read my letter to the Garde de Sceaux," Laval persisted.[16]

The presiding judge had had enough. This was becoming, he said, like a public meeting. There were noises, shouting, tumult in the courtroom. "One more such incident," Mongibeaux warned, "and I'll suspend the session."

"You want everything," Laval bitterly observed, "everything but the truth."[17]

15

Pierre Laval, Collaborator 2[1]

Whether in the dark and dismal prison cell that served as a reception room, or in Laval's own cramped quarters where his files and records were set out on the floor, Jaffré never flagged in his concern for Laval or in his task of being the human bond that connected Pierre Laval to his family, his lawyers and to the world outside.

Jaffré had learned to be direct, not to hesitate to ask those questions which weighed on his mind.

"Did you really, M. le President," he asked, "believe in a German victory?"[2]

Laval's habitual smile had a tinge of irony. He seemed to sense that Jaffré was referring to a phrase he had once spoken on the radio. Jaffré didn't ask why he might have said certain words—only if he had, until the end, the conviction that Germany would win the war.

Laval looked intently at Jaffré. He paused for a few seconds then said:

"To believe something will happen in the future, that's prophecy. I was never a prophet. But I always had to take into account what I saw. If I believed in a German victory in 1940, I wasn't the only one. Most of us French believed it then. That's why I went to Montoire to see Hitler. Because I wanted France to continue to live. Because I wanted a peace that wasn't a peace of destruction for my country. I wanted France to preserve those institutions that suited its temperament. I wanted to save the maximum of our liberties. I didn't know if I could. But I tried with all my might."[3]

But he understood, he said, that Jaffré's question didn't refer to 1940. It wouldn't have shocked or surprised anyone then.

"You were thinking," Laval said, "of that famous phrase I said on the radio."

"Yes, M. le President."

"Yes, and they're going to make that the heart of my trial."[4]

These are the words, and they proved to be fatal, that Pierre Laval uttered on the radio on June 22, 1942:

"I wish the victory of Germany, for without it Bolshevism would tomorrow be installed across Europe."

"But," Laval continued, "the real question is why I said what I said in 1942. Wouldn't it have been more natural, on the morrow of Montoire to say that the German victory seemed certain, more certain than in 1942, when I started to have doubts? That's what they ought to think about. Perhaps if they looked into the situation of France in 1942, they wouldn't need to ask the question."[5]

He explained why. "In 1940 there was no need to make such a statement. It was never my practice in any affair to go any farther than I had to." But he was sure of one thing. He would do whatever was necessary to obtain an advantage for France.

Conditions had been very different on his return to government in 1942. The indictment said he had been returned by the Germans. He denied it. It was a lie. He could prove it.

"I knew in 1942 that the Germans were changing their methods in France; their demands were becoming more and more draconian, and that France had to face the worst. When I returned in 1942, it wasn't to satisfy the Germans. It wasn't to revenge my dismissal of December 13, 1940. It was only to serve my country. My family were all against it. My friends were all against it. It was against my own interests. I met Goering in Paris. He warned me what was in store for France and advised me not to return under such conditions."[6]

"But those were only reasons to the contrary," he told Jaffré. He was, he felt, the only man in France who could undertake the responsibility, without adopting a posture of servility to the Germans. Which, he was quick to add, others would have done who aspired to the job.

"Think what they may," he told Jaffré, "even my adversaries knew I was neither naive nor impulsive. That famous phrase on which they want to hang me wasn't a matter of chance. It was perfectly premeditated. From the moment of my return, I knew the policy I would follow, the defense of France against the growing demands of the Germans." He paused to reflect adding: "And I knew what I might have to say."[7]

"Did you think it was with gaiety in my heart that I uttered that phrase? I had long reflected on it. It weighed on me. It was only that my country might suffer less, that and no personal consideration. I knew it would revolt the French and give rise to passionate responses."

"I knew all that. And I knew what use my enemies would make of it. But it was the sole means of avoiding the worst.

"They talk of courage. Sometimes courage is being glorious. But didn't," and he looked to Jaffré for reassurance, "didn't it take courage and determination to act as I did?"[8]

"And nothing in the world will make me regret what I said. And what happened after." A few months after his famous phrase, he claimed to have denied the military alliance Hitler sought. He had obstructed Sauckel's efforts to draft French labor. "If I had wanted a German victory," he asked rhetorically, "would I have rejected a military alliance with Germany? Would I have refused the workers? But if I had never spoken as I had, would I have been able to do what I did?"

He uttered again the demand that was the refrain of his defense: "Judge me, not by my words, but by my acts. Because my acts explain my words."

"There were others," he said, "who practiced the policy of communiqués. Their policies varied according to the latest news and the current likelihood of a German victory. It was natural enough. They were only human."

"But I didn't have the right to pursue such a policy, at least not openly. In my position I had to deal with the Germans as occupiers. Win or lose, they were there. And there was always the terrible possibility that as they began to lose the war they would become harder, more demanding. Well, one day, when you look at all the facts, you will see how many French lives I saved, beginning with many of those who are in power today."[9]

He said it again: "I wasn't a prophet. Now that Germany is beaten, it is easy to say that it was inevitable." But he had doubted it. There were the German secret weapons. He had heard about them, about tests. The Germans said they could produce weapons that would need only two or three to destroy London.[10]

"And apparently the German leaders believed in these weapons. Why did they pursue the war to the total destruction of their country if they hadn't believed? I could never understand why they didn't try to negotiate with one or another of their adversaries, cost what it might. But I could never exclude the hypothesis of their victory. It would have been terrible for France. That's why I hung on to the end."[11]

And that is why, he told Jaffré, he had to utter words indicating a belief in their victory. "But," he said again, "the real issue wasn't what

I believed or didn't believe as to the outcome of the war, but what I did in the face of terrible realities."

"But was it prudent?" Jaffré asked.

"It wasn't prudent," Laval replied. "But it was true. Bolshevism is on the march. Maybe the Americans (this was 1945) will stop it with their bomb."[12]

Laval grimaced. He was in pain. His health was failing. But his smile returned. He had an anecdote to tell.

He had discussed these very words with Marshal Pétain. Originally he had said that he foresaw a German victory. But Pétain said that as a civilian he was not qualified to express a military opinion. Hence the wish was substituted for the opinion.

"Well, that's the way the soldiers were," Laval said, with immense good humor. "They didn't hesitate to practice politics making admirals and colonels prefects and a ship's captain drafting a constitution. I never had any ambition to command a division, nor even a regiment." They accused him of wanting to lend military aid to Germany, but he had refused. "What would some of those generals and the admirals have done before they found safety in Algiers. I don't know if they hoped for a German victory. But I knew that they were ready to aid Germany militarily and I thought they were crazy."[13]

The same day he spoke those words, Charles Rochat, the secretary general of the Ministry of Foreign Affairs, told Laval: "But it's a needless risk." "Is it you who will be shot," Laval had replied, "or me?"[14]

Another of Laval's colleagues was Paul Morand. Laval gave him the revised text to read. "You ought to say you hope Germany isn't defeated, that the war will end and France will be the arbiter. Isn't that what you really believe?" Morand asked. "There are those who will put a period, not a comma after 'I hope for the victory of Germany.'"

Again Laval voiced his innermost feelings and concerns. "Do you think it would give me pleasure to see Germany win the war?" he asked. "But I would rather pay them in words than acts, because that costs France less. A phrase like that could mean the return of a hundred thousand prisoners. Those words could help me deny hundreds of thousands of workers to that brute, Sauckel. Well, my sword will be those words. Because I don't have any other."[15]

Two months later when Laval addressed a group of teachers in central France, he told them that his words, engaged only himself. They cost nothing to the French. Understand me, he told them. "I accept for my person all the risks so that I can give to France its chance."[16]

In a real trial, the whole policy of Laval, and not simply selected accusations would be carefully reviewed. And this would be true even in
a more limited proceeding where it should always be open to respond
to the charges by showing background and motive, not to mention ex-
tenuating circumstances.

What would such a proceeding look like?

"The indictment," Laval told Jaffré, "absolutely ignores everything
positive that I did. Others may dream of grand politics. I wanted, and I've
said it a hundred times, for France to suffer as little as possible."[17]

What were the problems with which he had dealt? First and foremost,
the problems of food supply. "Well, you didn't do that by destroying the
flour mills and the warehouses. You had to have food so the factories could
go on working, so that you could maintain a transport system. Would
I have served my country by wrecking the trains? They were the vital
organs of the country. They were needed to bring aid to the prisoners, to
bring them food and clothing, to keep up agriculture, things as humble
as seed and manure. Students needed to get to school. The public health
had to be safeguarded, the hospitals, the manufacture of pharmaceuticals.
And the public services had to continue to serve. These are things that
any government worthy of the name would do whether in war or in peace,
and even if it were under the boot of the occupant."[18]

Both while awaiting and during the trial Laval labored long and hard
on a memorandum which would present his case in its most positive
light to the Court. He indicated in his outline the colleagues to whom
he looked to support the various elements of his case. He labored alone
with only his memory to aid him.[19]

He recounted his protests, seventy-two in all against the annexation by
Germany of Alsace-Lorraine. He had acted to protect its citizens, establishing their university at Clermont, providing government subventions
to their organizations, sustaining their morale in exile.

In his brief he reviewed all the steps he had taken to protect the French
economy against German confiscation of French property and enterprises.
Yet the government had continued to meet its pension obligations and
family allowances, and that included the families of prisoners of war.

He was proud that the production of a great number of factories had
been reserved for France, more than ten thousand, and their workers were
thereby saved from deportation. And real production had been higher and
coal more available than in the post-Liberation winter of 1944.

His outline covered posts, telegraphs, prisoners of war, and the suppression of German operations in the black market, thereby conserving

important goods for France. His government had replaced the wheat lost from North Africa and had accumulated food stocks in Paris so that there would be no famine in the aftermath of the Liberation.

Pierre Laval loved his cattle and it was with special interest that he wrote that France was the only country in Europe whose livestock had been preserved from German exactions. The family allotments had always been paid, even to the families in France of soldiers fighting for the Free French under de Gaulle and Giraud.[20]

Stocks of arms had been hidden and never delivered to the Germans or the Italians.

He had always, he maintained, supported the republican cadres of the country's administration against the pro-Germans and their armed force, the Milice.

"They're ashamed to talk about all that," Laval told Jaffré. "They're ashamed to tell all that I've done. They want to pin everything on two or three spectacular things which hardly weigh in the whole balance of what I did."

He said it again "*Il faut que j'aie tort pour qu'ils aient raison.*" "I have to be wrong so they can be right. So there must be silence on my real record."[21]

"One day," he said of his outline, "my brief will serve as a starting point for a real inquiry into what happened during the Occupation. But right now it only serves to brake a little my trial by judges who want to condemn me but don't want to listen to me.

"They can kill me if they want but they can't suppress the truth indefinitely. What they're doing, at the same time, they're attacking millions of men who were loyal servants of France, men who served under terrible conditions. Men whom I often had to protect against the Germans and who were caught in the same pincers between the exactions of the Germans and the distrust of the French."[22]

"I know these men, their self sacrifice, their sense of duty. Like me, they often wanted to let everything go. But without them, without their firmness, the country would have fallen into anarchy and disorder. They maintained what could be maintained. And they're the ones who are attacked. It's more than stupid. It's atrocious."[23]

16

The Trial: October 6, 1945[1]

Pierre Laval was a veteran lawyer. Whatever his hopes might have been, Laval must have known when the preliminary examination was terminated and the trial date set that political necessity had overtaken justice and the search for truth. This had been confirmed by the Presiding Judge's charges to the jury of blackmail and horse trading and by the farce of the jury selection. Still, he could await the actual commencement of the trial proceeding with some bred-in-the-bone belief that the system he had served so long, the proud and durable traditions of the bar, the very concepts of liberty and equality before the law would serve to dampen passion and prejudice and inform the course of the trial. Given that it was the task of the Attorney General to strike hard for his side, yet the attitudes displayed by the Presiding Judge, upon whom any court must rely for its guidance in the tone and character of the proceedings, could only strike fear and trembling into the heart of the defendant. And this was compounded a hundredfold by the naked hostility of the jurors who did not hesitate to hurl insults and make their opinions, indeed their conclusions, clear long before they had heard any competent evidence.

All this ignited, from time to time during the trial, fiery outbursts from Pierre Laval, inspired in part by his own anger and disgust in the proceedings and in part from his command of the courtroom and his sense of the drama in which he played the central role. And yet, for all that, Jaffré noted Laval's "sang froid, his calm, his lucidity, his intelligence, and the presence of a truly remarkable spirit."

Laval had cried out for the light. The Presiding Judge's response had been to threaten to suspend the hearing. Laval had wished to reply to the Attorney General's charge that he had been condemned to death by a tribunal in Marseilles on the charge of having been an intermediary in the sale of a newspaper to the Germans. Yet the Court had denied him the right to respond, saying that it was irrelevant to the pending trial. The law provided an absolute right to reply, but the more practical question was the impact on the jury of such a charge left unanswered.

The Presiding Judge again demanded order in the courtroom.

"But, Your Honor," Laval protested, "you don't let me defend myself."[2]

"Answer the question I have put to you," Mongibeaux ordered. This was the question of Laval's continuing association with Pétain and the Vichy regime despite his distaste and his objections.

"But I want to reply to the Attorney General," Laval answered. "That's important."

"The Court," Mongibeaux said, "does not wish you to answer the Attorney General."

"But my defense requires that I answer the Attorney General. He has just denounced me before the jury on a very important matter. He said that I was condemned to death by the Military Tribunal in Marseilles for having been an arbitrator in the sale to a German group of *Le Petit Marseillaise*. It's all a lie, a lie, a lie."[3]

M. Biondi, the most vocal of the jurors intervened. The jury, as juries will, took its lead from the Court. "The jurors want you to answer the questions put to you."

"Listen, M. Biondi," Laval addressed him man-to-man. "Put yourself in my place. If you had an accusation like that, would you remain silent?"

"We've forgotten the accusation," Mongibeaux offered.

"You may have forgotten," Laval replied, "but what about me?"

Mongibeaux persisted. He wanted an answer. And so did the jury.

"I will answer clearly," Laval said. "But I say in all decency that my defense isn't facilitated either by an incomplete preliminary examination...."[4]

Mongibeaux finished Laval's sentence in stinging words:

"...nor by your acts during four years, which all France knows about."

Here it was in open Court, before all the jurors. Here was the accusation that came, not from the indictment, as it must, not from the Attorney General whose task it was, but from the presumed fountainhead of objectivity, fairness and of the defense of the rights of the accused, the Presiding Judge.

Laval gasped, stunned by this departure of the Presiding Judge from all of the rules, legal and moral, of his high calling. Yet he rallied quickly.

"I think it would be better if you were to take my place and answer the questions that you put."[5]

"You persist in that attitude?"

"Your Honor, you ask the question and answer it at the same time."

"In your position, do you think you have impunity?"

"I have no assurance of impunity. But there is one thing that is over all of us, over you, over me, and that is the truth. And that is justice of which you are the expression."

"Justice will be done," cried out juror Bedin.

"Justice will be done," another juror took up the cry.[6]

"And it will be French justice," shouted another.

"The High Court," Mongibeaux thundered, "will have the last word."

"You have it," Laval replied.

"You don't wish to answer?"

Laval was crisp and firm: "No."[7]

"Reflect well upon your answer. You won't answer my questions."

"No, Your Honor, in the face of your aggressiveness, in the face of the way in which you formulate both the questions and the answers."[8]

The tumult in the courtroom reached a crescendo. The Presiding Judge raised his voice to make himself heard.

"The hearing is suspended. Guards, take away the accused."

Mongibeaux rose. The jurors stood, too, and in the clamor the court stenographer tried with grave difficulty to record what was said and who said it. The words echo down the printed transcript:

"Salaud. Bastard."

"Twelve bullets."

"He's never changed."[9]

"No," Pierre Laval confronted them. "And I won't change now."

Mongibeaux called for order.

"But the jurors," Laval spluttered, "the jurors. Before judging me. It's formidable."

A juror now pronounced these fatal words: "We have already judged you. And France has judged you too."

The guards now removed Pierre Laval.[10]

What is most interesting and important in this pathetic scene is the failure of the Presiding Judge to administer any warning or any rebuke to the jury. In an American court, a juror who expressed his opinion on the case during the trial, who read reports or was in communication with the parties, witnesses, or court officers in violation of the judge's order would be dismissed and replaced. The judge would have instructed the jury that they were to hear all of the evidence and not to form judgments, and certainly not to discuss them with their fellow jurors, until they had heard all of the evidence and had retired to deliberate.

Whatever the difference in the legal systems, several things are clear. The jurors had expressed, in the most contemptuous terms, their hostility to the defendant and hence their inability to arrive at an honest judgment. More than that, one juror had stated, as plainly as he could, in open court, that he had already decided the case and none of the jurors had raised his voice in disagreement. And this had happened without a single word of warning or rebuke from the Presiding Judge and this had been the case in every other outbreak of passion or opinion by the jury. The jurors must then have clearly understood that such outbursts were officially sanctioned by the Court, represented the tendency of the Court, and that they could carry on in this mode unrestrained by any considerations of fairness, of decency, or of justice.

No such proceedings in any court system could have remained standing on appeal. But the law establishing the High Court provided no appeal.

Laval's stunned disbelief persisted when the lawyers conferred with their client. The words that came most frequently to Laval's lips were "C'est formidable." "Formidable" is, in the French language, a protean word. It means, in the English sense formidable, and also, in a standard French dictionary, dreadful or tremendous. But the word is infinitely capable of broader usage and finer shades of meaning. As Pierre Laval expressed it so often in this extraordinary court hearing, he might equally have wished to say, "It's incredible." "It's astounding." "I can't believe it."

He said what any lawyer might say under the circumstances. It's absolutely impossible that a judgment could be rendered under these conditions.

His lawyers counseled a demand to the Court to redress the injury suffered by the defendant. But what good will that do, Laval asked, since there's no appeal.

What about recusing the jury?

"And who would replace them?" Laval asked. They had all done him injury, he said. He had decided not to respond further. He was convinced that the trial could never go forward under normal conditions.

The suspension lasted for an hour and a half. The tumults subsided but there were bitter comments on the tenor of the proceedings. The Presiding Judge reopened the hearing.

"Accused, you have furnished long explanations during two days about the first charge which is a plot against the internal security of the state. I consider on this point that you have furnished all of the explanations that you have.

"There remains the second charge. You know it. It's intelligence with the enemy. You know on what it rests—the statements of the attorney general."[11]

"I invite you to address the second charge. As to the public, I warn you again as I have before that I will not only expel from the court room but I will arrest any demonstrators and send them to the correctional tribunal or to the High Court."

Turning to Pierre Laval:

"You have the word."[12]

Before hearing Laval's response, it is worthwhile to consider that Mongibeaux's disposition of the first charge of the indictment was in every way as extraordinary as his conduct in the face of the jury's misconduct. Beyond his own rambling statements and the shorter interventions of the Attorney General what was the evidence to support the charge?

Not a single witness had been presented. Not a single document had been placed on the record. Substantial elements of the original indictment had been dropped—Laval's-pre-war activities, his personal finances, the Armistice, the convening and the action of the National Assembly. There had been references to acts, to circulars, but these had never been identified or defined, no more than the specific factual basis underlying the charges.

How could the defendant defend himself unless the acts charged were specified and the prosecution had made out its case? None of this had been done.

Pierre Laval showed no trace of hesitation or fear as he faced the Presiding Judge. The self confidence that had marked his rise, that was one of his fundamental characteristics, did not desert him.

"Your Honor, the injurious way you have questioned me, the demonstration by certain jurors, make it clear to me that I am a victim of a judicial crime. I will not be an accomplice." "*J'aime mieux me taire.*" "I prefer to remain silent."[13]

The Presiding Judge did not pause for a moment to gauge the man who stood before him, to reflect even for a second upon the profound statement he had just heard. Unmoved he announced: "Call the first witness."[14]

But there was none. They had not as yet been called. No one had expected this dramatic turn of events. There would be four witnesses:

Albert Lebrun, the last president of the Third Republic, General Doyen, a member of the Armistice Commission, Ambassador Leon Noel, and M. de LaPommeraye of whom so much had earlier been heard. The Court recessed.[15]

"What will happen," Laval asked his lawyers, "if I don't appear?" They told him the Court would send him a summons ordering him to appear. "Not of my own will, "Laval said. He dictated a letter to the Court. It said that he conceived it his duty not to appear. It was impossible to present his defense, not only because of the lack of a preliminary examination, but because he was convinced he was not in the presence of true judges. He cited again the conduct that day of the judge and the jurors.

"The High Court may condemn me, but it will not have judged me. I leave to it all of its decisions and its responsibilities. I await the judgment of History, the judgment that is denied to me today."

When court resumed the presiding judge read sections 8 and 9 of the Law of September 9, 1835. If a party refused to appear, the Court would issue a summons. If the party did not answer the summons, he could be brought into Court by force or, after reading the record of refusal, the Court could proceed in his absence.

The Court announced that the trial would proceed in the absence of the accused. But it had failed to comply with the procedural step required by the law. Jaffré asked what Laval would do if forced to return to the Court. Laval was conscious of his dignity. He didn't want to be brought in on a stretcher. He would ask the gendarme if he had handcuffs and when he arrived in the courtroom, he would turn his back to the Court to signify that he would in no way be a part of their doings. But the Presiding Judge had elected to proceed in Laval's absence.

The next day was Sunday. Pierre Laval looked forward to a day, if not of rest and repose, a day in which to look deep inside himself and look equally deeply to the future.

Jaffré visited Laval at Fresnes. He expected gloom, perhaps despair. But Laval was jovial, full of anecdotes. He maintained his balance, the only sign of his distress was in the words he repeated again and again: "C'est formidable."[16]

He couldn't continue, he said, under such conditions. And he really wanted to testify about Alsace-Lorraine. That was the only phase of his defense that he had had time to prepare.

But Laval had more serious concerns. He dictated to Jaffré another letter addressed to the Garde des Sceaux. In it he told of the injuries, the indignities, the breaches of law and procedure of which he had been the victim. How could those judges, how could those jurors competently pursue his case?

"I had the honor nineteen years ago to occupy your high functions. I know the traditions of the judiciary of which you are the guardian. I cannot believe you would let such a scandal take place."[17]

The very enormity of the charges against him, he wrote, should guarantee the strictest and most impartial of trials. "Is it possible, on the morrow of the Liberation, to permit the silencing of a process that embraces the history of our country for so many years? Why refuse to France the means the trial offers to know who was really responsible for the country's unhappiness. Is there another country in the world that would permit such a scandal?"[18]

He refused to be a part of what he again called a judicial crime. He pleaded for a resolution consonant "with the sentiments of justice which you incarnate."

The next day, Jaffré, Baraduc and Naud called on the Garde des Sceaux, Pierre Henri-Teitgen. Jaffré took in the details, a somewhat rumpled blue suit, a striped tie and resting on a table a pair of shoes badly in need of a shine. But the first impression wasn't bad.[19]

Teitgen had received Laval's earlier letter. "Tell your client," he said, "without further ado, that I've read his letter. That I can't respond because of my official position. But tell him I highly advise him to return to court. If the trial proceeds without him and it will, he will certainly be condemned to death without having put in his defense."

But, the lawyers replied, an accused couldn't accept judges who attacked him and announced the verdict before the case had been tried. The only solution, they said, was to suspend the trial and resume with other judges. It could be done in another court where even if a sentence were entered, there could be an appeal. But there was no appeal from the High Court. So the only solution would be a new series of preliminary examinations.

"Impossible," said Teitgen. "Don't even think of it." But he had advice to give. They should return to the Court. Pétain had been convicted only by a small majority. If he had to judge Laval personally, he would have to take into account his intentions and his motives. In all honesty, he didn't know what his decision would be. "Tell your client," he said, "that he made a strong impression on the members of the Commission of Inquiry. He can do the same with his judges." Teitgen let them know the government was concerned. He had harsh words for the jurors. They had dishonored themselves. "I wouldn't shake hands with them," he said.

"But your client shouldn't exaggerate. He should lend dignity and calm to the proceedings." Laval had, Teitgen said, quit the proceedings with an uncomplimentary epithet. Or so it was reported in the press. Teitgen also had hard words for Mongibeaux and Mornet. He congratulated the lawyers for their civic courage in undertaking an unpopular cause.[20] All of these were encouraging, even honeyed words. They came with a probing question: "I know well what M. Laval has done for his country. The question is whether to defend the body of France it was necessary to lose its soul."[21]

In the end the lawyers concluded that Teitgen's concern had been, not for justice, but to protect the Government. The trial had become a scandal, especially in the foreign press. Public opinion seemed to be moving in Laval's favor. Many people were sick of the proceedings.[22]

The lawyers reported to Laval on their meeting with Teitgen. He dictated another letter to Teitgen. He wanted, he wrote, to respond to the wishes Teitgen had expressed. If he didn't appear, he would be condemned. He recited again the hostile attitudes of the judge and of the jurors who would be moved to solidarity with their fellows. His only recourse was to the Garde des Sceaux. "*Il faut permittre a la justice de faire toute la lumiere.*" Justice needed the light. A new examination was needed.

He respected, Laval continued, the high office of the Garde des Sceaux. A supplemental examination—time was of the essence—would permit him to defend his honor and he held his honor higher than his life.

"I await from your high authority a decision consonant with the inalienable rights of the defendant and my natural right, the no less inalienable right, to defend myself."[23]

Not to appear in court was a great gamble and Laval accepted it. He believed that if he didn't return to the Court, the government, driven by public opinion, would be forced to find a pretext to interrupt the trial. Jaffré, on the contrary, thought that the government wished to be done with Laval at all costs, even if justice were the real victim.

Mongibeaux, too, tried to prevail on the lawyers to return. "Think," he said, "of the repercussions upon justice in this country. The reputation of France is at stake." Mornet, too, tried to be affable. Mongibeaux told the ultimate truth: "It's General de Gaulle himself who insists that you return to your place at the bar."[24]

So, it had all been arranged. To restore the dignity of the High Court, the accused was asked to suffer and accept every indignity and his lawyers were to be the accomplices. When Jaffré reflected on all of this, a phrase kept recurring to him:

"C'est formidable."
It was on October 6 that Pierre Laval had decided he would no longer participate in the trial. This was the stuff of headlines as shown in *Combat* for October 7-8.

LAVAL DECIDES NOT TO APPEAR
THE DEFENSE ALSO RETIRES

The public was scrutinizing the proceedings. Apparently, so also were the editorial staff of *Combat* which offered the following:

> The Laval trial is nauseating France. What has been going on at the Palace of Justice doesn't resemble anything we would call reasonable. The session yesterday surpassed in odiousness its two predecessors without the relief furnished by those notes of bitter buffoonery which gave the previous sessions some cohesion. It was, this time, the worst, mediocrity confronting incoherence. It was just a brawl of the most sordid kind. In the middle of these cries and gestures, try to find the dignity of justice and its implacable hand.[25]

Combat depicted Laval as a pickpocket who creates an incident in the street in order to divert the attention of his prospective victims.

> He had to because his cause was desperate. He had to appear the victim of injustice. It had to appear that the jurors were going to injure him. It had to appear that it was he who retired, head high above his white tie so as 'not to be an accomplice in the denial of justice' but all of this did not make Laval any less criminal.

But still, there was Laval's plea:

> The revolting partiality of the proceedings has not allowed me to present my defense. The High Court as if it feared the truth, will condemn me but it will not have judged me.

"Is that," the editorialist, asked, "what we wanted? Certainly not."[26]

Figaro took note of the atmosphere of the court that day:

> The nervousness of the President, lacking the serenity which is indispensable to his functions, then the attitude of several jurors accusing the defendant ('twelve bullets'...'the rope') forgetting that they were before the judges finally created an intolerable atmosphere.[27]

On October 9, *La Croix* headlined:

VIOLENT INCIDENTS BREAK OUT DURING THE THIRD SESSION
THE DEFENDANT REFUSES OBSTINATELY TO APPEAR

> The third session of the trial opened with the interrogation of Pierre Laval. But this didn't succeed. The former head of government was inexhaustible, and it was only the

rare admonition of President Mongibeaux which could dam a flood of an eloquence both familiar and cunning. It would be surprising, under these conditions, if the trial ended at the expected date, at least if the President, who up to now has seemed incapable of it, does not succeed in containing the defendant within the limits of the question posed.

The newspaper then reported Laval's refusal to participate further in the trial.[28]

L'Humanité also headlined Laval's refusal to appear further.

The traitor Laval, after two days of maneuvers, has pushed to the foreground yesterday his plan of defense to try to make the normal progress of the proceedings impossible so that he can say that the proceeding has been aborted. Does he hope on this basis to obtain grace?

So Laval has tried, since the beginning of the affair, to multiply the incidents. He argues, he orates, he makes long digressions, then he feigns indignation which lets him insult the court.

Finally yesterday, after vivid incidents, he refused to appear again but the traitor is mistaken if he thinks that he can save his desperate cause. Everybody understands that if he has left the court, it's because he doesn't wish to answer questions.

Was it the members of the Paris bar of whom *L'Humanité* wrote:

But the group of Nazis in the back of the room murmured loudly. Perhaps the Prefect of Police can tell us how he recruited this audience. Because so far as we know, the jurors had no invitations at their disposal.[29]

Figaro reported Laval's refusal in this way:

Nothing is left but to pursue the case...though it is a case without the accused, without his lawyer, and without witnesses, an extraordinary situation.[30]

With Laval absent, the short parade of witnesses began not without difficulty. They looked for this first witness, as *Combat* reported on October 9.

But they couldn't find him. Under these conditions, M. Mornet asked for the deposition of M. Gazel to be read. The whole Court was bored to death…. The session ended pitifully. After having suffocated justice with ridicule, it was buried with boredom.[31]

The papers reported the verdict of the court on October 9. It is interesting to note that in reporting the judgment, *L'Humanité* quoted *Liberation-Soir* which wrote:

It is almost impossible to execute him without having him appear before a more serene jurisdiction.[32]

And *L'Humanité* of October 9 allowed that:

The whole press believed in grace for Laval after the grace that was given to Pétain.[33] Many newspapers agree with *Combat* that truly the High Court was too pressed. It's a done deal. Even in advance. Why so much haste? Let the bandit breathe. There will be plenty of time to chastize treason....[34]

After Laval had been condemned to death, *La Croix* on October 12 gave this valedictory:

> In a few hours the Laval trial will end. It is a page better left unwritten to preserve the good name of French justice. When the foreign press writes that Laval has been refused the guarantees which he had every reason to expect, that the forms of justice have not been observed we will be obliged to accept the judgment.[35]

And *Combat* reported on October 10 the reading of the verdict- death, national indignity and confiscation of his goods:

> The hall empties rapidly. One is in a hurry to quit these places where there was just handed down a justice which whatever else may be said, is not our justice.[36]

17

The Trial: October 6, 8, 9, 1945[1]

When Court resumed on October 6, Pierre Laval was, by his own decision, absent. The witness was Albert Lebrun, the last president of the Third Republic. His testimony in the trial, he said, would be modest. In so saying, Lebrun was himself more than modest. He was in fact a nonentity. In the crash and thunder of May and June, 1940, when the German armies overran France, Lebrun almost literally said nothing and did nothing. He was, it was true, the head of state and not the prime minister. But he took no initiative, he made no appeal, he led in nothing and meekly submitted his resignation when it was asked for.[2]

Mornet had asked Pierre Laval why he had not acted like Clemenceau on the Somme. In 1918, fighting desperate odds with no thought of yielding Clemenceau had summoned "*tout le monde a la bataille*." It was a question Mornet could better have addressed to Albert Lebrun.

Laval, Lebrun said, had entered the government on June 23, that is to say, after the Armistice had been signed. Lebrun himself had given up all of his official duties on the following July 12. After that, he said, all he knew was what he read in the papers.

During the period from June 23 to July 12, governmental activity centered on preparations for the National Assembly. The last cabinet meeting of the Third Republic was held on July 8 and Pierre Laval presented the proposed law which would be considered by the National Assembly. Questions had been asked by the ministers and Laval made changes in response to the questions. Everyone knew "*les jeux etaient faits*," what was planned, and thus the meetings were short.

Lebrun recounted how earlier, on June 21, he had received a visit from Laval and fifteen or twenty deputies. Their visit had followed a meeting of the four presidents, the president of the Republic, the president of the

Council of Ministers, that is to say the prime minister, and the presidents of the Chamber of Deputies and of the Senate. They had discussed a possible removal of the government to North Africa to escape the German armies.

Laval had come, Lebrun testified, to oppose such a move. He had been emphatic not to say vehement. If they left the soil of France, Laval had said, it would be a defection. It would be treason. And a new government would be established on French soil in which they would have no power. It would be as if the French government didn't exist.

It was the same message, Lebrun said, that Laval addressed to the members of Parliament who were arriving in Bordeaux and who were undecided what attitude to adopt.

What were Laval's motives, Lebrun asked himself. "In my opinion" he offered, from the safe harbor of victory, "it would have been better for France to be ruled directly by a German gauleiter than by a French government with only the appearance of power, a government the basic role of which would be to endorse the policies of the occupiers."[3]

And that was all he had to say. It was, to say the least, a remarkable statement that it would have been better for France to receive the full impact of a German administration and to suffer the fate, say of Poland. One might ask what were the activities of Albert Lebrun during the Occupation, with what defiance he had challenged the Occupier, what continuing and effective acts of resistance he had performed? Or did he instead pass the Occupation, if not in comfort and ease, then at least under the protection and in the debt of the Vichy government?

Mornet was not satisfied. "What more do you recall of Laval's visit. What did he say about the President of the Senate?" He elicited the answer by Lebrun he knew was forthcoming, and with great satisfaction he heard Lebrun say: I hate him. I hate him." Which words Mornet now repeated.[4]

Under Mornet's questioning, Lebrun told how Pétain had submitted to him, still president, a list of the proposed cabinet members in the new government. That list included Laval as foreign minister. But on the advice of the secretary of the Ministry of Foreign Affairs Laval's name had been dropped because it might be offensive to Britain. This had upset Laval and in his stead Badouin took the office.

Had Lebrun been surprised by the rapidity with which Pétain had submitted his proposed cabinet list? If surprised, it was an agreeable surprise to a president whose world had crumbled about him and who himself had no plan to address the immediate future. Mornet reached. "Wasn't Laval's name at the head of the list?" Lebrun couldn't remember.

Mornet's next goal was to induce Lebrun to testify to the illegality of Pétain's Constitutional Acts following the delegation of power to him by the National Assembly of July 10, 1940. Lebrun's first response was characteristic. He had signed the bill convoking the Chamber and the Senate but he didn't have anything to do with the National Assembly. It was all beyond him so he was not well placed to give an opinion.

But he did nonetheless. He pointed out that Pétain had been granted the power to frame a new constitution which would be submitted to the country for its approval. But there was a problem. A national vote could hardly be held under the circumstances of the Occupation. Clearly there had to be an interim regime. And that regime, he said, should depart as little as possible from the administration of France before the National Assembly.

Mornet described the Constitutional Acts and their effects. Lebrun again protested his total inaction following his resignation. But Mornet finally achieved his purpose in eliciting from Lebrun the opinion that Pétain's constitutional acts, insofar as they weren't a new constitution approved by the people and insofar as they weren't consonant with the prior regime, were illegal. And on their alleged illegality rested in substantial part the criminal charges lodged against Pierre Laval.

"It was an abuse of mandate?" Mornet asked Lebrun.

"*Si vous voulez.*"[5]

"*Si vous voulez,*" is a reply heard so often in so many contexts in French life. It is hardly a rigorous affirmation, but rather, "If you like," "If it pleases you."

Lebrun concluded with a disclaimer. "As I've said, really, aside from Laval's visit on June 21, there was nothing else in my mind that was important."

When Court convened on October 8, 1945, everyone looked to see if Pierre Laval would appear. The Presiding Judge reported he would not. "Once more I summoned him. He maintains his refusal to appear." Matter of factly he turned to the Attorney General. "Call the next witness."

The witness was General Doyen. He had been director of the French Armistice Commission from September 12, 1940. He had, therefore, been the representative of the defeated French military among the victorious German chiefs.[6]

"Before giving my testimony," Doyen said, "I would like to express my regret that the accused is not before me. I have grave charges to level against him and I would have liked to have him here so we could discuss them, man to man. But that's not my fault and I shall testify before you exactly as I would have if Pierre Laval were here."

Doyen described the terms of the 1940 Armistice: dismemberment of France by the Germans, three departments in Alsace annexed to Germany, two departments in the North separated and attached to the German command in Belgium. These had been, he said, German goals from the First World War. And the German administration of the Armistice, Doyen asserted "was far from what it should have been."

As a consequence, the general declared, "The safety of France could only come from those who continued the fight against Germany, Britain and later the Allies. Anything that aided the enemy—and Germany was the enemy and the Armistice wasn't peace—could only help Germany achieve her goal—the destruction of France. And any such policy, was criminal. One man was the father of that policy. And that man was Pierre Laval."[7]

What had happened at Montoire? He didn't know, but it resulted in something more than the word collaboration. And after Montoire had come Paris.

Doyen prided himself on the part he alleged himself to have played in preventing a ceremonial meeting of Hitler and Pétain in Paris to the rage, he said, of Laval. While the witness was at the Armistice Commission, from September to December 1940, Laval's intimacy with the Germans had been complete and indecent while two million French soldiers languished in German prison camps. And Laval, he said, had demolished all that he and his colleagues on the Armistice Commission had done to defend France.

He cited the sale to Germany of the French-owned Bor copper mines in Yugoslavia in which he had refused to participate. But Laval had done the deal and the Germans had gotten badly needed copper.[8] Then there was the affair of the publishing and news houses Hachette and Havas. Doyen said he had learned of the pending sale of these vital organs of communication to the Germans and had journeyed to Vichy to protest to Pétain. Pétain had reacted vigorously. And two days later, Laval left the Hotel du Parc between two gendarmes, dismissed. The Germans had reacted violently, but the policy of collaboration was ended, at least for a time.

"And to finish, I simply state what I said at the beginning, of the policy of collaboration as instigated by M. Laval. That policy was criminal. It could only lead to the dismemberment and destruction of France."[9]

The much talked about M. de Lapommeraye now made his appearance.[10] He was a spry enough septuagenarian, the honorary Secretary General of the Senate. No question was put to him. Fully primed, he launched into his testimony. He had been present at the Hotel du Parc on the evening of July 10 when the law passed by the National Assembly was being prepared for signature by the President of the Senate for transmission to Pétain. Five or six weeks later he had seen Laval at the Hotel du Parc giving some papers to Pétain. It was then, de Lapommeraye said, that Laval had remarked: "That's how one reverses a Republic." He had been astonished. Laval later said it was nothing more than a pleasantry. But de Lapommeraye recalled an earlier discussion with Laval on July 3. They had talked about how the constitution might be revised. Laval had spoken in favor of a large revision.

"We are beaten," the witness reported him saying. "As never before. And in six weeks, England will be on her knees and forced to capitulate. If we want a less onerous peace, we'll have to create a favorable climate and we'll have to adapt our constitution to the institutions of the Germans."[11]

Was the atmosphere on July 10 one of pleasantries, Mongibeaux asked the witness. "Certainly not," he replied. And was Laval bantering that evening. The witness hesitated. "I can't," he said, "look into the conscience of M. Laval."

There was a curious gap here. The witness had testified that Laval's remark about reversing the constitution had come five or six weeks after July 10. The Attorney General wished to advance the date. He asked de Lapommeraye about the law voted by the National Assembly, the need for its authentication by the President of the Senate before Pétain could promulgate his Constitutional Acts. Was it not instantly afterwards that Laval had appeared, with the Constitutional Acts in hand?

The witness who could not penetrate the conscience of Pierre Laval was reserved here, too. He was too discrete to know or even to ask what the papers were in Laval's hands. But it was there and then that he made his remark. The Attorney General was in deep waters. He failed to appreciate the difference between the law passed by the National Assembly, which needed the signature of the President of the Senate, and the Constitutional Acts which needed only Pétain's signature and he confused the timing of each, but he succeeded in having the phrase pronounced once more, and he revisited, too, the remarks of July 3 about creating a favorable climate and the need to adapt the constitution. Even here, the Attorney General got less than he sought.

"How did Laval say he would adapt the French Constitution to German institutions," Mornet asked. "He didn't say," was the reply.

"Did he not use the words National Socialism?" Mornet asked.

"He never said it to me."[12]

Laughter in the courtroom underlined the Attorney General's discomfort. He recovered by asking the witness once more to repeat as he did: "To create a favorable climate we must adapt our constitution..." He said no more and then retired.

M. Beauchamp was a youthful twenty eight.[13] He was secretary general of the National Federation of deported workers and their families. He represented four hundred thousand workers who had been drafted for work in German factories and fifty thousand who had not returned, victims of assorted violence. He detailed the hardships they had suffered. The worst of it, he said, had been the crisis of conscience of those who were requisitioned, whether to go or to evade. The basis of Laval's policy of the Releve was that for every two French workers sent to Germany, a French prisoner of war would be released. The cruel dilemma was that the young knew that if they did not answer the requisition, they would prevent a prisoner, a head of family, from returning.

Many youths chose to go underground to the maquis, despite Laval's efforts to prevent them. Indeed, the witness said, it was the labor regulations that made so many young Frenchmen into heroes of the Resistance. If there hadn't been the maquis at the end of 1942 and the beginning of 1943, it was the labor draft that later created them.

He had brought with him numerous circulars and communications detailing this program. The first was typical, addressed to the prefects dated April 22, 1943, calling for sending 220,000 workers to Germany by June 30.

"I call your attention," the circular read, "to the strict necessity of carrying out these operations on schedule. You should commence operations on receipt of this telegram so that by May 5 you will have sent to Germany ten percent of your quota. Intensify your efforts with those who were delinquent in previous operations. The grace for those who have not fulfilled their obligations will terminate on April 30."

"The distribution of food ration tickets in the month of May will be particularly severe."

"You should use all means possible to assure the success of these operations for the recruitment of labor."

The circular was signed by Pierre Laval. It was the word "recruitment" that stung the witness in this and similar circulars. It carried the imputation that these workers had gone to Germany voluntarily and this M. Beauchamp bitterly denied.

The testimony of M. Beauchamp concluded. There were no further witnesses on hand. M. Leon Noel would appear the next day. They would then proceed to hear the depositions of the absent witnesses Lamarle and Gazel, and then hear fifteen interrogatories which Pierre Laval had answered in the course of his preliminary examination.

Beauchamp's testimony raised a series of important questions. How did the labor draft originate? What was the origin of the Releve and its exchange of factory laborers for prisoners of war? What success had the Vichy government had in repatriating its prisoners? What, also, would have been the fate of France had there been no Vichy government and could that be tested against the experience of other nations captive to Nazi Germany?

More important, what were the actual facts? Circulars were one thing, the results perhaps quite another. Did the two hundred twenty thousand workers actually go to Germany, and if not, why not? Was it possible that the policy depicted in the circulars masked quite another program and a very different attitude on the part of the Vichy government? Only a serious sustained and dispassionate inquiry could begin to furnish answers to these questions.

M. Armand Gazel[14] whose deposition the clerk now commenced to read had been Counselor to the French Embassy in Spain in 1939 when Marshal Pétain had been the French Ambassador. As the clerk read, the audience departed, one by one, until the courtroom was nearly empty.

The reading of depositions to a court or jury is always dull, lacking the vivacity of real witnesses and what may be read from their appearance, their ambiance, their responses. In this case, the process was rendered duller by the disjointed character of the deposition and its essential irrelevance to the charges at hand.

M. Gazel had little of sensation or even of interest to tell. There had been a plot in the fall of 1939 in favor of a separate peace, but the name of Laval was never mentioned. Pétain had been asked by Prime Minister Daladier to join the government but he had declined. Pétain had shown Daladier a list of potential cabinet members should he be called to power. Gazel remembered the names of Laval and Lemery. But Pétain had told Gazel he would never accept to come to power through a coup d'état. Pétain had been a pessimist about the war. He had little confidence in the English.

All this was so uninspiring that Mornet's mind wandered afield. "Whose deposition are you reading?" he asked amid laughter. He then observed that there was nothing very interesting in the deposition but that the reading of it had all but finished.[15]

Was there anything of interest, the presiding judge asked, in the deposition of M. Lemarle? Only, the reply was, that Laval's name had appeared on Pétain's list of ministers and there was testimony about letters from M. Loustanou-Lacau to Pétain describing his interview with Laval.[16]

Mongibeaux asked the clerk to try to find the relevant passages. But the Presiding Judge was not tarrying. After a recess, he dispensed with the Lemarle deposition. He then called for the reading of portions of the pre-trial testimony of Laval before the examining magistrates. He hoped it would not be too long. Mornet assured him that he would, as the reader might imagine, read only selected portions, and the reader may further imagine that those portions would be the least helpful and the most damaging to the accused. "The portions," as Mornet put it, "that it is important for the jury to know." So the detached and impersonal process began of reading questions which had on August 18, 1945 been put to Laval and then reading his answers.

The first question put to Laval by the magistrates had been why his name had appeared on Pétain's proposed list of ministers.

"It's not the first time," Laval had replied, "that I have been the object of so flattering a choice. I have, after all, occupied many ministries and have been many times prime minister. I am surprised that M. Lebrun was surprised that Marshal Pétain had a list ready to hand. He was a military man, orderly in his habits. I knew nothing of the existence of the list, but I wasn't surprised when the Marshal counted me among his eventual colleagues. But I had nothing to do with drafting the list."[17]

In a lengthy question, Laval was asked his opinion of the change in the character of the new Pétain government in the wake of the vote of the National Assembly and especially the extraordinary new powers delegated to the Marshal. Didn't all that constitute an abuse of the Marshal's mandate?

Laval's response needs careful consideration. He was not about to answer off the cuff.

"The question is important," he had said. "If you will give me a copy (of the relevant documents) I will give you on my next interrogation a full and complete response which will tell exactly my thoughts on the Marshal's acts."[18]

The question, then, would be answered timely, but with due respect for its importance as a question and for the importance of the answer.

"The indictment charges that by intrigues and menaces you stopped the President and Parliament from removing to North Africa there to form a government which would have represented France before Europe and America, which would have affirmed the persistence of France as a sovereign nation."

"Another important question," Laval had replied, "which I will answer in the same terms as the preceding question."[19]

He would respond to a question about Montoire in the same way.

He was then asked to explain his dismissal from office on December 13, 1940 and the subsequent German pressure for his return. "You seemed to be the German's man and, according to certain witnesses the evil genius of the Marshal."

"I will reserve my reply on the same terms as the others. But there was a word which wounds me greatly and I take strenuous objection. I was never anything but a man of France, France's man and I'll prove it."

How had it been, the question was put, that he had returned to government in 1942 and the Marshal had said they stood together hand in hand all this after his humiliating dismissal in 1940?

He would answer it later Laval had replied. "But I can only say now that I wasn't humiliated in December 1940. Only those who dismissed me were humiliated."[20]

Why upon the British assault on Dieppe on August 24, 1942 had Pétain sent a telegram to the German command congratulating them on repelling the assault and offering military collaboration?

"I had," was Laval's response, "absolutely nothing to do with that telegram, neither the idea, nor the drafting, nor the sending of it. I had nothing to do with any congratulatory messages to the German command. I never dealt with them. If I had a message for them, it would have been sent through the Ambassador. But I knew nothing about it."

In an orderly procedure, Laval would, on his next session of the preliminary examination, have made his response and his record on all of the inquiries. He would have had the benefit of documents, reflection, the aid and advice of his counsel. And a nearer truth would have emerged from the process, precisely as it was designed to produce. But the further interrogation never took place.

The next question centered on the famous statement of June 27, 1941 "*Je souhaite*." "I wish for a German victory." "What anger, what stupor it must have caused to many French. Did you really believe that Germany would be victorious when England had been reinforced and the United States and the Soviet Union were coming to her aid with their formidable resources?"[21]

Laval deflected this critical question. He referred to his testimony in the Pétain trial and reserved the right to add to it. But even further, the next question probed, had he not said on November 29, 1942 that he was certain Germany would win and then, speaking of Britain, had he not recalled its egoism, its hardness in the past when it stole, one after another, French possessions in India, in Canada, those magnificent domains of Old France? And in the same speech had he not said that President Roosevelt through propaganda and corruption had weakened France's means of defense? And had he not added that Bolshevism was the real menace and that it should not come wrapped in Anglo-Saxon furs to extinguish the civilization of France?

Did Laval pronounce these words? And if so, why and how were questions of absorbing interest.

Mornet droned on, reading the interrogatories and the answers. Had not Laval said to workers departing for Germany on October 22, 1942 that their tools would recover what French arms had lost? And that they were working for France?

To this veritable cascade of questions, relating to separate times, events, circumstances and responses, Laval took the course of deferring his answer, knowing that answer he must.

Had he not said on December 15, 1942 at a press conference in Vichy: "Enough of hypocrisy. We must choose our camp without equivocation and without ambiguity. I want the victory of Germany?" To escape, had he not added, the menace of Bolshevism and had he not said that Roosevelt carried in his baggage the double triumph of the Jews and of the Communists, and he would break them at all costs?[22]

These were serious charges, Laval said, that like the others he would furnish his reply in the next session.

And had not, the drum beat of the interrogation continued, Laval congratulated the French volunteers who had gone off to fight in Russia, as defending the interests of France?

His general response, Laval said, would explain what seemed to be so shocking and his reasons at the moment when those words had been spoken.

Had he not, in the moment of the German disaster in North Africa warned of treason, and proclaimed that the Americans, the British, and the Gaullists were wrong to doubt that Germany was invincible? Was it necessary to say again that Germany was not beaten?[23]

Even in the reading of the questions and responses from Laval's preliminary examination, the words took on an urgency to which Laval was bound to respond. "I will explain all of that," Laval said. "But for the present, I will tell you that if I had not said certain words, I wouldn't have been able to resist many German demands and it would have been the worse for France." He made an important distinction. "I spoke only for myself. It enabled me to accomplish difficult tasks. I have only betrayed my own personal interests and I did it in the service of my country."

This was, of course, at the heart of Laval's defense: That what he had given, the Germans could have taken by force and with impunity, and by what he had under those circumstances given or said he had saved much more. The final question: In Tunisia in 1943, had not Admiral Esteva called for French forces to aid the Germans? Had not Laval authorized obligatory labor to help the Germans build fortifications?

He had never given military orders to Admiral Esteva, Laval replied. He would explain the Tunisian situation, but in the end, he had exercised no authority there because it was impossible to carry out any orders he might have given.[24]

The next set of interrogatories had been taken on August 23, 1945. They were curious in content. What connection did Laval have with a French information office in New York? The answer was none; but long before his marriage, his son-in-law, René de Chambrun, then a young lawyer in New York, had been involved in that office. To a question about his personal finances, he said he would review the expert's report that had been commissioned and he would furnish his own information. He wanted to be interrogated on this to put an end to legends and calumnies.[25]

What of the annexation of Alsace-Lorraine? When he had entered France from Spain, Laval replied, his valises had been seized and never returned to him. They contained notes and materials ample to answer that inquiry. From them, he could give a complete response.

Didn't the new regime ape the methods of the occupier? Were not the laws affecting the Jews a servile example of this?

He would reply by a note, Laval said. And to the question of the arrests of Jews in July and August 1942, he made the same reply.

The next question was highly cumulative and complex. Had Laval not adopted a German policy of persecution of the Jews, Freemasons, and the Communists. Were not the French police put at the service of the Germans, with 25,000 arrests the night of July 15-16. And had not Vichy adopted laws of exception, all contrary to the French tradition?[26] He would answer, Laval said, by a note.

Then there were the labor drafts, including a circular of July 13, 1943 threatening the lifting of the licenses of doctors who aided youths to evade the service as well as sanctions against their parents.

It would take a long time, Laval said, to answer all this. But he would.

To a question about the crimes of the Milice, Laval said that he would answer fully in the next interrogation and that he would say now that the Milice had been imposed upon him for the very reason that the Germans judged that he had failed in the work of repression. And on this issue, if he had quit, he would have left France in the hands of the adventurers who were tougher and more inhuman than the German occupiers. But naturally he had protested this ordinance that came from Hitler himself.[27]

Another labor circular was brought forward. Laval was disposed to answer more fully. Of course he had signed many circulars. They were *"papiers d'un epoch,"* papers of circumstance and he used them to retard or stop the departure of workers. It was, he said, a way of showing the Germans efforts to comply. And he had often succeeded in having these orders revoked or replaced with others that were less rigorous. Many of them were like warnings and they had given many the chance to escape.[28]

Finally, what about the sabotage of the French fleet at Toulon? Could it not have escaped to North Africa? That was Darlan's order, Laval replied, in which he had played no part. He never gave orders, either to the Army or to the Navy.[29]

The interrogatories of September 22, 1945 were now read. Their essence was the law of December 11, 1942 which he had signed requiring Jews to be categorized on their identification cards.

To this Laval had responded with a plea. He had been examined over nine hours that day. It was 5:45 and he was terribly tired. Before this session of the preliminary examination closed, he spoke up.

He had been shocked, he said, to learn that the preliminary examination had been closed. He ran through a litany that became more and more familiar—the subjects key to the indictment on which he had never been examined. He was accused of a plot against the security of the state, but he had never been examined on the National Assembly. He had been accused of intelligence with the enemy and never examined about Montoire, nor about his negotiations with the Germans. He was, he said, sending a letter of protest to the Garde des Sceaux. He demanded a continuation of the examination so he could exercise his natural right of self-defense.[30]

But, his plea notwithstanding, he was examined again that same day. As to the Bor Mines he said that the transaction was related to other important negotiations, that the government had approved it, and that the Germans had paid 3,000 francs each for shares that were then selling at 1,800 francs. That might have seemed to Pierre Laval like able horse trading.

For the moment the reading of Laval's deposition was done. Mornet said other points would be made in other readings. The other portions would deal with the cession of the French merchant fleet, the sabotage of French warships in the Antilles, telegrams in November, 1942, about the German use of air fields in North Africa. Mornet said he would relate all this. But under the circumstances, he asked, did the jurors desire a further reading of the testimony of Laval? The Presiding Judge put the question to the jurors. M. Lempe asked if all of the notes submitted by Laval in reply were available. They were all in the file Mongibeaux replied. They are all in the dossier, Mornet added. But they didn't add anything to the answers he had already read.[31]

It was on the next day, October 9 that the next witness appeared. He brought elegance to the proceedings. He was Leon Noël who had been France's ambassador to Poland. Before taking the oath he had a statement to make.[32]

He had testified in the Pétain trial. He had given his deposition in the Laval case. He had there passed a harsh judgment on Laval's policy. He had indeed, and he said this with pride, been the first in the Paris region after the Armistice to take a public stand against the policy of collaboration and it had broken his career.

But, he wished to add, he had in earlier years been a colleague of Laval's in the Ministry of Foreign Affairs. He did not forget what he owed to Pierre Laval in the advancement of his career. What he next said was more than a straw in the wind. When in 1942 one of his close friends in the resistance had been arrested and held in secret at Fresnes, Laval had intervened on his behalf.

The sometime ambassador spoke with thoughtful precision. It was not his habit to shirk his responsibilities. He had not changed his opinion on the wartime policies of Laval. He had nothing to add or detract from what he had already said. But the accused was not in Court. Under the circumstances, he found it morally impossible to give evidence, whatever might be the reasons for the absence of the defendant. He hoped the Court would appreciate an attitude dictated by conscience.

In an extended colloquy, the Presiding Judge and the Attorney General found no moral objection to using Noël's previous testimony in the Pétain trial in the present proceeding.

The final witness was M. Edmond Fouret,[33] chairman of the Hachette publishing house. He testified to continuing pressure by the Germans to buy a majority position in his enterprise and the continuing resistance of the Hachette board.

In January, 1943, Laval had indicated to Fouret that he would form a new French state enterprise if Hachette would yield to the Germans. But the Board had again refused and Hachette remained exclusively French as it had been since 1939.

"Pressure accompanied by promises and threats?" Mornet summarized.

The witness replied that he had told the facts as he knew them and would say no more.

18

Pierre Laval's Decision[1]

Pierre Laval had made the fateful determination not to participate further in his trial. But he read in the papers stories of the October 8 testimony of General Doyen and M. de Lapommeraye. He wrote a letter to the Court which was read to the jury the following day, October 9.[2]

He regretted, Laval wrote, that he had not been present in Court to confront General Doyen. He would have referred to the testimony he had given about the Bor Mines before the examining magistrates Langier, Gibert, and Martin. General Doyen would then have known the true facts.

"I am surprised," Laval wrote, "that, given the sentiments he expressed in court, General Doyen remained at the head of the French Armistice delegation at Wiesbaden and had not resigned. How could he have remained so long and participated in a policy which he now condemned so harshly? I never heard any indignation from Doyen while the general was serving at Wiesbaden."

"How could he, as president of the Armistice Commission, not have known of the engagement undertaken by General Huntziger never to let the Bor Mines pass into British hands? It was his duty as President to know of this understanding with the Germans. Wasn't that an agreement designed to injure the Allies in which Doyen participated?"[3]

The statement he had made to the examining magistrate, Laval went on, about the ceding of the shares of the Bor Mines was surely clear enough to contradict the assertions of General Doyen.

The witness had incriminated Laval on the sale to the Germans of the shares of Hachette and Havas. But the shares of Hachette had in fact never been sold and a minority interest in Havas had been sold in 1941 by Admiral Darlan when Laval was in retirement. And, that, by the way, was when General Doyen was with the Armistice Commission at Wiesbaden.[4]

The general had talked about Alsace. As president of the Armistice Commission, it was precisely his duty to protest to the Germans against any breaches of the Armistice convention. Perhaps he did so, but he never got any response.

Had he been in court, Laval wrote, he would, without the slightest difficulty, have destroyed completely Doyen's erroneous testimony.[5]

Laval further wrote that M. de Lapommeraye had not been content to repeat his testimony at the Pétain trial as to what Laval had said in Vichy on July 10 about the reversal of institutions. He had since then elaborated his testimony with some other propositions about the need to conform French institutions to those of Germany. Laval absolutely denied making such statements. His relationship with the witness was never close enough to engage in political conversations.[6]

He once again focused his letter on the heart and soul of his case: "All the public statements I made during the Occupation, about the Republic, about the hope to recover lost liberties, contradict the positions charged against me. I have all those statements in my files. I was too often attacked by the newspapers in Paris that were intimate with the Germans, and precisely because of my republican sentiments and statements, to need to respond to the fantastic statements of M. de Lapommeraye."

He regretted, he wrote, his inability to confront the witness because he would have asked about another incident he was sure the witness would remember—when de Lapommeraye had come, after his retirement, to one of Laval's colleagues to ask for a job. He had supported his request by citing the services he had rendered to procure the July 10 vote of the National Assembly. Laval had two witnesses who would refresh his memory on that point.[7]

In the course of the court session, Laval further wrote, the Attorney general had said that he, Laval, had furnished notes to the examining magistrates and that these notes proved nothing and added nothing. He would make it clear that he had submitted one note only, on his dismissal on December 13, 1940 and that concerning the really important matters he hadn't submitted any other. Indeed, he hadn't answered and he wanted to answer, not by a note, but by a preliminary examination conducted in the usual way. A formal judicial proceeding, he wrote, was carried out by questions and answers and not by notes. It would be completed by hearing witnesses and by confrontations between the witnesses and Laval. That was not what had been done. It is just that that he had been refused.[8]

This letter attested to Laval's fighting spirit. It also raised some interesting questions. What indeed had been the testimony in the preliminary examination? And how were the jury to decide whose claim concerning such testimony was correct when they had not themselves had the benefit of it? What written notes had Laval submitted to the examining magistrates, and, if he had, what was in them? If the trial were a pursuit of the truth, how was it to be determined, and by whom? The jury to be sure, had the ultimate power to convict or acquit, but on what basis was difficult indeed to perceive in this stage of the proceedings.

Whatever optimism Laval may have had during the preliminary stages had yielded to harsh reality. He had been accustomed to say: "I have to be wrong so they can be right." Now he grimly smiled and said: "*Pour qu'ils aient raison, il faut que je sois fusilé.*" "I have to be shot so they can be right."[9]

He nevertheless maintained his perspective. "After all," he told Jaffré, "the judges of the High Court aren't brutes. They aren't idiots. I don't know them, but I knew others like them who were in Parliament under the Third Republic. They weren't crazy." They took him for a traitor. But, at the heart of it all, what could they know of his actions, of how he had dealt with the Germans? They wanted to judge him in haste and have done with it, sincerely believing that they were doing a patriotic duty. If they would only let him explain...[10]

But he saw no sign that they would. And there was always the injustice of not having had a preliminary examination before magistrates who would have understood the historical nature of the case. Not, he said, like the cannibals on the jury who the other day wanted to silence him.

One day, earlier in the proceedings, Jaffré had joined his colleagues in a visit to Mornet. Mornet was agreeable enough and he dispensed advice. They should plead their case, he said. And in doing so they should pair Laval's policy of presence and of negotiations with the policy of intransigence and combat of de Gaulle. He had then added: "Outside of the policy he represents, Laval is a curious and interesting person."[11]

On leaving, Jaffré had said to his colleagues: "He isn't all that bad." But when he told all of this to Laval, Laval said: "But he's the one who drafted the indictment and you couldn't call that a document very friendly to me. Your Attorney General Mornet has sharp teeth."

Laval motioned to Jaffré to listen carefully. He spoke in low tones devoid of passion. "I'm not counting on anything good from him. And yet," he paused, "he owes me a debt of gratitude. I'm going to tell you something you don't know. During the Occupation, Mornet was a member of a commission which had for its task the denaturalization of certain Jews. One day I received a letter from a member of the commission. He was notoriously pro-German. It was a denunciation of Mornet, and accused him of sabotaging the work of the commission. Whether Mornet had in fact done that, it wasn't for me to find fault. In fact I found so little fault there that I threw the letter in the wastebasket without answering. Now suppose the letter, instead of coming to me, had fallen into the hands of some excited pro-Germans. Mornet would have been in plenty of trouble."[12]

"Why doesn't anyone ask Mornet to explain why he belonged to an anti-Semitic commission and why he solicited the honor of sitting on the Court at Riom" (where former Prime Minister Leon Blum, Edouard Daladier, and other personalities of the Third Republic had been unsuccessfully prosecuted for failing to prevent and then to prepare for war.) "I understand well enough what he says today—that he did it to serve the cause of France and to protect the French. Did I do anything different? And today it is M. Mornet who drafts the indictment against me and who asks for my head. It's madness."

He had another anecdote. After the First World War, Mornet had been named to the Court of Cassation, an appeals court. A judge and his friend emerging from the Court were discussing this appointment. "What do you think of your new colleague?" the lawyer asked. "Nothing!" said the judge. "And me," said the lawyer, "if I were accused of a crime, I wouldn't want to appear before him-even if I were innocent."[13]

"He's aged," Laval observed, "but he hasn't changed."

Nothing could better illustrate the issues and the perplexities, the practical and the moral problems that faced the French people in four years of German Occupation. Mornet had been a member of a German inspired commission whose express purpose was to strip French Jews of their French citizenship. The cruel consequences were that their property could be seized and they could be deported, in effect a death sentence. The commission of which Mornet had been a member was an arm of the Vichy government which he now so violently attacked as an abuse of the vote of the National Assembly and illegal, unconstitutional and criminal into the bargain.

And yet the accusation had been leveled against Mornet that he was sabotaging the work of the Commission. Apparently, then, where Frenchmen stood was neither all black nor all white. Mornet could participate in the work of the Commission and at the same time work, or be thought to work, in the opposing cause. As Laval perceived, Mornet could today claim he had worked on the Commission to defend French people and interests, the very claim upon which Laval's defense rested.

The accusation against Mornet at a time when he was serving on the anti-Semitic Commission had been addressed to Laval, Mornet's accused, and it was Laval who had put an end to the inquiry in defense of Mornet. The same Laval was here accused by Mornet of an anti-Jewish policy when in fact Laval had many times labored to sabotage German demands for anti-Semitic measures and for Jewish deportations.

To sort out issues so tangled, so dense, so concrete yet at the same time so arcane would require a careful examination of all of the facts, of motivations, of intentions and of results that would need the services, not only of a judge and jury but of a veritable Solomon or a philosopher king.

19

The Trial: October 9, 1945[1]

It is interesting that in the trial record, Mornet's final argument is labeled "Requisitoire," which the dictionary defines as "indictment." In the Anglo-American system of law, the indictment states the crimes charged against the accused. The final argument on the other hand, is a summary of the evidence that supports the indictment.

There was no question that Mornet, a veteran prosecutor with many a celebrated scalp hanging from his belt, would make a powerful final appeal to the jury. The question was to what extent that appeal would consist of a list of charges and to what extent it would review competent and material evidence that the jury had actually heard.

The courtroom was, as always, packed with those spectators fortunate enough to gain admission: with the press, and members of the Paris bar who came and went as their schedules permitted and who were of all this assemblage among the most critical. The jury was alert and attentive as Mornet launched his statement.

"I would have wished," he told the jurors, "for the trial to proceed in a more serene atmosphere. But could it have been otherwise with a defendant who from the start did not wish to be judged, who left the courtroom followed by his lawyers? The court is obliged to assure the presence of defense counsel and the court has complied. The court hoped to see defense counsel here today with their client. But they refused."

"And I regret it."[2]

"As for myself, whatever robe I wear, I am only a party before the High Court. My task is to explain how and why you ought to judge Pierre Laval."

"I've said it many times. This is the trial of a policy, a policy, may I add, that was root and branch criminal and that policy was concretized in the man you are to judge."

"A political trial, yes. But there are two kinds of policies. There is internal policy which is criminal only in an attempt to overthrow a legal regime. But a foreign policy can be criminal in and of itself."

"I leave aside those policies, however disastrous, which proceed from error and in good faith. But there are those policies, criminal in themselves, which spring from a willful disregard of the duty every citizen owes to his country."

"That policy, criminal in itself, can take two forms. The first consists of humiliating one's country, accepting its diminution, its downfall, when the enemy occupies a large part of your country, to collaborate, to accept the fait accompli. The second is not only the humiliation of a country but leading it to dishonor, lending aid and comfort to the enemy, not only in spirit, but also material and military aid against an old ally fighting in a common cause."[3]

"Here is dishonor. Yes the dishonor of the nation. Except...except when that nation, like France, proves by the blood of its martyrs and its arms that it was never tainted by that pseudo-government. It is a crime rooted in insouciance, in amorality, like those crimes which are against the common law."[4]

This appeal to honor was indeed a remarkable sentiment coming from a man who had loyally served the Vichy regime, solicited a place on the Riom court and sat on the panel charged with denaturalizing his fellow citizens of Jewish faith. Perhaps that was why Mornet was so quick to cloak his address in the bloody rags of an exalted patriotism.

Was it necessary, Mornet asked, to establish the criminality by witnesses, by confrontations, by inquests? The question, the reader must note, betrays his sensitivity to the absence of such common elements of proof of a crime.

"No, there were the acts of a government of which the accused was at the head, its decrees, its laws, its circulars, its declarations, which were in themselves confessions, stripped of any artifice. So it was with Pierre Laval. The case against him rests on the laws he signed, the circulars addressed to the various services, the declarations, the documents, and none of them were contested except for two. I won't take advantage of either of them" -but he now took care to state them- "that phrase reported by the English radio that the hour of deliverance of the prisoners would not sound until the hour of German victory and the other at Mayet-et-Montagne. Everything else is undeniable and was never denied."[5]

So, in the end, the problem remained the same. There were laws, there were to be sure circulars, there were declarations. But what, one might ask, was the context? What was the background, what were the circumstances, what were the options, what were the possibilities, what were the intentions, what was the balance between the threatened evil and the chance of avoidance, what was the balance between what had been lost and what had been saved and between those who had been lost and those who had been saved? To what degree did the inculpation rest on words and to what degree upon acts, and when and where and how had the words taken the place of acts that might otherwise have been compelled? All this was at the heart of the defense of Pierre Laval, the defense that the Court had heard only in bits and snatches before Laval had given up the trial as hopeless in the face of the conduct of the Court and jury.

Mornet addressed the insufficiency of the preliminary proceedings. They had continued, he said, since the day the High Court was established in November, 1944, and they included a supplemental instruction. And if Laval believed he was entitled to a longer preliminary examination, well, the problem was that the examining magistrates had quickly perceived that whatever the question was, Laval would not respond. Mornet added a remarkable coda. "When the higher interests of the country are at stake, when there is an accusation of treason over four years, when the charges are established [were they?], then it is time to judge. And the sooner the better."[6]

If Mornet had betrayed some sense that the evidence had been less than comprehensive, he showed an equal apprehension about the documents. They had all been available to the defendant, he told the jury; and if they hadn't, defense counsel had only to ask for them and they would have been supplied. The fact was that the trial dossier had been locked up in Beteille's cabinet while he was off on his holiday. But, Mornet insisted, he had done everything that the law required. If fault there were, once again Mornet charged it to the defendant and his counsel.

The state of Mornet's conscience that day was indicated by his next remark. "If Pierre Laval had been arrested a year ago, he wouldn't have enjoyed all of these guarantees." In other words, if the proceedings were deficient, they were better than nothing.[7]

Mornet would now get down to business. The first segment of the case against Pierre Laval started with the war in 1939 and lasted until May, 1940, a period of anticipation for those who lurked in the shadows, awaiting the grave events of the morrow when they would step forward.

Then there were the tragic events of May and June, 1940, when Pierre Laval had emerged from the darkness of France's defeat. They were for him the hour of revenge, under the banner of Marshal Pétain, who inspired a confidence among the French which he, Pierre Laval, never could.

Next came the period from June to July 10, 1940, followed by the constitutional acts of July 11, the suppression of the republican regime, and the policy of collaboration personified by Laval. Thereafter, when he was temporarily out of power, there had been a powerful campaign in the Axis press for his return. He then returned to power and his words and authority were symbolized in the famous phrase, "I wish the victory of Germany..." Not only had he wished it, he had prepared for it.[8]

"There are men," Mornet said, "whose role, whose influence must disconcert not only the moralist but also the historian. History would not say that Laval was one of those who quit power poorer than he had entered."

This gratuitous remark was the measure of Mornet's prosecutorial ethic. He had clearly said that the issue was no part of his case against Laval. So it was with another twist of the knife that Mornet cooed, "I don't say anything else, the facts are uncontested."[9]

Mornet now reviewed Laval's career, his rise, his high offices, and his hatred of democracy. To this was added a hatred of Great Britain because of the failure of the Hoare-Laval plan to end the Abyssinian War. There were the violent diatribes against Britain; at the National Assembly of July 10, 1940, he had said Britain had propelled France into a war and treated the French as mercenaries.

"Laval and Pétain. France shouldn't have been surprised to see these two, linked together, come to the fore." Mornet now reviewed documents, the letters of Loustanau-Lacau, which imputed to Laval the promotion of a Pétain government. There was, he said, the testimony of M. Lamarle to the same effect (though the jury had never heard it). And, remarkably, he told the jury, there had been the testimony in the Pétain trial (which of course was outside the record of the Laval trial) of a young woman (unidentified), secretary to the Italian journalist Giobbe (who never appeared at the trial), to the effect that in November, 1939, Laval, had said that he, not Daladier, was the man of the hour, in a Pétain ministry. The same mysterious source had reported in May, 1940, that Giobbe thought that France should move closer to Germany and Italy, leaving Paul Reynaud to form his ministry in London while in France there was a revolution headed by Pétain and Laval.[10]

For once Mornet was fair. These were not properly arguments against Laval but they showed a climate of opinion in which the names of Pétain and Laval were linked. To the same effect was the testimony of Gazel, attached to Pétain's embassy in Spain, that Pétain had showed him lists of prospective members of a Pétain government in which the name of Pierre Laval was always included.[11]

The jury must have wondered why Mornet lingered so long over these exiguous testimonies. As Mornet admitted, Laval would say he wasn't responsible for what other people wrote and said. But Mornet continued. When President Lebrun invited Pétain to form a government, Pétain had taken out of his pocket a list of members and Laval's name was on that list. But in fact, Mornet was constrained to admit, Laval had not entered the Marshal's government at its debut but only days later, on June 23, 1940, as minister without portfolio.

Was there a crime here? Laval's name had been linked with Pétain's and it had appeared on a list of prospective members of a Pétain government. Laval would never deny that he thought Pétain indispensable to France as head of state and he had worked mightily, but far from alone, to that end, which was, in the event, overwhelmingly voted by the National Assembly. Where was the crime? Mornet did not say. Instead, he moved on to what he conceived to be a substantive charge.

This was the charge that Laval had exercised a decisive influence which had prevented the president of the Republic, the presidents of the Senate and the Chamber of Deputies and important members of Parliament from departing for North Africa, there to carry on the government of France. That would have avoided, Mornet said, the formal capitulation of France, the end of the republican regime, and the policy of collaboration. But Laval, he charged, had frustrated this, leading to the formation of the Vichy regime in the absence of what would have been the real government of France.

It is hardly necessary to review the testimony of President Lebrun as characterized by Mornet. No historian today would believe that Laval single handedly could prevent members of the government or other members of Parliament from acting in accordance with their beliefs, their principles, their consciences, and their estimate of the situation. To believe that would impute to Laval extraordinary powers of persuasion, of seduction, not to say of control. It would at the same time impute to the president of the Republic—granted not a rock of determination and fixed purpose in the hour of crisis- and to the members of the government and of Parliament a total absence of perception, of critical thinking, of conscience, and of a sense of duty which neither then nor today reflects the situation as it was and how men responded to it. Nor would it seem today anything other than fortunate that the French government did not move to North Africa where a German response might have fundamentally altered the course of the war in the Mediterranean to Hitler's great strategic advantage.

However clear these things may seem two generations later, it was certainly an appealing picture that Mornet suggested to the jurors: a France, steadfast and determined, a France without Vichy, a France fully participating in the ultimate triumph. What that appealing picture omitted is what France would have been and what France would have suffered under a very different kind of German occupation.

Mornet now attacked the Vichy regime, which he labeled the new order. "And you know what that new order meant—the abolition of the Parliamentary regime, the entente with a conqueror, a new order instituted by a coup d'état—for what else can I call the three constitutional acts of July 11, 1940?—a coup d'état founded on an abuse of confidence, a defiance of the mandate given to the Marshal..."[12]

Of all this, Pierre Laval as vice president of the council, was the accomplice, the co-author. And what had he said at the Pétain trial? That the constitutional acts were null and void because they had never been approved by the Council of Ministers and therefore he was free to serve in the government. Well, then he participated in a government that arose out of invalid acts. And he had ironically said to de Lapommeraye, "That's how one reverses a Republic," and later that France would need to adapt its institutions to those of the victor.

M. Noel, out of conscience, had declined to testify against Laval. But Mornet referred to a deposition he had given in which he said France could have stood on the Armistice terms and rejected anything else. If forced to obey the exactions of the occupant, the French government could have publicly protested and so safeguarded the dignity of the nation.[13]

This was another argument attractive in the retrospect of 1945, but a difficult case to sustain if serious consideration were given to the actual facts of 1940. What indeed would have stopped the Germans from doing quite as they pleased? There were examples of what that meant and Poland was only one of them.

But, Mornet knew as well as we know today that the Pétain regime had been inaugurated with the overwhelming support of the nation and the 569 to 80 vote of the National Assembly, and that among those votes were Jeanneney president of the Senate, Herriot, president of the Chamber of Deputies and the former socialist premier and icon of the left, Leon Blum. It was a government to which the administration of France gave its loyal and continuing support and among their supporters was the Attorney General, Mornet. If Pierre Laval, in participating in the formation of the Vichy government and later in serving it were guilty of a capital crime, then his co-defendants in France would have been legion.

Mornet now turned to a more agonizing subject. There were decrees of October 3, 1940 severely restricting the Jews in various professions and the decree of December 11, 1942 requiring "Jew" to be stamped on their identity cards and ration cards. All of this would make the Gestapo's job easier.[14]

What was most curious is that these two decrees, and these alone were charged. What indeed had happened during the long nightmare of Hitler's war of extermination against the Jews that came to be known as the Holocaust? What had been the fate of French Jews, of Jews in France and why was Mornet silent beyond what scant reference he had made? Was it his own guilty knowledge of his participation in the denaturalization panels? Or was there a record he did not wish to bring to the attention of the jury?

All these were matters which Pierre Laval and his counsel might have addressed in their final argument to the jury if indeed there had been one. But there was not, and, if there had been one, how would Laval have responded?

There was, Mornet continued, the sale of the Bor Copper Mines to Germany, the pressure on Hachette to sell. If the share price for the Bor Mines had been more than twice the market quotation, the Germans could simply pay for those shares out of the Occupation charges that were levied daily. Mornet did not say how the French government could have prevented German seizure of the mines and the shares, too, and what France's remedy might be if they had.[15]

Mornet next charged Laval with failing to protest the German annexation of Alsace-Lorraine. We have already seen Laval's vigorous riposte to this charge, the list of his protests, the extensive action in favor of Alsace-Lorraine and its inhabitants, and his pregnant question how the witness, General Doyen, could so long have retained his post as president of the Armistice Commission in the face of his own testimony.

What, Mornet asked, had been Laval's response to the annexation of Alsace-Lorraine? It had been to meet with Hitler at Montoire. The very name Montoire had dark connotations. It stood, Mornet said, for slavery to Germany.

But what had actually happened when Pétain and Laval met Hitler and Ribbentrop?[16] Montoire was, after all, only a name, a place. Mornet clearly thought the name was enough. What indeed, would have been

Laval's view of the meeting at Montoire as expressed in the final argument that was never made?

Mornet continued by relating Laval's return, after his December, 1940 dismissal, to government in April, 1942, and the broad authority he then enjoyed. It was then he uttered the fateful words: "*Je souhaite...*" "I wish for the victory of Germany..." "Words which are acts," Mornet concluded.[17]

Mornet returned to the chase. There had been 700,000 deportees, even though they had been called volunteers and 50,000 had never returned. This was a sore and difficult subject and Mornet reviewed Germany's desperate need for manpower and Laval's efforts to supply it. French workers in Germany were, he was quoted, working for France. And when the "volunteers" failed to report, there were threats against parents and doctors who helped young men to evade compulsory labor service.

Mornet anticipated Laval's defense. Far proportionally fewer had gone from France to Germany than from Belgium. If this were true, Mornet tried to turn the argument to his advantage. It was because in France young men could join the maquis, hard to do in the cramped and flat terrain of Belgium.[18]

There were numbers here. But what was the truth behind the numbers? How many workers had been demanded, how many had been supplied? The question was like so many others: What was lost, what was it possible to save and what had been saved? The issue remained the same: what force had been applied, what means were there to resist; had the demands been resisted; had the resistance succeeded; and, if so, to what extent? To require that the German demands for labor be rebuffed in all places and at all times without yielding a single man was not within the realm of reality. But what was? And, again, what would have been Laval's response if he had chosen to respond?

Mornet now turned to military matters and the support which, he said, the Vichy regime had given to the German armed forces. He cited a telegram of congratulations in the name of Pétain on the German repulse of the Dieppe raid of August 19, 1942. But he admitted that it was by no means certain that Laval had signed the telegram and that Laval had denied all knowledge of it.

This was followed by the Allied landings in North Africa of November, 1942. Amid all of the confusions and conflicts of orders and of loyalties, Mornet fastened on an exchange of telegrams whereby French forces were ordered not to interfere with German aircraft flying over France's Unoccupied Zone toward the Mediterranean. There were other telegrams indicating that the French authorities had permitted German aircraft to land at French bases in North Africa and then to participate in its defense against the Allied invasion.[19]

Why were these incidents, modest, even trivial, all that Mornet chose to present to the jury on the issue of military collaboration?

Mornet now admitted that in the matter of the scuttling of the French fleet at Toulon in November, 1942, the primary responsibility had rested not with Laval, but with Pétain, who had congratulated Admiral Laborde for obeying his orders. But Mornet could not refrain from adding that Laval and Pétain, Pétain and Laval, "marched hand in hand and the communion between them was complete." As might have been expected, it was the sinking of the French fleet that had precipitated the German occupation of all France.[20]

Mornet then reviewed the fate of the French naval forces in the Antilles, and the conflicting orders that had been sent there; but in the end, the ships and the treasure they carried had all been saved for France.

Mornet was on sounder ground in reading Laval's letter to Hitler of November 22, 1942, offering to place the French merchant fleet at the disposal of the Germans. An act, the letter continued, indicating the will of France to take part in Germany's gigantic struggle and to defeat Bolshevism. What the purpose of this may have been is indicated in the last paragraph by the request for a meeting with the Fuhrer, but whether such a meeting ever took place and with what results Mornet did not see fit to tell the jury. What he did say was that Laval would claim that he had made this offer to encourage reciprocal benefits and the good graces of the victor. But that was, he said, "a policy of petty profit, in the end a petty profit at the price of a great injury to France, as much moral as material."[21]

Laval, he charged, had continued to believe in a German victory and uttered menaces against those who did not share that opinion. He had praised Pétain's appointment of Joseph Darnand as head of the repressive Service de Maintien de l'Ordre (Service for the Maintenance of Order) and he had not hesitated to sign an order in March, 1944, that in case of military operations on French territory, the mission of the Service de Maintien de l'Ordre would be to contribute to the security of units of the German Army which were not engaged in combat and to oppose the forces of the Resistance. "An army against the nation," Mornet cried. "What a monstrous error, an error not only of reason but of the heart."[22]

Leaving aside questions which would normally be raised in a capital case as to the provenance and authenticity of this document and of the role of Laval in issuing it, it is a vivid example of the selective technique of a prosecutor in a case in which only his side will be represented. Was this all Laval had said on the subject and if not, what else had he said, and when, that might fairly present the matter?

Mornet now grandly summarized his case. Why had Laval so departed from elemental morality? There was the parvenu, arrived at an astonishing fortune, there was the taste for power, the gambler's instinct which had served him so well, except when the Senate and the nation had rejected him. It was all of a piece, the hatred of the parliamentary regime, the hatred of England.[23]

The alliance with Pétain had been foreshadowed and they emerged out of the shadows of disaster to do what? To play the German card and play it to the end. And what did that mean? It meant a France subservient to Germany, its political system, its elites destroyed or in exile.

"And what would Laval say if he were here? He would say that in 1940 no man of sense would believe Germany would be defeated, that he was a man of sense, that there was no other policy possible in the interests of France."

"But the interest of France was not to accept defeat and to preach it. That was a crime. You might ask—to be mistaken, is that a crime? It was a crime," Mornet answered his own question, "when there was a want of conscience, of duty to the country. That was a common crime."

"But, Laval would say to you, if he had not been there, it would have been worse. And he would have had facts and figures to support that." Maybe, Mornet observed, France wasn't Poland or the Ukraine where there had been systematic attempts to annihilate the population. But there was suffering and blood enough in France—120,000 deported on grounds of race of whom only 1,500 returned, 120,000 political deportees, of whom many died at Dachau, at Buchenwald, and in the gas chambers, not counting the 150,000 executed on French soil. How then could Laval say if he had not been there it would have been worse?[24]

"But there were higher considerations. The policy of Laval exposed France to a suspicion of treason to France's allies. It had put France's honor at stake. To doubt the faith of an ally is to doubt its honor."

"There has been talk here of History. There have been reversals of alliances before. But how can you talk of reversal of alliances when those who presided over it were so completely at odds with the nation?"[25]

Completely at odds? The overwhelming vote of the French Parliament to install the Pétain regime, the overwhelming support it received and maintained across the nation, occupied and unoccupied, were all submerged in Mornet's bold assertion that the nation had been a stranger to the Vichy regime. The charge of treason might have raised a question among jurors with longer memories.

The final appeal was inevitable and Mornet did it handsomely. "France is washed clean of suspicion. France is redeemed by the blood of martyrs, the Maquis, the Resistants, the common victories in Normandy and Brittany. The crimes of Vichy are inexpiable, inexcusable crimes against the Motherland and against its martyrs. There can only be one penalty. Death."[26]

The defendant had refused to present his case. "That was his supreme resource, that was his supreme tactic. You have seen," Mornet told the jury, "that when questions were put to Laval, he refused to answer or said he would submit a note. Here was your gambler, and what he was saying was: 'You wouldn't dare.'[27]

"Well, for my part," Mornet thundered, "under the circumstances and seeing my duty, I will dare. And I do dare." What he added did him less honor. If, he said, popular justice had been done to Laval in August 1944, he would have dared then to applaud. Justice would have been done. Justice for which France had waited for five years. The final words inevitably rolled out: "I demand that you pronounce the sentence of death on Pierre Laval."[28]

It was anticlimax indeed when the court now read to the jury the letter Pierre Laval had written the day before. The defendant and his counsel were not present in court. Save for this letter there was no other response to Mornet's final argument.[29]

20

Pierre Laval's Defense

The court and jury had heard Mornet's fiery final argument and his demand for the death penalty. In regular French trial practice, Mornet's *requisitoire* would have been followed by the *plaidorie*, the accused's final argument. But in the absence of Pierre Laval and his lawyers, there could be no reply to Mornet's assertions of fact, arguments of law or appeals to emotion. It is useful therefore to make some accounting of the charges so vividly presented, and the facts that might have been presented but never were.

Large chunks of the prosecution's case had fallen of their own weight, or had been abandoned by the prosecutor. No evidence had ever been presented of financial improprieties and there was the pointed omission of any reference to the report of the financial examiner, M. Caujolle. Only the insinuation remained.

The prosecution had abandoned any charges based upon Laval's prewar politics or diplomacy. Historians continue to debate the merits of his policy as Foreign Minister and then Prime Minister in 1934 and 1935. There is a growing body of historical opinion that Laval's efforts, with Sir Samuel Hoare, the British foreign secretary, to resolve the crisis caused by Mussolini's aggression in Abyssinia, once universally condemned, were a sound policy which could have preserved Italy as the ally of Britain and France in the containment of Nazi Germany. It was Mussolini's tilt away from Britain and France in late 1935 and early 1936 that gave Hitler the signal to march back into the demilitarized zone of the Rhineland in March, 1936. Mussolini had been Austria's protector and defender. With Mussolini now his ally, Hitler annexed Austria in 1938 leaving Czechoslovakia literally surrounded, to fall to Germany first at Munich in 1938, then in the final takeover in 1939. This was the fatal train of events that led to the Nazi blitzkreigs of 1939 in Poland, in 1940 in the West and all of the horrors of the Second World War.

However that might be, whatever his views, no historian today would find anything criminal in the policy which Pierre Laval then so openly, pursued.

The prosecution had also abandoned any charges relating to Laval's policy or conduct during the so-called Phony War, the period between the onset of the war in September, 1939, and the German assault on the West that began on May 10, 1940. Even in the tumultuous atmosphere of October, 1945, when memories of defeat and occupation were still fresh and scars livid and unhealed, the prosecution was forced to concede that Laval had nothing to do with the Armistice, which had been decided upon, negotiated and signed before he became a member of the Pétain government. There was no doubt, as he freely stated, that he was convinced of the necessity of an armistice and that he had vigorously advocated it. But in this he was at one with the overwhelming majority of the French people, Parliament, military, citizens and all, surely including his judges and the Attorney General. But he had the Lavalian audacity to say that had the matter been in his hands, he would have negotiated better terms.

It had been charged that Laval had prevented the French government from leaving France and establishing itself in North Africa, there to maintain French sovereignty and to carry on the war. But the absurdity must have been self-evident, even in 1945, that one man, holding no other office than as a member of Parliament, could single-handedly have prevented the duly empowered and acting representatives of the French people from taking action on a matter of life and death other than as their judgment, their consciences, and their sense of duty dictated. Surely Marshal Pétain needed no urging from Pierre Laval to remain in France and accept the burdens of defeat and the same was true of the vast majority of the French. The prosecution had freely conceded that this charge no longer formed any part of its case.

There had followed the events of July 9 and 10, 1940 when the two houses of Parliament had convoked the National Assembly which had, in its turn, and surely under the guidance of Pierre Laval, delegated the powers of the Third Republic to the new regime of Marshal Pétain. The charges were vivid, that Laval by threats and menaces, maneuvers and intrigues, had foisted an illegal order upon a stoutly resisting National Assembly. The truth was that the procedures were scrupulously in accord with the Constitution and overwhelmingly approved by a free and fair vote in Parliament on July 9, 1940 and by a vote of 569 to 80 in the National Assembly the next day. No historian today would sustain the colorful charges of the indictment and Laval himself so ably demolished such claims that the prosecution conceded and the issue was dropped from the charges but as we shall see, reinstated in the judgment.

Julian Jackson concludes of the votes of July 9 and July 10, 1940:

> Essentially the vote was born out of despair and defeat. It revealed an erosion of faith in the institution of the Republic across the entire political spectrum....Such people were not voting for what we have come to know as the Vichy regime. The size of the majority was essentially a vote of confidence in Pétain and is entirely explicable without involving the black arts of Laval.[1]

There were various minor charges that appeared, either in the indictment or the testimony of the various witnesses, none of which would, on reflection, seem to rise to the level of a capital crime. There was, for instance, the sale of the stock in the Bor copper mines. The first question was how the French government could prevent the Germans from simply taking over a mine in Yugoslavia when they could not prevent the occupying power's expropriations in France. Moreover, the shares had been sold at twice the current stock market quotation. Laval was essentially a negotiator, a wheeler-dealer, with a shrewd peasant's eye for an advantageous piece of business. He might well have concluded that he had brought off a smart deal getting, to France's advantage, twice the value for property the Germans could simply have had for the taking. This was reminiscent of his statement on his return from Rome in January, 1935, after signing a treaty of alliance with Italy, that he had brought home Mussolini's shirt and studs.

In the overall scheme of things, in Laval's efforts to deal with the Germans over every issue of political margin, of the life and sustenance of France, the Bor mines were not a major issue. Against what background did the transaction play out, what were the other issues on the table and how important, and what chits, what goodwill did Laval gain against his other needs and demands on behalf of his country? All these would illuminate the intent with which the transaction was arranged and the results obtained.

It must be remembered that France was utterly prostrate at the feet of the Germans. Laval had no physical force to interpose against the occupier whose displeasure could have tragic consequences. Laval had basically only words at his disposal, his skill as a negotiator, as the player, albeit with high confidence, in a risky game. He would, he said, always prefer to give papers rather than men. He told his close colleague Pierre Cathala: "Sauckel wants men. I shall give him legal texts."[2]

If it was necessary to make certain representations, or indeed promises, they might be useful in forestalling what the Germans demanded. Judge me not by my words but by my acts was Laval's frequent plea.

There were orders, there were counter-orders. There were conferences and communiqués. But in the end, the French fleet and French gold remained safe in the West Indies and Admiral Robert returned to thank Laval for his support.

In a similar vein, there had been much talk, there had been requests and demands, but in the end, the shares of Hachette were never sold into German ownership.

Montoire was another case of much talk and little consequence. Collaboration did not begin at Montoire. It was required by the Armistice agreement. Laval's goals were surely in the interest of France. They included reducing the occupation costs, a more favorable ratio of the franc to the reichsmark, relaxing the line of demarcation between the Occupied and Unoccupied Zones and placing the departments of the Nord and Pas de Calais under the German military command in France rather than Belgium. The return of the prisoners was always in the forefront of Laval's thinking.

The Germans wanted a French declaration of war against Britain or at least meaningful military help. The French wanted a real amelioration of the Armistice terms. As Laval's biographer, Professor Warner summarizes it:

> The results at Montoire were a disappointment to both sides. They did not lead to Anglo-French hostilities in North Africa, let alone to a French declaration of war against England, as the Germans had hoped. Still less did they bring any significant improvement in France's relations with her conqueror, as the French had hoped.[3]

And it was, of course, Pétain who took full responsibility. He said in his statement to the nation on his return from Montoire: "I responded freely to the Fuhrer's invitation. I underwent no diktat, no pressure from him." Pétain had concluded his declaration: "The members of the government are responsible to me. It is I alone whom History will judge."[4]

Both sides were clearly disappointed in the end and little came to pass as a result of Montoire. None of the French requests were ever met and, more important, Germany did not get the French declaration of war on Britain. The whole matter would seem, in an objective light, to furnish no basis for criminal charges, even less for the death penalty.

How Pierre Laval collaborated with the Occupant has already been related in chapters 13 and 15.

There remained, in the indictment and some of the testimony of the witnesses, important issues. What role did Pierre Laval and the Vichy government play in the persecution and the deportation of the Jews?

Did Vichy lend military aid to Germany and, if so, where and when and to what extent?

What was the role of Vichy in general and Pierre Laval in particular in the drafting of French labor for work in German factories? And to what extent did Vichy and Pierre Laval accede to the German annexation of Alsace-Lorraine and to what extent did they protect and defend its population against German oppression and the loss of their homes, their livelihoods, their language and their nationality?

In order to answer any of these questions, it is necessary first to ask in each case what was possible. Could the Vichy government or the French people impose their will on the Nazi conquerors? Could they simply reject out of hand German demands for occupation costs, for labor, for goods and services, for the deportation of the Jews? And if they tried, what would be the gain and what would be the cost? If they could not impose their will, if they could not flatly reject German demands, then how much room for maneuver did Vichy have? To what extent was it possible for Vichy to protect and defend French lives, French liberties, French property, and French values against the crushing force and insistent demands of their Nazi overlords? And how, then, is one to rate both the efforts and the degree of success of those efforts; how is one to keep score in this grim game?

In considering these issues it is important again to remember that Laval declined to participate in the trial in its third day. The defense had been deprived of the normal preliminary proceedings, the court, prosecution and jury were openly hostile and had openly declared that hostility and the dossier of the prosecution was hidden from the defense. Under these circumstances, we do not know what the true defense of Pierre Laval might have been. We can attempt to consider the case that might have been made by the defense. Not a definitive study of these contentious and complicated issues, a consideration of the defense that Laval might have made helps to balance the scales in any analysis of the record and on any thoughtful appraisal of the demands, both of justice and history.

Pierre Laval and the Jews

There can be no better issue to examine for the answers to these challenging questions than the sad and often tragic story of the fate of the Jews in France from the day of the Nazi triumph until the day of the Liberation.

Roots

The story of the fate of the Jews in Vichy France did not begin in 1940 and end in 1944-45. It is part of a longer history, indeed the history of modern France. The English Revolution of the seventeenth century and the American Revolution of the eighteenth century achieved resolution of the issues over which they were fought and a consensus that has proved a remarkably durable base for both government and society.

France has not been so fortunate. The French Revolution overthrew the *ancien régime* but the issues it raised and the antagonisms it aroused reverberate in France today. The kingdom became via the Directory and the Consulate Napoleon's First Empire. It was in turn followed by a Bourbon restoration, its overthrow, an Orleans restoration and its overthrow. The Second Republic rather quickly gave way to Louis Napoleon's Second Empire from which emerged, albeit shakily, the Third Republic which survived until it was swept away in the debacle of 1940.

So it was that Pétain's État Française was preceded by the Third Republic and followed, after a provisional government, by the Fourth Republic and then the Fifth Republic which governs today. These successive regimes responded to and represented very different elements of French society. There were on the one hand the upholders of tradition, the royalists, the Bonapartists, the aristocracy, who clung to their titles, their prerogatives and their prejudices insofar as they could. The church and the military were their allies as the business establishment became. This was the circle from which Pétain drew advisors, colleagues and inspiration.

A very different vision of society moved the workers represented by the labor unions. They paid allegiance to republican principles and were either anti-clerical or at least suspicious of a role for religion in the affairs of state. These were Pierre Laval's people and he was the small-town lad, the labor lawyer, the perennial mayor of a blue collar suburb who paid frequent and sincere tribute to the republic which had educated him and raised him up from his father's inn to the Elysée Palace.

The case of Captain Alfred Dreyfus, a Jewish officer in the French army falsely accused of espionage, had been a turn of the century cause célèbre and a bitter manifestation of this clash of philosophies and sympathies. Long before 1940 it was evidence of an active strain of anti-Semitism in French life, an anti-Semitism that came quite naturally to the upholders of the old tradition. Their complaint was not that the Jews were Jews but that they weren't French, that they possessed a complementary culture, an outlook that was cosmopolitan and therefore less than French. They were, as many French saw it, "other." It is clear that these attitudes could readily be found in Marshal Pétain and many of his coterie.

It is equally clear that Pierre Laval had never shared such sentiments. He had intimate associations with Jews both in politics and in business. In government Georges Mandel had been his mentor. René Mayer was his close political associate. Indeed the anti-Semitic press accused him of being a Jew; there was in his swarthy complexion and dark eyes an air of the Middle East. And his name spelled backward the same as forward, a sign some found suspicious.[5] To all this he would only reply, "I am neither an Arab nor a Jew, nor a Freemason, and if I were, I would say so because each is perfectly honorable. But I have to tell you, I have one flaw. I'm an Auvergnat."[6] Stung to anger and grief by the assassination of Georges Mandel, Laval took special care to protect Leon Blum from a similar fate. The presses of his newspaper, *Le Moniteur* were active in the Vichy years in producing baptismal certificates and false identity cards for Jews and the enterprise on Laval's orders sheltered many in difficulties or in flight. Laval, with the help of his son-in-law, René de Chambrun, was active in procuring visas and facilitating the safe exit from France of such leading Jewish figures as Franz Werfel, Golo Mann, René Clair and René Mayer.[7]

The Jewish presence in France was complicated by the relatively recent arrival in France of large numbers of Jews during the 1920s and the 1930s. France had welcomed immigrants in the 1920s to compensate the losses of manpower in the First World War. The 1930s saw the rise of the dictators, generating refugees from hostile regimes in Central and Eastern Europe and most notably those who fled the increasing repression of Hitler's Germany and the losers in the victory of fascism in Franco's Spain. No country had been more generous than France in accepting these strangers. Yet the newcomers suffered under the dual disability of being seen not only as aliens but, in a time of depression and high unemployment, as rivals for scarce jobs.

The demographics tell the story. There were in France in 1939 some 330,000 Jews. Of these 190,000-200,000 were of French nationality, of varying lengths of residence in France, some of old French families, some quite recently arrived. There were also some 130,000-140,000 Jews who were foreigners or stateless.[8] It is against these numbers that the fate of the Jews in France in 1940-45 must be measured.

The French governments of the 1930s were well aware of the issues raised by the refugees. There were regulations and restrictions, limitations on the numbers of foreigners in professions and both modifications of the liberal citizenship law of 1927 and the authority to strip naturalized citizens of their citizenship if they were judged "unworthy."[9]

Michael Marrus and Robert O. Paxton, preeminent scholars of Vichy and its Jewish policies, give us this summary:

> Vichy's anti-Jewish program was neither new nor limited to a small minority on the extreme Right. It fed on a decade long obsession with the alien menace. Even moderates had learned during the 1930's to think of foreign refugees—and Jews predominantly among them—as a threat to jobs, to the purity of French culture, to peace.[10]

It was against this background that the Vichy government, the shadow of the Nazi conqueror looming always in the background, addressed the Jewish issue.

1940

The Vichy government had first enacted ordinances denominating Jews and placing them under various disabilities on October 3, 1940.[11] It was this ordinance to which Mornet had pointed and stressed what he thought the self-evident fact of Laval's signature. But the truth is that Laval not only had no part in elaborating this law but he had vigorously opposed it, and that it took several sessions of the Council of Ministers to adopt it.[12] Its proponents did not act out of sheer malice; they claimed a French law would forestall the imposition of far harsher measures by the Germans like those in the Occupied Zone. Here, then, at the beginning of this sad saga, the issue of relativism vs. absolutes raises itself for our consideration.

The same was true with respect to the German ordinance of October 18, 1940 placing Jewish enterprises in trusteeships. Vichy promptly established its own system of provisional administrators to keep matters in French hands and to protect the French economy.[13]

As Marrus and Paxton relate, "Vichy's measures were not intended to kill."[14] Instead, they had among their ends to repatriate recent arrivals to France and to submerge French Jews in a newly homogenized French nation.

No better example of these principles may be found than in the October, 1940 statement of Paul Baudouin, vice president in Pétain's government. He wanted the American public to know that Vichy had no intention to persecute. "Neither persons nor property will be touched and in the domains from which they (the Jews) will be excluded there will be no humiliating discrimination."[15]

Comforting words, but they proved all too easily obliterated in the maelstrom that France and the Jews in France were about to face.

The Interim

Pierre Laval had been dismissed by Pétain from his ministerial posts on December 13, 1940 to be succeeded briefly by Pierre-Etienne Flandin and then by Admiral Francois Darlan. He was in retirement at Chateldon until his return to government on April 26, 1942. This was the period which saw the passage of significant anti-Jewish legislation and the erection of an administrative framework and a bureaucracy for addressing Jewish questions.

Mornet had referred to the statute of October 3, 1940 defining Jews and limiting their activities. The only other statute to which Mornet had referred was the statute of July 22, 1941 in which Laval had no part placing Jewish property and enterprises under so-called Aryan administration.[16] This was far from the only such legislation of the period. Those to which Mornet made no reference included the June 2, 1941 law permitting the assignment of refugees and foreigners to the camps inherited from the Third Republic,[17] the aryanization law of June 19, 1941;[18] the Statut des Juifs of June 2, 1941 defining Jews by religion[19] which was followed in October, 1941 by provisions for the issuance of a certificate of non-appurtenance, or non-belonging; the law of November 17, 1941 further restricting participation of Jews in businesses and professions,[20] and the law of November 29, 1941 establishing the Union General des Israelites Françaises, a compulsory device for restricting Jews and subjecting the Jewish community to collective damages and fines.[21] Administrative structures included the formation in the spring of 1941 of the General Commission on Jewish affairs (CGQJ), headed by the rabidly anti-Semitic Xavier Vallat and the Police for Jewish Affairs (PQJ)[22] which was set up in the fall of 1941.[23] The first mass arrests of Jewish professionals and intellectuals took place in Paris in December, 1941.[24] In the same month, a fine of billion francs was levied on the Jewish community in the Occupied Zone.[25] And, fatally, the first deportation train left France on March 27, 1942.[26]

It is interesting to note that the passage of these laws and the establishment of these structures and these actions caused no ripple of dissent or resignation among the corps of civil servants and administrators who were at the daily center of the government of France. Jules Jeanneney had been president of the Senate in 1940. He had been a leader in the transfer of power from the Third Republic to the Pétain regime. He told the Marshal:

> I disapprove of the Jewish statute, for all the ways in which it is contrary to respect for the human person, and to French tradition, as well as because the Germans imposed it on you. But it is the law. It must be obeyed.[27]

Certainly, in the administration of justice, no hint of disapproval was heard from Mongibeaux and Mornet who continued in the exercise of their functions in a system that denied justice. Recent scholarship has emphasized the degree to which, contrary to Jeanneney's assertion—and it was a common one—the French statutes were the result, not of German importuning but of French initiative.

What is important in this analysis is that during the time all these events occurred, these laws were passed, these institutions were established, Pierre Laval was in private life amid his fields, his vineyards, his herds and his flocks in Chateldon. From this we may conclude that he did not inspire these laws and institutions, that he had no part in their creation and elaboration and indeed neither his advocacy nor his concurrence were necessary to do all that was done. And, save for the statute of October 3, 1940 which he had vigorously opposed, Mornet made no specific charge that he ever had.

When Pierre Laval assumed the grave responsibility of government on his return on April 26, 1942, there was therefore in place a body of law and institutions which he had not only to take into account, but to deal with as best he could. How he did so was part of the defense he never made.

1942-1944

What exacerbated Pierre Laval's task was that his return to office in April, 1942 was preceded on January 26, 1942 by the Wannsee Conference which promulgated the infamous Final Solution.

It was shortly thereafter that the first plans were made to implement the "solution" in France. On June 23, 1942, Heinrich Himmler gave the order for the deportation of *all* Jews from France. He was seconded by Adolf Eichman who was in Paris on June 30, 1942 demanding that *all* Jews be deported from France without distinction as to nationality or citizenship. The first step was to be the arrest by French police and deportation of 22,000 Jews from the Paris metropolitan area, of whom forty percent would be French citizens. The inducement offered for French collaboration was the future establishment of the French police administration in the Occupied as well as the Unoccupied Zone. This would represent a much desired recognition of the sovereignty of Vichy in both zones.[28]

Laval was informed of the proposed operation. What could he do? What was it possible to do?

He protested to the German ambassador. He interceded with SS Brigade Führer Karl Oberg. "The trains are ready," Oberg told him. "They have to be filled at any price. The Jewish problem has no frontiers for us. The police must help us or we shall do the arresting without any distinction between French Jews and others."

Laval concluded that if he could not save all, he would save as many as possible. He negotiated with the devil—it would be a familiar role—to protect and safeguard from deportation the Jews of French nationality. The German plan called for victims between the ages of sixteen and forty-five. Laval insisted that children should not be separated from their parents. He issued a plea to the embassies of the nations represented at Vichy- Spain, Hungary, Bulgaria, Portugal and Turkey—and indeed many of these were able to intervene successfully on behalf of their nationals.

He also addressed the Papal Nuncio. He urged his administration to place what obstacles they could in the way of the proposed operation. He secured exceptions for foreigners married to French Jews and all Jews who had rendered exceptional services to France.[29]

The roundups, the arrests, the deportation took place on July 16 and 17, 1942 and are remembered as the Gran Rafle du Vel d' Hiv, scenes of horror, of terror, of inhumanity, of terrified and abandoned children, which France can never forget and scenes which aroused a fervent resistance against their repetition. The fate of these children weighs heavily against the conscience and the memory of Pierre Laval.

It has nowhere been suggested that Vichy or Laval intended the extermination of these innocents. Yet considerable evidence points to other motives. The children were not only an administrative problem, but also an acute embarassment to Vichy as their plight became known. Further, their numbers could be counted against German deportation quotas.[30]

Conan and Rousso pass this judgment:

> As in the case of the children, which the Nazis were not then demanding but who were handed over, its (Vichy's) reasoning did not follow a logic of extermination but of cold politics and bureaucracy inconsiderate of human life.[31]

In the end, the results were far less than the Germans had intended. Instead of 22,000 there were arrested 12,884 foreign Jews, the majority women and children. Laval's wish for children to stay with their parents bespoke his belief that they could remain united and betrayed no consciousness of the death camps that would be their destination.[32]

Nevertheless, according to Conan and Rousso the mass roundups of 1942 weren't taken "upon the sole initiative of Vichy for ideological reasons in the logic of state anti-Semitism." They were a consequence of the Final Solution, "a demented plan that was not its (France's) own," but to which it lent the decisive aid of the French police and government.

"The Vichy regime never had the intent of exterminating the Jews. It was content to exclude Jews and to give itself the possibility of detaining – often in inhumane and deadly conditions – foreign Jews."[33]

What did Laval know? What indeed did anyone or any government know? It is easy to assume that everything we know today was known then. The Germans took care to conceal the horrors of the extermination camps, reports were fragmentary and governments and people had a natural reluctance to believe any government could institute and carry on mass murder of the innocent. So much is evident from the hesitant record of response of Allied governments to the Final Solution.

According to Marrus and Paxton,

> For one thing, the Nazis did their best to hide from all but a few administrators and security officials, the murder of millions of Jews.[34]

Born and raised in Vienna, Gitta Sereny became one of the keenest analysts of the Nazis and their era. What did she know as a young woman living in wartime France?

> Looking back now on our lives under the Germans after June 1940, the fact that we knew or guessed nothing of what the future held for this huge group of Europeans of all nationalities, demonstrates yet again how effective the Nazis were well before and indeed after they embarked on genocide, in keeping their intentions secret.[35]

She continues:

> I emphasize this because even now, as I write [in 2000], many people still believe that the fatal threat to Europe's Jews—which if it had been understood, would have confronted us with a moral imperative –was obvious almost from the start and startlingly unopposed, not only by 'all Germans'...but in the United States and Britain, and in all countries occupied by the Germans, that is, most of Europe.[36]

According to Julian Jackson,

> In the end "Who knew what is one of the most vexed questions about the Holocaust. Evidence about the extermination of the Jews was filtering out by the middle of 1942. But what does knowing mean? The images of Auschwitz which labor our imagination did not exist. Raymond Aron, who spent the war in London, where much information was available, wrote later, 'What did we know of the genocide?' I must confess that I had not imagined it and because I could not imagine it, I did not know.[37]

As to Laval, he consistently maintained that he did not know. He questioned the Germans, he said, who replied the transports were bound for Poland and a Jewish state there. He was, as usual, candid: "I was well aware that this meant working there in terrible conditions, most often to suffer and die there."[38]

Laval had, as many others, been deeply affected by this episode. He would no longer cooperate with such operations. He defended the Jews vigorously, often using as a shield the person of the Marshal who was moved by the protests of the Catholic Church. When the Germans made new demands, Laval said he had done enough and that to do more would imperil the stability of the Vichy regime.[39]

Of course the Germans did not relent. They sought to achieve their ends by a process of denaturalization of French Jews. Laval met this with a mastery of bureaucratic maneuver. He gave to both René Bosquet and Darquier de Pellepoix, Vallat's successor as head of a new anti-Jewish agency, the mission of preparing a denaturalization law. On June 20, 1943, he signed Darquier's text but conveniently forgot to pass it on to the Germans. He told them on August 7 that he had signed Darquier's law by mistake thinking it was Bosquet's. To the incredulity of his interlocutors he then told them that Darquier's law could not be promulgated because it had never been discussed at the Council of Ministers. And why, he demanded to know, should the police be dealing with denaturalization when they had far more urgent security work to do?[40]

Laval then retreated to a minute examination of the dossiers, one by one, month by month, producing in the end a list of 2,500 rather than 20,000.[41]

What, Laval asked, did the Germans intend to do with the lists? The Germans told him of their plans for further arrests. Laval took a stand, draped in moral principle. He could not do it. They had to see the Marshal, who alone could give his consent. When on August 14, 1943, Laval was given the denaturalization law to sign, he again cited the opposition of Pétain. Anyway, he said, the law could not go into effect for three months during which no arrests could be made and then not by the French police. He asked why the German policy was so different from the policy of the Italians in their zone of occupation. Finally, on August 26, Laval explained to the Germans that the Marshal could not accept the law because "The Pope was personally concerned for the well-being of the soul of the Marshal."[42]

Such opposition could not achieve total success. But the rate of arrests and deportations of both French and foreign Jews sharply diminished, as did the rate of participation by the French police, especially after November, 1942 when Germany occupied what had been the Unoccupied Zone. Thus, in 1943, of 44,000 arrests of Jews and non-Jews for political activity, German police arrested 35,000.[43] Professor Warner is Laval's not particularly laudatory biographer. He says: "On the other hand it cannot be denied that Laval fought very hard for the French Jews."[44] The records suggest that the fight was not limited to the French Jews.

At the same time, as Professor Warner writes, "There is evidence that Laval did his best to sabotage other anti-Jewish measures."[45] This aroused the bitter complaints of Darquier de Pellepoix, who told German agents that Laval had delayed the signing of anti-Jewish measures by nine months.[46] And in October, 1943 military authorities told the SS that there were reports that Laval had issued secret instructions that the anti-Jewish laws no longer be applied. Whether or not the SS had such knowledge, they confirmed that "it is certainly the case that the attitude of the French government and the French authorities toward the Jewish question has hardened in recent months."[48]

That their suspicions were justified is illustrated by a speech Laval gave on September 21, 1943 to the assembled regional prefects. He told them they should protest the arrests of Jews and that the French police should not lend any helping hand in the arrest of French Jews. And prefects did in fact follow the order leaving the Germans to fend for themselves.[49] The Germans complained bitterly but the rhythm of the deportations showed a steady decline.

Laval's attitude may also be seen in the successful resistance to incessant German demands to segregate Jewish prisoners of war. They were neither segregated nor treated differently from other fellow French prisoners of war, a tribute both to the attitude and the action of the government that shielded them.[50]

The Numbers

We have already noted that in 1939, there were some 330,000 Jews in France of whom 190,000-200,000 were of French nationality and 130,000-140,000 were foreigners. Citing the authority of Serge Klarsfeld, French historian and Laval biographer Jean-Paul Contet reports that of these 80,000 fell victim of whom French Jews were 24,500, foreign Jews 56,500.[50]

These figures show a survival rate of 87.5 percent of French Jews who had been exposed for four full years to the furor Teutonicus. The survival rate of the foreign and stateless Jews was between 58 percent and 60 percent. These figures must be considered in the light of the fate of other European Jews.

No one can establish with certitude the exact numbers of Jews murdered in the course of the Final Solution." The *Holocaust Encyclopedia*, published in 2001 tabulates by country the Jewish population of Europe in 1933 and the death toll in the end. The statistics subtract for emigration but are surely affected by population flows and boundary changes after 1933.

The balance shown is a 1933 Jewish population of 8,754 million. The death toll was 6,147 million, leaving a postwar population of 2,607 million or a survival rate of 29.8 percent.

The *Holocaust Encyclopedia* gives earlier estimates by the Institute of Jewish Affairs in New York of a 1939 European Jewish population of 9.5 million reduced in 1945 to 3.1 million and a 1959 study by Jacob Lestschinsky showing 6 million dead and 2.95[51] million living in 1950.[52]

Lucy S. Dawidowicz in *The War Against the Jews*, gives on Table 1 a panoramic view of this tragic accounting.[53]

The overall estimates are weighted by the nearly total annihilation of Polish Jewry. They tend to show that approximately two-thirds of Europe's Jews perished, and one-third survived. It is against these figures that the experience of France must be measured.

It should first be noted that Dawidowicz' figures for France include both Jews of French nationality and foreign or stateless Jews. That said,

Table 1

Country	Estimated pre-Final Solution Population	Estimated Jewish Population Annihilated	Percent
Poland	3,300,000	3,000,000	90
Baltic Countries	253,000	228,000	90
Germany/Austria	240,000	210,000	90
Czechoslovakia	180,000	155,000	86
Greece	70,000	54,000	77
Netherlands	140,000	105,000	75
Hungary	650,000	450,000	70
White Russian SSR	375,000	245,000	65
Ukrainian SSR	1,500,000	900,000	60
Belgium	65,000	40,000	60
Yugoslavia	43,000	26,000	60
Romania	600,000	300,000	50
Norway	1,800	900	50
France	350,000	90,000	26
Bulgaria	64,000	14,000	22
Italy	40,000	8,000	20
Luxemburg	5,000	1,000	20
Russian RSFSR*	975,000	170,000	11
Denmark	8,000	-	-
Finland	2,000	-	-
	8,861,800	5,933,900	67

*not fully occupied

the experience of France was the reverse or the reciprocal of the rest of Europe. We have seen that 76.5 percent of all Jews in France survived, approximately 60 percent of foreign and stateless Jews and a remarkable 87.5 percent of Jews of French nationality.[54]

Michael Curtis accepts the number of 77,000 Jews from France, including citizens and foreigners, who fell victim to the Final Solution. He then asks,

> Only 77,000? Only 22.9 per cent of the Jewish population? It is no defence of Vichy to compare these figures with comparable ones in neighbouring countries. The Netherlands lost 75 per cent, and Belgium 42 per cent of its Jews. A number of factors explain the disparity; the changing military situation after 1942, which led to more caution on the part of the French; the geographical extent of France and its sizeable mountainous areas, which made it harder to round up Jews; the unavailability of German police; the scarcity of rolling stock causing transport shortages; the greater assimilation of native Jews in the general population; the fact that Jews now lived a more clandestine life and changed identities; the lower percentage of foreign Jews than in the Low Countries; the growing sense of shame among non-Jews as knowledge of the atrocities and the wearing of the yellow star by Jews made them conscious of the problem; the help by righteous individuals, both secular and religious; the resistance groups and Jewish organizations that hid people; and the delay of the Italians in implementing discriminatory measures.

The reader with note the pointed omission of reference to any action by the Vichy government, or of individuals who played a role in that government in holding the tragic loss to "only 77,000" of 330,000 Jews in all, "only" 22.9 percent of the Jewish population and indeed "only" 12.5 percent of Jews holding French citizenship.[55] Yet in the same work Curtis observes:

> If Vichy sacrificed a high proportion of foreign Jews living in its territory, it did try, with some limited success, to save French Jews and to protect them because they were citizens, if not because they were Jews.... If Vichy did engage in and initiate discriminatory legislation and actions against Jews, with some exceptions the government did not favor, support or encourage deportation or extermination. In any case, for apologists, Vichy did not know the destination or fate of the deported Jews, whom it said were being 'relocated' in eastern Europe.[56]

Of course, in the chaotic circumstances in which the trial took place, a few months after V-E Day and literally days after V-J day, these statistics could hardly have been available – that would take time and scholarship. Nevertheless, they are presented here as a background to the appreciation of the trial as it was.

Clearly something was different in France, in Vichy France. It is not recorded that German aims, ideology, and demands were different in France than in the rest of conquered Europe. Indeed, the ambition to deport all Jews from France was firmly and often stated. This raises the question whether, if Pierre Laval is to be condemned for what was lost, is he not also entitled to some credit for what was saved.[57]

The novelist Serge Doubrovsky, reflecting on his childhood in wartime France, observed that while the anti-Jewish measures of Vichy were the work of the French people, every Jew who survived in France during 1942 to 1944 owed his life to some French man or woman who helped, or at least kept a secret.[58]

For many Jews and indeed for many others, the person who helped was Pierre Laval. His care for the life of Leon Blum is emblematic. Another whose life he saved from almost certain condemnation to death by a German tribunal was Henri Teitgen, Batonnier of the Nancy bar. He was the father of none other than the Garde des Sceaux, P. H. Teitgen, who denied the plea of his predecessor, Pierre Laval, for elemental justice.[59] Yet another whose life and career against a dangerous accusation Pierre Laval was at pains at a critical time to protect was his implacable prosecutor, Mornet.

Pierre Laval and German Labor Requisitions

It was not only the Jews that the Germans pursued. The demands of a rapidly expanding war, especially on the Russian front, strained German manpower resources. As more and more men were fed into the armed forces to make up the heavy losses, corresponding shortages of labor inevitably developed at home.

Germany looked to France as a rich pool of labor, especially skilled labor. At first the appeal was for volunteers, lured by salaries exceeding pay levels in France, but their numbers never exceeded 100,000. The task of raising a vastly larger labor force was entrusted by Hitler to his long time colleague and fervent Nazi, Fritz Sauckel. Short, stout, his head shaven, Sauckel had been a longshoreman in Hamburg. Before that, he had been a World War I prisoner of the French, whom he detested. For cruelty and malevolence, Sauckel was outstanding even among the Nazi leadership.

His first demands were issued in June, 1942: 250,000 workers by the end of July on pain of sending back to Germany 600,000 French prisoners of war who had earlier been repatriated.[60] Laval had been newly restored to office in April. How, then, to address this imperious command? He used his accustomed tactics of negotiation, of delay, of temporizing. Always fertile in ideas, always searching for the quid pro quo, he now suggested to Sauckel a system whereby one French prisoner of war would be released for every worker sent to Germany. In the end, Sauckel agreed to a ratio of one repatriated prisoner to three workers.[61] At the same time he used all of the administrative resources at hand, encouraging the prefects to support his negotiating efforts. All this in the end materially limited the flow of workers to German factories. The result was that from June 1, 1942 to the beginning of September, 1942, only 17,000 of the planned 250,000 workers had been recruited.[62]

Faced with such meager results, Sauckel struck back. In August, 1942 he published a decree under which all men and women in countries occupied or administered by Germany would be liable for compulsory labor service. This raised two issues, the inclusion of women, and the status of France under the Armistice. Laval protested sharply that under the Armistice, France, both occupied and unoccupied, was not a German administered territory and he threatened resignation. His next move was reminiscent of the anti-Jewish legislation. He sought greater room to maneuver by operating under French enactments and French administrative law rather than under German edicts administered by the Occupant. So it was that, after vigorous debate, the French Council of Ministers promulgated the law of September 4, 1942 making all French men of eighteen to fifty and women of twenty-one to thirty-five liable for work which the government deemed "useful in the higher interest of the nation."[63]

This was the hated STO, Service de Travail Obligatoire or compulsory labor law that brought down the wrath of the French people upon Laval. But there was a quid pro quo. It was a substantial reduction in the age/sex groups first stipulated in Sauckel's exactions. Furthermore, instead of the blanket demand for everyone in specified age groups, the numbers were reduced to 250,000 for Germany and another 100,000 to work in France for the Todt organization, Germany's major military contractor.[64] But somehow, these numbers were never reached. Laval secured more inducements. If 100,000 skilled workers agreed to go to Germany, wives of prisoners of war would be allowed to join their husbands.[65] The numbers still dwindled. This was when Laval made his celebrated remark: "Sauckel wants men. I shall give him legal texts."[66] Laval's colleague Jacques Barnaud reported that the French administration: "...put as many spokes in the wheel as possible... Laval... was well aware of the fact that we were using delaying tactics, but he never asked us to change our method and accept the views of the enemy."[67]

But Sauckel's demands continued, in January, 1943 for 150,000 specialists and 100,000 others, in April 1943, for 200,000 skilled workers. Again he was met by tactics of delay and obfuscation. Dr. Elmer Michel,

Chief of German Economic Services in Paris wrote, "In a skillful manner, Pierre Laval pursued evasive and dilatory tactics to reserve to the French authorities the execution of the labor measures." Laval's program could only succeed, he said, by enlisting the support of other German authorities who were opposed to Sauckel's demands.[68]

This support Laval found in the Speer organization. It supervised French factories that produced goods for Germany. The number of workers in these so-called S Enterprises was subtracted from Sauckel's quotas. The system was later extended to agriculture and forestry and reduced by hundreds of thousands the forced exodus of French workers to Germany.

By July only 130,000 of Sauckel's 200,000 April quota had been met, none of them women. Dismayed but persistent, Sauckel met with Laval at 4 P.M. on August 6, 1943 at the German Embassy in Paris. Also present were Rudolf Schleier, chargé d' affaires at the Embassy, Vichy Ambassador Ferdinand de Brinon and Jean Bichelonne, Vichy Minister for Industrial Production.[69]

The meeting, Laval later said, was the toughest and most painful negotiation in a long career of negotiations. This time Sauckel raised the stakes. He demanded 500,000 workers at the rate of 100,000 a month by year-end 1943, and that the draft finally include women.[70]

Laval's attitude was negative from the start. France, he said, did not know what fate awaited it in a peace treaty. Though beaten France had to guard its prestige. Sauckel's demands would create disorder in France. The government had to keep in mind public opinion. And, Laval said, "as to me, the only reason I occupy my post is to defend France and in defending France I am defending Europe." Indeed, he added, he wouldn't be worthy of his position if he accepted Sauckel's demand. What follows is a report of the Laval-Sauckel dialogue condensed and edited so as to reflect not only the substance but also the tone and temper of this bruising encounter.

Sauckel: "I have received formal and non-negotiable orders from Hitler: 500,000 workers will leave for Germany at the rate of 100,000 a month before December 31."

Laval: "I would like to say yes but that's impossible."

Sauckel: "I demand a yes or no answer."

Laval: "I stand on my refusal."

Sauckel: "It's impossible for me to tell Chancellor Hitler that France cannot find 500,000 workers while Germany is carrying on the struggle on both the economic and the military fronts."

Laval: "I know perfectly well the consequences France will suffer for its refusal which I regret, but I think the consequences would be evil for everyone and so far as I'm concerned I can't do anything."

Sauckel demanded that a telegram be sent to Chancellor Hitler to tell him that the French government was ready to send 500,000 workers before December 31.

Laval: "You stubbornly ask me the question. I am obliged equally stubbornly to give you the same answer. I've told you what I can do."

Sauckel: "This can't go on. You must telegraph Hitler. Tell him either the French government is in agreement or tell him that the French government refuses."

Laval: "I can neither say more nor modify my answer."

Sauckel: "I cannot understand why the French can't agree to send 500,000 workers to Germany."

Laval: "The answer is clear; it's because French workers want to work in France and because the political climate doesn't allow the French government to undertake engagements which it cannot fulfill."

Sauckel: "Do I understand that you are refusing?"

Laval: "I repeat: It's impossible."

Sauckel: "Well, Germany itself will go out and find those 500,000 workers."

Laval: "I don't contest that you can find 500,000 men. What I can't accept is the principle of their departure."

Again Laval pled the uncertainty of France's fate and the pressures of public opinion.

Sauckel now moderated his demand. He no longer insisted on a guarantee of 500,000 workers, but only requested that the French government lend its best efforts to find and recruit these workers.

Sauckel: "In the situation today, France can't say that what I demand is impossible. The word impossible doesn't exist in the National-Socialist vocabulary."

Sauckel then stated that he expected Laval's answer that evening or the following evening.[71]

It was at this point, whether from pressure, fatigue, or distress, that Laval collapsed. At 8 P.M. Laval's daughter and son-in-law, Josée and René de Chambrun, arrived at the Matignon Palace, the seat of the French prime minister, where they expected to dine with Laval. They were met by Laval's private secretary, André Guenier. He was breathless. "Achenbach called me at about 7 o'clock from the German embassy. Laval had just fainted. I ran as fast as I could to the Rue de Lille where Laval was stretched out on a sofa in the salon with only Achenbach to keep him company. I gave him a glass of brandy. He downed it in one gulp. Pretty soon he regained some color and was resting. The meeting with Sauckel starts again in a quarter of an hour."

The de Chambruns waited in the dining room of the Matignon. They watched the clock. The hours passed slowly – 9 P.M., 10, 11.

Finally, at 11:30 Laval arrived. His face was pale with fatigue, his tie was undone, his vest unbuttoned. He fell into a chair. Josée dabbed his forehead with eau de cologne.

Laval glanced at his watch. "It's like talking to a piece of furniture. A real brute. For seven hours he demanded workers and for seven hours I offered him texts of law. I've already gained several months." There was a moment of silence. Then: "Let's have something to eat."[72]

Two days later Sauckel sent a secret report to Hitler:

> The French Prime Minister has energetically refused to start up a program for the recruitment of 500,000 French workers before the end of 1943. The discussion lasted more than 6 hours. Laval couldn't furnish reasons to justify his refusal...

All of his efforts, Sauckel reported, seemed to tend to obtaining political advantage for France. An argument Laval constantly made was the danger of political troubles in France if the workers marked for Germany took to the mountains and the forests, setting up bands of terrorists.

Sauckel complained bitterly that Laval never applied the laws which he passed, an observation made by many others on both sides of this struggle. It was, as Laval himself observed, that Sauckel demanded men and Laval gave him legal texts.

Sauckel concluded that Laval's failure to deliver important new contingents of workers put the Reich in an embarrassing position. "One cannot escape the conclusion," Sauckel closed, "that Laval is specifically exploiting that very situation."[73]

Sauckel then wrote to Schleier, chargé d' affaires of the Germany Embassy, in like terms:

> After having reflected calmly I must tell you that I have totally lost faith in the honesty and goodwill of President of the French Council Laval. His refusal constitutes a sabotage, pure and total, of the struggle for life by Germany against Bolshevism. At the same time, notably at the end of our talks, by declarations which were devoid of logic and incoherent in response to my clear and precise questions, he made the worst possible impression.[74]

At his trial in Nuremburg in 1948 Abetz was interrogated about the attitude of the French government to Sauckel's demands. He responded:

The French government put up a vigorous resistance to the recruitment of manpower other than voluntary. It seized every occasion to try to obtain recompense from Germany in particular in the matter of the liberation of prisoners of war. For the rest, it tried to oppose the recruitment demands by Sauckel in proposing the sending of French works to S Enterprises. That is to say privileged factories and these efforts were crowned with a certain success.[75]

At Nuremburg, Abetz recounted that in late 1943 Sauckel came to Paris. "You, Abetz," he accused, "You have organized the resistance to the mobilization of French manpower. I came to Paris with an order from the Fuhrer and heads will fall."

To this Abetz replied:

The first head will be mine. I would rather lose my life than to consent to an affair against the interest of Germany.

Abetz was not done.

If the maquis erect monuments in France, the most important will bear the inscription: "To our principal recruiter, the Gauleiter Sauckel from the grateful maquis."[76]

Laval's biographer, Geoffrey Warner, writes of this incident, "Laval refused point blank to any further figure for the dispatch of workers." The 500,000 workers demanded by Sauckel on August 6 never went to Germany.

Sauckel modified his program and in October, 1943 he told Laval that Germany would make no more demands until the end of the year. The ostensible reason was the availability of Italian labor. The real reason may well have been the inability of the Germans to enforce their labor drafts against recalcitrants and evaders. And this could hardly have been possible without the total lack of cooperation with the Germans by the French government. At its head stood Pierre Laval who was capable of point blank refusal, but of whom it was said, in a day-to-day context, "that he seemed to find the non-execution of his orders perfectly normal."[77]

Sauckel returned in January, 1944, with demands for a million workers at the rate of 91,000 per month. The same game was played out. Laval agreed to draft legislation. But instead, he proposed a "priority" program which involved a risible number of workers who had failed to return to Germany after their leave had expired. The Germans responded with their own priority program of 273,000 by April.[78] There were further discussions, further complaints by Sauckel about the S Enterprises which, he said, were "nothing but a protection from the clutches of Sauckel."[79] What counted in the end were the results, and for all of his grandiose demands, Sauckel obtained, between January and June, 1944, 42,000 workers. By

June, the Allied invasion of Normandy had brought to a virtual close this chapter in the history of Vichy France.[80]

Pierre Laval regarded himself as a realist. Judge me not by my words but by my acts was his frequent challenge. What, then, was the balance, what was the ultimate result of insistent German demands for French labor?

Certainly the numbers of French workers who went to Germany, voluntarily or involuntarily, fell dramatically short of Sauckel's demands and Germany's needs. The German demands from 1942 to 1944 totaled 2,625,000 men. It should be noted that no French woman was ever drafted and sent to labor in Germany, as was the case in all other German occupied countries. Against the 2,625,000 demand, France sent 723,162 men to labor in Germany. This number should be measured against a 1940 population of 41.9 million. By way of comparison, the Netherlands with a population of 8.5 million sent 530,000 men and women to labor in Germany and Belgium sent 278,000 men and women out of a population of 8.1 million.[81]

The labor issue is illustrative of Pierre Laval's methods. First and foremost, to put the matter insofar as possible into French hands and under French administration. There the execution of the laws would be under far more lenient and understanding authorities and indeed with rich possibilities of frustrating German ends and goals. And when a German exaction could not be resisted, then to negotiate something of value in return. Laval would have preferred one repatriated prisoner of war for each worker sent to Germany, but one in three was something and to the family of the returned prisoner, everything.

There was, finally, both in the case of the Jews and of labor the point blank refusal to proceed. How and when this could be applied, and with what risks and what reprisals must always be the most delicate of questions, answerable only by weighing in the balance a myriad of facts, personalities, timing, events, prejudices and passions which must render the judgment difficult for succeeding generations to divine. At least it should counsel caution that the final judgment is not to be found in a single document, a single circular, a single law, a single statement or a press report, but in an attempt to understand the position and the attitude of those charged with dealings with the Occupier on a day-to-day basis as the representatives and the protectors of the French people.

Finally, it may be asked what would have been the fate of France, of the Jews, of labor, had there been no French authority interposed between them and the Nazi machine, if France had been another Poland?

Pierre Laval and Military Aid to Germany

With Germany victorious in 1940 and French arms in a state of collapse, French military aid to or alliance with Germany did not seem a lively issue. Nevertheless Laval, addressing the joint meeting of the Senate and the Chamber of Deputies on the morning of July 10, 1940 that was the prelude to the meeting that afternoon of the National Assembly said that France would not declare war on Britain, indeed would not declare war on anybody. And when the constitutional acts of the Pétain regime were approved by the cabinet on the next day, although the Marshal was given broad powers, he could not declare war "without the prior assent of the Legislative Assemblies."[82]

Indeed, when in October, 1940 Pétain and Laval met Hitler at Montoire to discuss a program of collaboration, Laval reminded Hitler of this express limitation. He went even further, venturing the opinion that if the legislative assemblies were asked for a declaration of war, they would refuse.[83]

When Laval returned to government in April 1942, the United States was at war with Germany. Laval had close ties with America. His son-in-law, René de Chambrun, was the son of the former Clara Longworth of Cincinnati. Her brother was Nicholas Longworth, sometime speaker of the U.S. House of Representatives. Longworth's wife was none other than Alice Roosevelt Longworth, with whom René de Chambrun maintained warm ties and ties as well, to Franklin Delano Roosevelt and to Eleanor Roosevelt who was Alice Longworth's cousin. Laval continued to assure the American ambassador to Vichy, Admiral Leahy, that he would support no unfriendly word or act against the U.S. In a message to Robert Murphy, Roosevelt's special representative in French North Africa Laval wrote,

> Tell him that President Roosevelt and the Americans...can insult me and drag me in the mud, but I will never utter a word nor commit an act which can be unfavorably interpreted by America whose friendship is so vital to France.[84]

This was put to the test in November, 1942, when the Anglo-American assault on North Africa, which Murphy had done so much to prepare, took place. Laval approved Pétain's letter of protest to President Roosevelt against the attack upon French territory defended by French forces. But at the same time, he strongly advised in the cabinet against any meaningful military operations at the side of the enemy by the not inconsiderable French forces in North Africa.[85]

This was precisely what the Germans wanted. On the afternoon of November 8, Laval received peremptory orders via Abetz:

Chancellor Hitler demands to know if the French government is ready to fight at the side of Germany against the Anglo-Saxons. There must be a declaration of war against the English and the Americans. If the government of France takes this position, Germany is ready to march with it 'Durch dick, und dunn.'

"Durch dick, und dunn" was understood by Laval to mean "through thick and thin" or "for better or worse."[86]

Not only Laval but the whole of the Vichy administration had a continuing concern for France's large overseas empire and how it would emerge at war's end. They had continually sought from Hitler guarantees of its preservation and he had as continuously rebuffed such approaches. It was characteristic that Laval saw Hitler's demand as an opportunity for further negotiations of France's position in Hitler's world.

Krug von Nidda, the German representative, urged Laval to accept Hitler's proposal. Laval later wrote that he "seemed very disappointed at my extremely reserved attitude," adding "I confined myself to polite remarks and there could be no doubt about my refusal."[87]

Laval used Hitler's demand and his reserved response to gain a meeting with Hitler which was set for November 9. In the meanwhile, Admiral Darlan, fortuitously in North Africa at the bedside of his gravely ill son, had given orders for a cease fire in North Africa of which Laval, aware of the danger on the eve of his meeting with Hitler, procured the reversal.

René de Chambrun has given us a picture of Laval on the eve of his departure from Chateldon for Munich where he would meet with Hitler. Not knowing if he would return, Laval had gathered together the important documents which he always carried with him. His family, Madame Laval, René and Josée de Chambrun begged him to leave the government. He refused. His daughter insisted that his continued presence would achieve nothing. He replied that she did not understand. The Germans were about to become very hard.

"To leave now," he told them, "would be to desert. I have to stay to protect the prisoners of war who have been repatriated, the refugees, the Alsatians, the Lorrainers, the Jews, the Communists, the Freemasons."[88] Did he take with him a vial of cyanide for use when needed?

The journey to Munich was long and arduous. The meeting with Hitler was brief. Mussolini's son-in-law, Count Galeazzo Ciano, the Italian foreign minister, was also present and a debate evolved about Italian claims to Tunis.

Laval's biographer, Cointet, has summarized the practical results of this meeting: "Laval had certainly refused any co-belligerence by France at the side of the Axis in North Africa, and refused to declare war on the

United States." But the price was the end of Laval's policy of collaboration by France in a Europe dominated by victorious Germany.[89]

Mornet had brought to the jury's attention an exchange of telegrams following the Allied landings in North Africa in which French forces were ordered not to interfere with German aircraft flying over the Unoccupied Zone of France toward the Mediterranean. There were other telegrams indicating that the French authorities had permitted German aircraft to land at French bases in North Africa and then to participate in its defense against the Allied invasion.

However these exchanges may have sounded to a jury in 1945, a few minutes of reflection would yield another point of view. Whether there were French forces which could have stopped German overflights is dubious indeed, and the inevitable loss of life and failure difficult to justify. Beyond this the French government must have been aware that the direct and immediate consequence of such an attack on German planes would have been the total occupation of France and the' loss of the cherished freedoms, such as they were, of the Unoccupied Zone.

As to the North African airbases, Professor Warner is succinct. The Germans had sent an ultimatum:

> This gave the French government one hour in which to agree to Axis aircraft using bases in Tunisia and Eastern Algeria, failing which 'the OKW (the German high command) would take the measures which it deems appropriate of its own accord.'
>   The French had no alternative but to accept and the commanders in Tunisia were duly informed.[90]

Events were moving fast in North Africa leading to a cease-fire and the reversion of French forces to the Allied cause. The immediate response was the German invasion of the Unoccupied Zone on November 11, placing all of France, including the France the Vichy regime had had the pretensions to govern, under total German occupation.

The Vichy government was informed once more, on November 14, 1942 that Ribbentrop had demanded a declaration of war on America and Britain. Further discussion indicated that the demand was less than peremptory and that what was sought was a recognition of the facts of the conflict as they existed on the ground, and in the end even this declaration was deflected.[91]

Laval emerged from these events with increased powers. Darlan, obviously, could no longer could be Pétain's successor after he had gone over to the Allies. Laval was named Pétain's successor in the event of Pétain's death or inability to serve, but only for an interim period of one month, after which the cabinet would name a successor. More important,

Laval was now given power by a new constitutional act to promulgate laws and decrees but not constitutional acts over his own signature. But there was an important reservation. Under the terms of a secret letter to Pétain, Laval could not declare war even though he could order measures of self-defense in the event of an attack on the country.

He would moreover "respect the spiritual traditions of France," guarantee the personal and material security of the Alsatians and the Lorrainers, and "political detainees and those who have found refuge in our country."[92]

Even with these limitations, with this new accession of power Laval came to be seen as the very embodiment of the Vichy regime which, however diminished and weakened by resignations, persisted.

Laval met with Hitler once more on May 2, 1943, always pursuing his quest for more advantages for France in Germany's Europe. But nothing real was accomplished; rather the meeting sounded the death knell of the policy of collaboration. Nothing was said of France as a co-belligerent.[93]

The issue became very real upon the Normandy invasion of June 6, 1944. Laval's position was clear. To the French people he broadcast: "We are not in the war. You must not take part in the fighting. If you do not observe this rule, you will provoke reprisals, the harshness of which the government would be powerless to moderate. You would suffer both physically and materially and you would add to your country's misfortunes."[94]

This message had two audiences. The provocation of reprisals spoke to the likely German response to the Resistance. But it also spoke to another group. They were called the Ultras. Laval and his policy of collaboration had represented a middle road. The Ultras were those French who were the convinced and fervent partisans and supporters of Nazi Germany. Headquartered in Paris, they never ceased in their press to heap abuse on Laval. He resisted as long as he could their entrance into the government and when he was forced to yield, as in the case of Marcel Deat, he assigned unpopular tasks and even then hedged them around with safeguards. The Ultras included Jacques Doriot, head of the Parti Populaire Francaise (PPF), Ferdinand de Brinon, Vichy's ambassador to Germany, Jean Bichelonne, Minister of Industrial Production and Abel Bonnard, Minister of Education.

They produced on July 9, 1944 under the leadership of Admiral Charles-René Platon a manifesto against Laval's neutralist stance, demanding that the government, including the Ultras, move to Paris and

calling for the government to assert its authority, invoking severe penalties, including the death penalty, for those "whose action encourages civil
war or jeopardizes the European position of France."[95]

Laval took them on in the cabinet meeting of July 12. He understood
what they really wanted. They wanted France to enter the war on
Germany's side. "With what weapons?" he asked. "M. Deat says he's
not neutral. All right, then, let him join up. It's easy. M. Deat would
also like the LVF and the Waffen SS to go and fight in Normandy.
Today, therefore, I maintain my position in full. My only opponents
are a few maniacs who are, moreover, in no hurry to go and fight themselves."

Laval demolished the positions and pretensions of his adversaries, who
one by one shamefacedly retreated. He then procured a vote affirming
his position of June 6 that "We are not in the war."

There was more. Laval was furious at the murder of his mentor
Georges Mandel. "I have no blood on my hands," he said, "and I never
will have...these are methods which I utterly deplore." He referred to
the assassination of Jean Zay, the Popular Front minister of education.
"Two is enough, more than enough...let anyone who disagrees with me
say so." No one having spoken, Laval concluded: "I note the cabinet's
unanimity in favor of refusing to hand over any hostages in the future
and (to condone) reprisals of this nature."[96]

Time was running out on the Vichy government. With the Allies on the
outskirts of Paris, Laval made a final attempt, with Herriot, to reconvene
Parliament and to restore the Third Republic. It failed when they were
both arrested by the Germans and carried into captivity where Laval
refused to exercise any further government function. France had never
become Germany's co-belligerent.

Pierre Laval and Alsace-Lorraine

There should be little doubt of the Vichy government's firm and continuing position on Alsace-Lorraine. Unlike the Versailles Treaty which
specifically restored these provinces to France, the 1940 Armistice made
no special provision for and indeed no mention of Alsace-Lorraine. From
the standpoint of Vichy, they were as much an integral part of France as
any other department.

This did not prevent the Germans from applying a series of increasingly
severe measures in the three departments of Haut Rhin, Bas Rhin, and
Moselle. French administrators were evicted. Residents deemed loyal to
France were expelled. German became the official language, the 1914

frontier was re-established and later came labor drafts and obligatory military service.

The record shows more than 114 protests to the Armistice Commission at Wiesbaden without results.[97]

Such was the lengthy protest of September 3, 1940 detailing the expulsions of residents, the evictions of clergy and the appointment of a *gauleiter* for Lorraine and Alsace with the civil administration, railroads, posts and customs integrated with Germany and the introduction of German racial measures. "Assured of the righteousness of its position, the French government raises a solemn protest against measures taken in violation of the armistice convention to cleanse the departments of Alsace and Lorraine of their inhabitants, which constitutes a de facto annexation of these territories."[98]

The point is not whether this protest or others succeeded. The point is whether they were made and whether they responded to the implicit charge in the supplement to the indictment that Laval had failed to protect the citizens of Alsace-Lorraine.

The protest of September 19, 1940 confirmed that of September 3 and in November 1940 Laval made a personal protest to Abetz. Four trainloads of Lorrainers had been sent to Lyon.

By order of my government [Laval wrote],

I am charged with raising a solemn protest against these expulsions which, for whatever reason claimed are absolutely contrary to human rights, to universally recognized rules of equity and humanity and are without justification in principle or in execution. In winter, unprepared, families are forced to leave their homes with only a strict minimum of goods.[99]

Laval was in retirement from December, 1940 to April, 1942. On his return, he continued to protest on May 19, 1942 against expulsions to Poland,[100] on September 3, 1942 against the deportation of Alsatians and Lorrainers to Germany and the German colonization of the departments.[101]

More protests followed: against the conscription of Alsatians into the SS; against drafts of labor for the Speer organization; against military conscription.[102]

Vichy did what was within its power to aid and comfort the refugees. All of the staff of the French administration of the three departments was retained on the rolls of the Ministry of Interior. The Senators and Deputies retained their titles even though they could no longer play an active role in their departments.

The faculty of the University of Strasbourg transferred to Clermont-Ferrand where they continued their distinct and separate existence.

Alsatian refugees were exempted when obligatory labor service was enacted. Mornet claimed that the sole response to the annexation of Alsace-Lorraine was Montoire. This was an allegation unsupported by the evidence. Evidence to the contrary could readily have been produced had not Pierre Laval chosen not to defend himself further against what he conceived to be a verdict that would be determined without reference to the evidence.

Pierre Laval and his lawyers had made their decision. They would not participate in a trial that to them revolted every principle of fairness and justice and broke every rule of established law and procedure. In their minds, the jurors had given ample evidence of their determination to convict, whatever the evidence and the court had refused Laval the opportunity to speak out, to defend himself.

We may now, at the distance of more than half a century, look at each and every issue included in the indictment, calmly assess the evidence and conclude that a substantial case could have been made in defense of Pierre Laval. Whether that defense, in that time and that place, in that court, before that jury would have brought about a different result we may doubt, but, of course, we can never know.

21

The Judgment[1]: October 9, 1945

While the jury deliberated on October 9, Baraduc and Jaffré visited with Pierre Laval in his cell at Fresnes. Laval was unusually nervous. He asked if he should return to the courtroom. Baraduc then left. Jaffré remained.

It seemed clear to Jaffré that Laval was hesitant, not knowing which course to take. He seemed tempted to return. He was tormented by the idea that he would be condemned before he could speak his part.[2]

"I ask myself," he said, "whether to return. If they condemn me to death, it will be all over and they'll kill me without my opening my mouth. Well, that's what they want."[3]

He had received no summons to the court that afternoon. That was, Jaffré observed, a violation of the law. What, he wondered, would Laval have done had he received the summons. He wouldn't, be surprised to see Laval return.[4]

Laval's lawyers knew that the Garde des Sceaux had called the Batonnier to urge Laval to return. The Batonnier had replied that Laval's counsel could not go against their client's wishes. As they saw it the powers-that-be wanted Laval's lawyers to associate themselves with a parody of justice.[5]

Because he hadn't received a summons, Laval thought that the Court had not opened and that there would be a continuance. He was surprised when he learned that the Court was in session. He hoped against hope that the jury would not dare to pronounce a sentence of death in his absence.

He was wrong.

Baraduc came back with the news.

Laval spoke: "Alors?"

"The verdict is in," said Baraduc.

"What is it?" Laval asked.

"Death."

Laval took the news without blanching. Baraduc and Jaffré clasped his hands.

He gave his counsel instructions as to the future proceedings. The lawyers left to carry out their tasks.[6]

It was by the light of a carbon lamp, the electricity temporarily out of service, that Pierre Laval was officially notified of the sentence.

"Under Articles 8.7 and 7.5 of the Penal Code, and the Ordinance of November 18, 1944, he is condemned to death, sentenced to national indignity and to the confiscation of all of his property."[7]

In an extraordinary trial, the most extraordinary document was the judgment and sentence of the Court. It found Pierre Laval guilty and condemned him to death on a charge that the Attorney General had voluntarily withdrawn. On the first charge of a plot against the state, the Court found that Laval had taken an active part in the "enterprises, intrigues and maneuvers" by which, on July 10, 1940, and succeeding days, the legal government of France had been evicted.

Not only was this far from the truth, but the Attorney General, on October 5, had clearly and precisely said that he laid no charge against Laval for the proceedings of the National Assembly on July 10, but only for the subversion of its action by the Vichy regime to which the Third Republic had delegated its powers.

Far from being evicted under difficult circumstances of defeat and chaos, the Parliament of the Third Republic had scrupulously followed the letter of the 1875 Constitution and entrusted its powers to the new regime. And all of this had been done with overwhelming majorities in the Senate and the Chamber of Deputies and in the National Assembly and to the overwhelming approval of the French people.

The judgment of the Court went on to say that as vice president of the Council of Ministers of State Laval had presided or participated in operations which replaced the organs of the Third Republic with organs created by the new regime such as the National Council, the Departmental Councils, and the Municipal Councils. It is interesting that this conclusion speaks only of the period from July 11 to December 13, 1940 when Laval was vice president of the Council and a minister of state and not the later period when he was prime minister or head of state.[8]

What the Court was concluding, then, was that participation in the Vichy government was a capital crime. Yet that regime had counted innumerable cabinet ministers, administrators, indeed the whole of the administrative cadre of the French state, and not only the members of the National Council, the Departmental Councils, and the Municipal Councils specified in the Court's judgment. The Vichy regime included the entire judicial system—indeed all of the judges, the magistrates, the prosecutors, and the police. It also included the Presiding Judge and the Attorney General. And it included the armed forces. Among all these Pierre Laval was condemned to death for serving the same state and the same people all these had served.

The second count of intelligence with the enemy found Laval guilty of serving the cause of Germany, allowing the annexation of Alsace-Lorraine, attempting to adapt the institutions of France to those of Germany. It covered all these topics: Montoire, the Bor mines, the shares of Hachette and Havas.[9]

He had been dismissed, the judgment said, in December 1940 and while in retirement he worked for collaboration "a cause rejected unanimously by all good French."

This portion of the judgment is noteworthy on two grounds. First, having condemned him to death for being in government, Laval was now condemned to death for not being in government. Second, nothing could more clearly illuminate the state of mind, the emotional needs of the Court, the jury, and perhaps the populace than the statement that Vichy had been rejected by "all good French."[10] The fact was that in the period from December 13, 1940 to April 18, 1942 when Laval was out of government (and long after) if there were unanimity among the good citizens of France it was a unanimity in favor of the Vichy regime. The regime had been avidly welcomed and strongly supported by most French people before, during and after Laval's period of retirement. But there was a compelling psychological need, after the collapse of France and the subsequent victory of the Allies to pronounce that the good citizens of France, unanimously, had rejected Vichy, that they had been heroes, all of them, and that there was only one *lupus in fabula*, one wolf in the story, one villain, one prime mover of all that was evil and all that was inglorious and that he had, single-handed, imposed his will upon all these valiant folk.

The judgment continued that Laval had been restored to government by German pressure; that he had sent a telegram to the Germans congratulating them on repelling the Dieppe raid. It was a telegram that was not in evidence, has never been found, and was stoutly denied by Laval.

There were the persecution of the Jews, the events surrounding the Allied landings in North Africa, and the scuttling of the fleet at Toulon.[11]

As with so many other charges, there might have been a very different record if Pierre Laval had been permitted to make a well prepared, ably presented case to an impartial court and jury. As an instance, Laval never had authority over the military and gave no military orders, and certainly not the longstanding order by which the Toulon fleet sank itself. Another story could have been told of the fleet in Martinique, the merchant marine and of the Milice, the internal police and its leader, Darnand, forced upon Laval but used by him to mitigate the greater extremes of the Germans and the Ultras.

The judgment then cited the massive deportation of workers to Germany.[12] As was the case with the persecution of the Jews, the judgment did not discriminate between what was lost (and why and how) and what had been saved.

Quite the contrary, the judgment found that although Laval had maintained that his policies furthered the interest of France, in a sweeping dismissal it concluded that France had received not one benefit of any kind from his policies and actions.

Pro-German pronouncements were cited, including the famous "I wish for a German victory..." He had, the judgment said, lent his influence in the service of another country with which, it insisted, France had continued to be at war, the Armistice notwithstanding.[13] Here again was the portrayal of a France, unvanquished, defiant, that accorded so well with the new self-image of the France of 1945.

For all of these actions, these crimes, Laval was condemned to death, to national indignity and degradation and to the confiscation of all his goods and properties.[14]

It is easy to imagine the heartbreak of young Jaffré at the moment he learned in Laval's presence of the sentence. His youthful ideals of justice were intact and he could not accept or understand the difference between his ideal and the reality of the trial which had just concluded.

He tormented himself in the aftermath, wondering if the lawyers shouldn't have taken a different tack. He knew that Laval would have wished to count solely on himself. That would have been natural enough, Jaffré thought, if the trial had been before the Senate, Laval's natural element. Moreover, Laval was convinced of his innocence and that he had served his country well in awful times and circumstances. He thought that when thoughtful judges heard the evidence, however adverse they may have been at the outset, they would render a verdict in accordance with the evidence.[15]

Laval had thought, Jaffré ruminated, that it was not the man but the policy that would be tried, that his good faith would be recognized even by those who disagreed with his policy, and that if the worst came to worst, the penalty would be a political penalty, like banishment.

"I'm not a traitor," Laval would say, "or some vulgar agent of the Gestapo. I conducted a policy I thought was for the good of my country." He thought the continuing presence of a French government essential. De Gaulle would benefit in recovering a country which surely had suffered, but whose administration and finances were all in working order.[16]

Perhaps, Jaffré thought, Laval should have had other lawyers, giants of the bar, with an authority and experience that he and his colleagues lacked. Perhaps they could have protested vigorously, reached out to the public, made a stronger showing before the Garde des Sceaux and before de Gaulle.[17]

Perhaps, Jaffré fretted, they should have been at Laval's side in court from the start. Perhaps they should have protested more. Jaffré lay awake nights pondering these questions. But in the end, he concluded that whatever else they might have done and whoever else might have done it, the result would have been the same.

Jaffré had believed with all his heart, as many others did, that after such a trial it would be morally impossible to execute Pierre Laval. But he was wrong, the best evidence, Jaffré concluded, that the aim of the trial was not to do justice but to do away with Pierre Laval.[18]

22

On the Eve[1]

Baraduc and Jaffré visited Laval at Fresnes on Wednesday, October 10 the day after the sentence had been handed down. He was on death row. Jaffré was troubled by the silence, broken only by the noises of the prisoners' chains.

The door to Laval's cell was open. The man who had been so many times the Prime Minister of France wore the rough urine-colored garb of a convict. His feet were in chains. He was smoking. He lacked neither humor nor irony. "Not so bad," he said, "my tuxedo."[2]

His voice was low, a bit feeble. But he made no complaint. He was glad that they had left him the tri-color scarf which he wore around his neck. To Jaffré, although he was thin his aspect had not changed. His eyes retained their vivacity, their responsiveness, their keen intelligence. It was, he thought, a visage both serene and noble but in its serenity even more expressive than ever before. It was the calm and detachment of one who has accepted his fate without revolt. He smiled. "*Comment ca va?*" He extended his hand. His chains hobbled him. He walked in tiny steps as if on a slippery surface. The chains dragged behind making a cruel noise. Jaffré was shocked. They could have spared him that, if only out of consideration for his age.

Laval's first thought was of his family. He wanted to know how they had reacted to the sentence. He was more concerned for them than for himself. Jaffré replied that they kept up hope. He gave Laval a note hastily scribbled by his wife: "We are prouder of you than ever." "And look at me now," Laval said, "like a chained bear."[3]

An attendant entered with a basket of books. Laval declined, saying he was conferring with his lawyer. But he took a book, and then he said: "Really, they think of everything. Wine and now novels. Perhaps chosen by the General."[4]

A guard escorted them to a conference cell. Laval walked in his little steps, his chains dragging behind him. "It reminds me," he mused, "of the sack races in the square at Chateldon." The guard opened the door. "Does my costume make you laugh?" he asked.

"I know what it is," the guard said, "I was a prisoner."

"Of the Germans?"

"Yes."

"Here, during the Occupation?"

"In Germany."

"Deported?"

"No, prisoner of war."

"And did you get packages?"

"Yes."

"And tobacco."

"Yes."

"And food."

"Yes."

"And books?"

"Oh, yes, it was the Red Cross that sent us all that."

"The Red Cross? You think it was the Red Cross? It was me."

Laval smiled a small, sad smile. "I hope you never know my situation. But it honors me. My costume may make you laugh, but it honors me. It only dishonors those who sent me here. Look well. You will never again see a President of the Council dressed like this."[5]

Laval later said the same to Jaffré. "Look at me Jaffré. You will see in your time other Presidents of the Council. But you will never see a President of the Council in my position. But," and he lingered over the words that self-defined him: "*Je ne me suis jamais senti aussi grand.*"

"I have never felt so great."[6]

"Have I examined my conscience since they sent me here? They will kill me. I know they will... I tell you, the more I search my conscience, the more I feel that I have nothing to reproach myself. And that is why I have never felt so great."

"They accuse me of having humiliated France. My conscience reminds me of what I have endured for France and what I endure now. But that's nothing, nothing. My soul is serene because I know that one day justice will sound for me, whether I'm living or dead. That's all I have to say. And now, to work."[7]

He never stopped working. It was as if the whole trial had nothing to do with real justice. His death would only be an episode he told Jaffré, in the march toward truth. So he continued to work on the document that could have no impact on his immediate fate. And he worked with the same precision, the same sang froid, in the same regular script that he had two weeks earlier used to respond to the accusations of the indictment. He seemed to forget he was condemned to death and, the prison garb and the chains notwithstanding, Jaffré could almost forget that, too.[8]

He would not apply for clemency. Marshal Pétain had not. A President of the French Council ought never, he said, ask grace of anyone. All he would ask for was a new trial.[9]

But he still nourished faint hopes. Could anyone have imagined such a trial? Mongibeaux! Had any magistrate in the past acted with a quarter of the partiality Mongibeaux had shown, he would have been dishonored.

"Do you really think," he asked Jaffré, "after a trial like that they can execute me?" Jaffré, of course said no. He thought those who did would be condemned by history, and that they would give a second thought before arriving at the fatal decision.[10]

And Jaffré was not simply lending comfort. He believed it with all of his ardent heart. He wasn't the only one. Even many who condemned his policies thought that the trial had been a scandal and that it would be monstrous to execute Laval under such conditions.

That was what his family believed and felt. They lived in a fever, where agony was mixed with hope. They were busy with pleas, interviews, telephone calls, whatever they could do to save Laval from death.[11]

Josée de Chambrun called upon the celebrated writer Francois Mauriac.

"I shall never forget," he wrote, "the admirable daughter of Pierre Laval coming to me one evening as if I could save her father. Also, if ever there were a desperate case this was it. Pierre Laval had in a way assumed all of the hatreds, even those of the partisans of the Marshal. Never was a scapegoat more bitterly condemned—less for what he did then for what he said."[12]

Mauriac then wrote this letter to Tietgen, the Garde des Sceaux:

It is not for me to tell you, a jurist, the reasons to halt the execution. I can only say that if I were in your place, I wouldn't hesitate a moment. Especially abroad the trial must be seen as judged clearly, in the serenity of justice.[13]

Jaffré was caught up in this whirlwind. He lived in a nightmare, his nerves stretched taut, up to the limits of his strength, returning home each night exhausted and arising with the dawn. It was the same with Baraduc and Naud. They were certain their efforts wouldn't be in vain.[13]

The next day, October 11, Baraduc was the first to come to Fresnes. Laval had been irritated by a visit from the chaplain.

"In the evening," he told Baraduc, "in my little cell, when I look out and see the stars, I think that there is one who created it all." He smiled, silent, turned to the window and said: "I don't need priests." He paused. "I'm in direct communication with God."[14]

Jaffré and Naud joined Baraduc and Laval. They were worried about Laval's morale. Like Baraduc, they found him calm. Laval continued to talk of religion. The priest would come and say mass in his cell. But... he preferred to pray alone.

Laval had learned, like so many other convicts, to manage his chains. With a cord he could hold them up while he walked and escape the rasping sound they made on the floor.

Jaffré recalled to Laval Victor Hugo's description of a visit to the condemned man's cell. But that cell was spacious and there was a stove. There was no mention of chains, a detail Victor Hugo wouldn't have omitted.

"Well," said Laval, "I'm sorry I didn't live then. I would have had a little more comfort in my last days. At least I would have been warm. Here, you could die of the cold before they kill you. Back then, they would have let me defend myself. Men like Victor Hugo would never have countenanced silencing the voice of the accused. Some progress justice has made!"[15]

Laval had only the schoolboy's pen furnished by the prison. He asked if Jaffré had a fountain pen. It would help him speed his work. It was precise, as skilled as before, but Jaffré found in his writing a new conciseness, a loftiness of thought by a man who had no other means to defend his memory.[16]

During the day, Baraduc and Naud had visited Leon Blum in his elegant apartment in the Petit Luxembourg. Laval had taken great care to protect Blum throughout the Occupation, especially after the assassination of Georges Mandel. Blum quickly understood their goal, a revision of the trial. Blum hesitated. He didn't see what he could do for the man who had done so much for him. Finally, he authorized the lawyers to publish his opinion: that the trial, as it had been conducted, was a scandal and an error. They told Blum that Laval was in chains.

"But, who," Blum exclaimed, "who could have ordered that?" Blum waxed philosophical. When he and his wife had been deported, when they felt themselves in danger of death, it was then that they had found the greatest tranquility.

What the lawyers did not know was that on Sunday, October 14, Blum would write to de Gaulle an eloquent plea on behalf of Pierre Laval:

My dear General.

I have just returned to Paris and phoned Palewski [de Gaulle's chef de cabinet] who told me there was yet time for a final appeal to you.

You know my sentiment, but it is my duty to express it once again. I do not think you can carry out a capital sentence after a trial like this. It's not a question of grace but of justice.

We have never had any mutual sympathy or community of views and you know that it is not because of the gratitude I owe you but I have rendered justice in another time. I respect it and I wish it to be respected.

Excuse me and believe in my profound attachment.

P.S. I have reread this letter written in haste and I do not wish to be misunderstood. I do not ask grace but a new trial—or rather a trial.[17]

In the evening Baraduc saw Laval again. They walked in the corridors, Laval managing, as best he could, his chains. He had been forbidden to see his wife and daughter. They were uppermost in his mind. He entrusted a message to Baraduc. How grand they were in the face of sorrow. He tried to hide his tears. He took off his eyeglasses. "Mon Dieu," he said, "my eyes aren't working so well tonight."[18]

The next day was Friday, October 12. Laval told Baraduc it was imperative to save all of his papers. Otherwise, after the execution, the cell would be cleaned out and his documents lost forever. His narrative, he said, hardly satisfied him; there had been so little time. But he asked Baraduc to publish it in a book, a handsome book, as soon as possible. He told Baraduc in measured tones, "You can't save my life. But you can save my memory. And that I value more than my life." So, at his little table, in chains, he sat in silence. Had he aged, Baraduc asked himself, had he paled in the past days? Surely. But Baraduc saw only calm, never a complaint, never fear. "*Il faut vivre debout devant le malheur.*" "A man must stand erect," Laval wrote, " in the face of sorrow."[19]

"At sixty-two," Laval said, "I've had a full life. I can go." But he thought of another denouement. If they wanted to be rid of him, they could banish him. He could find a small place, a river where he could fish. But no, they wanted him dead.

"Promise me you won't laugh," Baraduc asked. A woman had sent a miraculous medal to Laval.

"I don't need to laugh," Laval replied. He looked at the medal. "Put it on me," he asked, "not outside," but inside his shirt. Laval rose. For the first time he took Baraduc in his arms and embraced him. All this without a word. Then, in a low tone, he ordered Baraduc to be about his business.[20]

The lawyers were now informed that they would have an audience with de Gaulle. They visited Professor Hugueney of the criminal law faculty of Paris. Jaffré returned to Fresnes where he told Laval the visit had not been encouraging. Things were about to happen. "Not tomorrow," Laval cried. "It's the thirteenth. The thirteenth has always been unlucky for me." He asked if the execution would be on the morrow, the thirteenth. Jaffré thought not.

Laval repeated a familiar phrase: *"Mon affaire n'est pas une affaire comme les autres."*[21]

Eynoux, the chief guard passed by. Laval asked the same question. Eynoux gave him his word of honor that there was no order for the morrow. The administration had to be notified in advance; they had measures to take. But Laval was not reassured. They could always change the procedure. *"Mon affaire n'est pas une affaire comme les autres."* He entrusted a large quantity of documents to Jaffré and put in his hands a letter *"A mes avocats pour les informer. A mes borreaux pour les reponder."* "To my lawyers, to inform them. To my execution-ers, to answer them."

"If it isn't tomorrow," he asked Jaffré, "be here at the earliest hour." Jaffré had no car that day. He walked two kilometers to the railroad station, heavily laden with Laval's documents. Night was falling. He was uneasy. He turned around from time to time to see if someone were following him, to rob him of his documents. He briefly visited with the family, then joined his colleagues to meet at seven in the evening with General de Gaulle who would hold the life and fate of Pierre Laval in his hands.[22]

The lawyers met first with M. Patain, the director of Criminal Services who in turn conveyed them to the rue St. Dominique where they were received by de Gaulle. To Jaffré he appeared a giant who had to bend almost in two to greet Naud, the shortest. Without being invited, the lawyers sat down. Naud described the defects of the trial, Baraduc the errors and especially the omissions of the pre-trial proceeding.

De Gaulle took out a cigarette and lit it. From time to time he glanced at the lawyers. Most of the time his eyes were fixed on the wall. Not a muscle in his face moved. Baraduc asked Jaffré to speak.

Jaffré took history as his theme. There had never been such a trial in France. Not even at the height of the Terror had an accused been so insulted by the judges. There were incidents of the trial that would reverberate to the end of time. Never had a prime minister been executed. It was a dangerous precedent.

It seemed to Jaffré that with this phrase de Gaulle made a slight movement. Nothing more. He thanked the lawyers. The whole procedure had been brief and glacial.[23]

M. Patain reappeared. He said that before deciding, de Gaulle wished to consult with the Garde des Sceaux who was off campaigning but would return on the morrow. M. Patain was far from optimistic. If Laval were to be executed, the sooner it happened the less he would suffer. He asked for them to be ready for a further meeting.[24]

What the lawyers did not know was that before receiving them, de Gaulle had given a press conference in which he had announced that the Laval verdict would not be revised.[25]

The next day, Saturday the 13, Jaffré found Laval cordially bantering with the guards. The night before his chains had been removed. Laval seemed to Jaffré very tired, as if he had passed a wakeful night. He had written letters discovered only after his death, among the most beautiful, Jaffré thought, he had ever penned.[26]

Laval asked about the details of his execution. He had a horror of being disfigured. He hated all violence. He had a profound respect for human life.

War was the worst of all follies, he told Jaffré, both for the victor and for the vanquished. What had France, what had Germany gained? War had to stop for the benefit of generations to come. That's what he had thought before the war, after the debacle, today, whatever the changes of the political tides. "Listen to me, Jaffré. I say this even on the verge of execution, Germany and France must unite if they want to live."[27]

Baraduc visited Laval in the afternoon. Laval was discussing potato culture with the guard, simply and without affectation. He was calm, at ease. He was sad that his daughter had no child. One day there would have been a little de Chambrun "and it would have been me."

He again expressed his fear of disfigurement. "I shall make, as the Chinese say, my last salute to the world. My work is finished. My eternity commences. It commences here in this little cell." He looked at the walls and smiled. "Funny little cell." He talked of his childhood in Chateldon, his friends, their games. "I don't know if it would be possible but I would like to be buried in the little church at Chateldon."[28]

Sunday, October 14, Jaffré spent most of the day with Laval. It had been agreed among the lawyers that he should spend as much time as possible with Laval while they attended to other appeals and proceedings. It was a great comfort to Laval's family to know that he had not been abandoned to solitude.

During the course of the day, many of the condemned men passed by on their way to see their lawyers. They stopped at Laval's cell. "You come to see me," he told them, "because you know I'm going to die. But we're all going to die one day."

There were those who knew Laval and who would embrace him with heartfelt words, "Courage, President."

Laval had a smile for them and he would thank them. "Don't worry about me," he would say, "I'll show them how a French prime minister dies."[29]

The tireless Josée de Chambrun had learned of the intimacy of Monsigneur Chevrot with de Gaulle. He was indeed de Gaulle's confessor. She heard his last mass and sought his help. He did not hesitate and then and there wrote to Mlle. de Miribel, de Gaulle's secretary: "You cannot think of the trial of Pierre Laval as anything but a veritable comedy."[30]

Tragedy would have been more apt. The letter continued: "The trial should be revised. Laval should be judged. I beg de Gaulle to stop this denial of justice."[31]

Baraduc visited Laval at noon. He found him calm, sorting his papers. He had a letter for each of the lawyers, "For you, for Naud, for little Jaffré." Baraduc stuffed the letters in his pocket. "Don't you want to read it?" Baraduc opened his letter. It was headed "On the Eve of Death."[32]

They wanted to silence him, the letter said, to hide the truth. If he had had the opportunity, he would have destroyed the lies and vindicated the truth. They called him clever and sly. But he was simply a child of the people. They called him an enemy of the people and he had always defended them.

"I am entering the eternal sleep. My conscience is at peace. Remorse will torment those who did not know me, who soiled and tortured me.... I do not hate them because the hate which inspires them has no place in my soul. I weep for my family because I have made them suffer."

"I wish happiness for the country I love and the liberty which has been taken away. It will find it one day in another spirit and with other guides."

"I await death with serenity because my soul will live. I prefer death to chains."[33]

When Baraduc had left, Jaffré tried to maintain his spirits. But he was crushed by the knowledge that this man whom he admired, whom he had come to love, would shortly suffer a violent death after a parody of a trial. His mood did not escape Laval. "Are you sure you told me everything?" Laval asked. Jaffré insisted that he had; he had no right to hide anything from Laval.

"The law," Laval told Jaffré, "is a wonderful profession, especially when it's practiced with conscience and with ardor. How I have been touched by the devotion of my lawyers even though they never knew me before." He was sure that they were convinced of his innocence. They had been courageous throughout the trial and he was profoundly grateful.[34]

Laval's eyes shone and he fixed his gaze on Jaffré with unwonted intensity. His voice betrayed no excessive emotion and if he started when he heard a footstep in the corridor, the clanging of a door, he mastered his feelings admirably.

Courage, Jaffré thought, consisted not in being unmoved by the specter of death but to be sensible of it and to overcome that sensibility.[35]

It was in the afternoon that Baraduc received a telephone call at his office. An anonymous voice asked him to be ready at the entrance to the Palace of Justice at 8 A.M. the next day. A car would take him to Fresnes.

He now had the sad duty to go with Naud to the Place Palais Bourbon. They were met by Josée de Chambrun. There was no need to speak. She greeted them and pronounced the words they could not. They stood rooted to the spot, unable to move. Madame Laval whispered "*Mon pauvre petit*." Naud saw Josée stricken like a wounded animal. The brilliant light of those extraordinary eyes was suddenly extinguished as she stared blankly at all those around her and at a fate she could not accept. René de Chambrun wept.[36]

En route to Fresnes, the lawyers left Josée de Chambrun at Mlle. de Miribel's door.

The director of the prison awaited their arrival. Laval was calm he said, but he insisted it would be a terrible thing to tell him the truth before the morrow. Baraduc and Naud entered the cell. Jaffré's heart stopped when he saw them. They were trying to keep up a good countenance but Jaffré saw the news must be bad.[37]

"What news?" Laval asked.

"Not brilliant."

"Has anything been decided?"

They were not sure. They had no news from de Gaulle. Laval thought all hope was not lost. He asked Jaffré to sit at the table and write. Jaffré could hardly see the paper in the dim light. They asked to move to Laval's cell where the light was better. While Laval moved documents, Jaffré turned to Naud. Was it for tomorrow? Naud nodded silently.[38]

"Then you have to tell him," Jaffré said. "We can't," Naud replied. "We don't have the moral right."

Jaffré reflected. Alone, he would have. But he had to stand by his colleagues.

Laval started to dictate. To Jaffré the scene was unforgettable. He was overwrought, unable to continue. He struggled on. Laval was unsatisfied with the result and asked him to rewrite. Naud intervened. He could re-copy the letter later at home. Naud took the letter, crumpled it and threw it into his pocket. "What good is it?" Jaffré thought.

They clasped hands. "Come tomorrow."

"We will be here at eight," Naud answered.

"But the doors don't open 'til 8:30," Laval said.

"But we'll be here at eight," Naud replied.

"Ah," Laval simply breathed.

The guard led the lawyers out. Pierre Laval was left alone with his thoughts.[39]

Those thoughts centered on those he loved most. To Josée he wrote:

My dearest little one, I hold you in my arms. You know how much I loved you in my own way... I think of you when you were little with your bear. I remember how I teased you to make you laugh, to make you angry... And when you hid under my table. Remember these things, not to weep, but to remind you how much your father loved you...How I wish I could take your sorrow away with me. How much more at peace I would be if I knew I hadn't made you unhappy with my own unhappiness.

He added words of consolation:

You are blessed to have Bunny. He loves me as if I were his own father. I'm proud of him, happy he's your husband. He loves you passionately. He will protect you. You will never be alone. You have your mother... She has suffered so much because of me. She loves you so much. When you have a care, think of me. I will be there. I will be in your heart to console you.[40]

Of his last letter to his wife, only a portion remains. The rest Josée placed years later in her coffin. But those brief words tell all:

I am with you. I embrace you, I hold your hand. I love you desperately. We will meet again. Never leave Josée...I will be with you always. Always.[41]

23

Dernier Cri[1]

Years after, Jaffré penned a graceful appreciation of Laval:

Laval loved life. He loved men. He loved the French. He had a tenderness for the common folk. He loved the fields, the peasants, his farm at Chateldon. He loved politics, discussions, negotiation. He loved power, but not out of pride—he never sought popularity but for the satisfaction of rendering service to his country. He loved his family... he loved France.

His vitality was extraordinary. You could read it on his countenance; it poured out in his talk and he showed all this until his final breath.[2]

On the fatal morning of Monday, October 15, the lawyers joined the cortege on its way to Fresnes.[3] Troops and police guarded every intersection. It was like the funeral of a sovereign Baraduc thought; and he remembered Jaffré's words: "Not since Louis XIV."[3]

The courtyard at Fresnes was black with guards. The prison director greeted them wordlessly. Their footsteps echoed in the silence of the corridor. They entered Laval's cell.

He was stretched out on his bed, resting on a shoulder, face to the wall. He looked up, silent.

Naud spoke. "*M. le Président, pour l'Histoire, pour vos avocats, ayez du courage.*" "For History, for your lawyers, have courage."

Softly, Laval replied: "Don't say such a thing to me."

He pulled the cover up to his face and from his hand there dropped an ampule which bore the label Azym. Dr. Paul picked it up and held it to his nose. "Cyanide!"[4]

Laval gasped. Baraduc held his hand. Laval passed into convulsions, the covers cast aside. Dr. Paul expected immediate death.

Where had Laval gotten the cyanide? Jaffré firmly believed he had for a long time had it and that he had carried it to his meeting with Hit-

245

ler in November, 1942 when Hitler had demanded a declaration of war against the Allies.[5]

The world crowded into the cell. Laval's cigarettes were on the table and photographs of Chateldon, of Mme. Laval receiving guests on the terrace with Josée. They were carefully arranged so that he could look at them for the last time.[6]

There were letters on the table. Naud read aloud the letter to his lawyers. They had forbidden him, he wrote, to talk at his trial. Now they were trying to silence his voice forever. He would not accept an execution, which was tantamount to murder. In the Roman manner, he would take poison, a final protest against savagery.

The soldiers, he wrote, would do their duty. They ought not to be compelled to shoot a man who died because he loved his country too much. "I ask that they leave me my tri-colored scarf. I want to wear it for the great voyage. I address my last salute to the France I have served. My last thought is for her."[7]

Nothing could have been more characteristic of Laval than another short note in which he thanked the prison personnel, the little people, for their kindnesses.[8]

The medical staff busied themselves with pumping Laval's stomach. Dr. Paul declared that if he did not die within the hour, he might survive, but paralyzed. Bouchardon, who had given assurance of an ample preliminary examination, was there. When he saw the ampule, he declared that Laval couldn't have hidden it, that someone had brought it to him. Totally insensible to what he saw, the same magistrate now suggested that Laval could be shot in a chair or on a stretcher.[9]

At 11:30 Laval showed signs of consciousness. He was tortured by thirst. He asked for water. Father Mourin approached him. Did he wish to receive the sacrament? "Yes," Laval replied. The crowd retired, leaving the priest alone to give the absolution.[10]

Mornet and Bouchardon had come and gone. It was said that they had telephoned de Gaulle in the rue St. Dominique. When they returned, they bore the instruction that Laval should be executed on a stretcher. "Impossible," said Dr. Paul. "The code forbids it."

Laval was regaining lucidity. "I didn't wish to die," he said, "by French bullets."[11] The time of execution was set. Laval was dressed with difficulty. A search of his valises produced his final white tie. He asked for a comb and carefully arranged his hair with the help of a small pocket mirror. He was suffering from nausea, retching, heaving, unable to throw up. "Fantastic," he said, "after the poison I took. I must be a real Auvergnat."[12]

He asked for the Colonel commanding. He would be an obedient condemned man, but wished no brutality. "You will not suffer, I guarantee," the Colonel replied. Laval wished to give the command to fire. This was denied. He asked not to have his hands tied. This, too was denied. He asked not to be blindfolded. That was granted. Conscious, however wracked by pain and thirst, of his dignity, he asked for his hat and cane.[13]

The door of the cell opened. A voice cried out, "Dress him quickly!" It was a prison administrator. Laval looked at him calmly. "Are you late for lunch?" he inquired. The man left abruptly before Laval could say: "You don't know how a President of the Council dies?"[14]

They were ready to leave. Jaffré carried a bottle of water for Laval. The prison director forbade him to carry it. One of the guards tugged at Jaffré's sleeve. He could, he said, put the bottle in his pocket. Jaffré had only to ask for it.

Laval walked, supported by his lawyers. He was extremely feeble. A guard carried a chair. Laval stopped at ten meters to sip some water. They mounted a police vehicle. "I accept to die," he said, "but my heart goes out to my wife and daughter." They occupied his thoughts during the brief journey. "Tell my wife and daughter," he asked Baraduc, "that my last thoughts were for them. Tell them I didn't suffer. They won't believe it, but no matter."[15]

The vehicle stopped between a hearse and the stake to which Laval was to be tied. Laval descended. "Where are the magistrates?" he demanded. "Where are the magistrates?" he repeated. Mornet and Bouchardon crept out from behind the hearse. They clasped their hats to their breasts. They trembled. "They have given you a sad duty," Laval told them. He advanced a few steps to the stake saying: "I die because I loved my country too much."[16]

He asked his lawyers to help him step forward. Jaffré embraced him. "Au revoir Monsieur le President." Naud too, said, "Au revoir Monsieur le President." Laval embraced and spoke to Baraduc and Father Maurin who gave him a crucifix. Laval's hands were tied. An officer approached Jaffré "Please return to M. Laval. He wants his last look to be at his lawyers."[17]

The officer raised his sabre. Laval cried "Vive la France." The sabre was lowered the volley exploded. Laval fell to his knees, his eyes fixed on his defenders. He was wearing his tri-color foulard. As if in a dream,

Jaffré saw the officer administer the coup de grace to the temple. Pierre Laval was no more.[18]

From throughout the prison came raucous cries: "Assassins, assassins. Vive Laval." Baraduc, Naud, and Jaffré left in silence to fulfill a last duty, and to bring the sad news to the family at Place Palais Bourbon.

24

Aftermath

Trials and history share a common goal—the truth. But judicial proceedings are limited by subject matter, by procedure and by finite boundaries of time. Trial, judgment and appeal are intended to produce finality. History, on the other hand, is never final.

The trial of Pierre Laval, instead of revealing the truth, did much to conceal it. This was widely recognized at the time. After its performance in the trial of Pierre Laval, the government of France continued the policy of concealment. The truth could no longer affect the outcome of the trial. But history still had its claims to truth and it was those claims that were only slowly, and by persistence, courage and loyalty, overcome.

Stoic in her grief, Madame Laval maintained her accustomed silence until her death in 1958. Fiercely loyal to the name, the reputation and the memory of Pierre Laval, Josée and René de Chambrun never ceased in their efforts to vindicate him. Laval's faithful defenders, Naud, Baraduc, and Jaffré were equally dedicated.

In December, 1947, de Chambrun was approached by a colleague from his days at the New York bar who had participated in the Nuremberg trials of Reich Marshal Hermann Goering and General Field Marshals Erhard Milch and Hugo Sperrle, the leaders of the Luftwaffe. He alerted Chambrun to the existence of substantial German documentation concerning the role of Pierre Laval in Vichy's dealings with Germany. These documents portrayed Laval as tenacious, wily, and, from the German point of view, too successful in opposing German demands and exigencies, whether they concerned the French aviation industry, banking, manpower or other issues.[1]

Baraduc assembled the documents which were published in 1949 under the title *Tout Çe qu'on vous a Caché* and in English as *From the Secret Archives of the Reich*.

Decades later, in July, 1987, a Laval biographer, Fred Kupferman, directed a mysterious visitor to René de Chambrun. He wore the ribbon of the Legion of Honor. He had occupied a semi-official post in Germany. For many years, he explained, he had had in his possession documents relating to Pierre Laval which rightfully belonged to the family. They were written during Laval's last days. When de Chambrun looked at the documents, he immediately recognized Laval's hand. Most poignant was a copy of the sentence of death on which Laval had written a critique. It was written in the third person, combining passion and objectivity, as if Laval were the attorney and not the condemned. Two weeks later, de Chambrun received, not a visitor, but a cache of documents left with the doorman at his office building. Here were the notes Laval had composed in his cell at Fresnes, letters from his wife and daughter bearing the prison censorship stamp, manuscript copies of letters to the Batonnier Poignard, lists of witnesses and questions to be put to them. There were notes from de Chambrun via Baraduc and Jaffré and there were notes written by Laval to his lawyers which they never received. Most important was the schema, the outline of his defense in which Laval responded in detail to all of the charges against him.[2]

Most of these documents had been concealed from the searching eyes of history for more than forty years. René de Chambrun's cheeks were damp with tears as he recognized the tight, precise, slanted handwriting of his father-in-law on the execrable paper of the epoch. He read Laval's appeal to de Gaulle:

> I am not discouraged, I have made no protest even when my honor and my very life were made the plaything of a strange justice...I have been a submissive defendant, calm and correct in the face of the threat of sanctions.
>
> I had hoped at the trial that there would be a full investigation of the facts to replace the preliminary examination which was refused...
>
> I cannot ignore the fate that awaits me. I prefer to run the risk rather than to associate by my presence at a proceeding so grossly arbitrary and brutal without precedent...[3]

Had there been a trial consonant with its historical importance, Laval wrote, the facts would have been revealed, the explanations, excuses, and responsibilities clarified. He would have spoken without fear and without hate. "A free France judges, but does not assassinate. You are the chief. I have confidence in your decision."[4]

There was no reply.

Once more de Chambrun lingered over Laval's words captioned "On the Eve of Death."[5]

"Nothing will prevent France from learning what has been hidden... France is not free if France does not know the truth."

"I will sleep the eternal sleep. My conscience is at peace... I do not hate those that condemn me because the hate that drives them has no place in my soul."

"I weep for my family whom I have made to suffer. For my country which I love I wish the happiness and honor which have been snatched from it. It will one day find them, in another spirit, with other guides."

"I await death with serenity because my soul will survive. I prefer death to chains."[6]

It had always seemed clear to René de Chambrun that more truth would be found in the trial dossier of the prosecution than anywhere else. Having already filed a written request with M. Louis Joxe, then Garde des Sceaux, he discussed the matter with Prime Minister Georges Pompidou. They talked at length about Pierre Laval. "Your father-in-law," Pompidou told de Chambrun, "united a superior intelligence with exceptional courage—a rare combination."[7]

He spoke of the Auvergnats. They often undertook tasks that were beyond them, whether for their farm, their village, their province or their country. They were accused of self-interest. But they also accomplished challenging tasks. "The great merit of Laval," he said, "was to undertake the impossible—to protect France from the enemy, and to accomplish that, to bear unpopularity even to the ultimate sacrifice." "History will one day do him justice."[8]

Pompidou assured de Chambrun that permission to see the prosecution's files would be granted. He did not seek de Gaulle's approval, which de Chambrun was sure would have been refused. It was a time when much was happening. There were the celebrated events of 1968, the departure of de Gaulle, Pompidou's becoming president. There were also the workings of the French bureaucracy to be overcome. So it was only in August, 1970 that de Chambrun was received at the Palais Soubise, the archives of France, by the chief conservator, M. Cezard. Twenty-five years after the trial of Pierre Laval, de Chambrun looked with awe and emotion upon the eight cartons which comprised the dossier of the prosecution.[9]

He secured permission to transcribe and then to photograph the documents. He made three sets of five separate dossiers, each containing the documents he felt were most significant. One he deposited in the French National Archives, a second at the Hoover Institution at Stanford University and the third at the Fondation Josée and René de Chambrun.

Nevertheless, it was agreed that all of the documents would remain under seal until the fiftieth anniversary in 1995 of the trial of Pierre Laval.[10]

While in German captivity, Pierre Laval had started to prepare his defense for the trial he knew must come. All of the documents representing this immense labor were seized and confiscated at the moment of Laval's return to France in August 1945. It was these materials that René de Chambrun saw for the first time.[11]

Here was a statement of general policy: "My interest was to remain at home. My duty was to do what I did." "And there had to be a government to face victorious Germany to defend the position of our country." There were detailed notes on Montoire, Laval's March, 1942 meeting with Goering, on the famous statement "*Je souhaite*," on Alsace-Lorraine. Jean Bichelonne, Vichy's minister of industrial production had prepared studies of labor supply and economic policy and results. M. Guerard had contributed a summary of the visit of the Grand Rabbi of France to Laval to discuss protection of the Jews. There were Laval's notes on the origin of the Milice and the *Petit Marseillais*, the newspaper which had been alluded to in the trial. All this laboriously compiled documentation was seized and withheld. The only purpose could have been to disable Laval's defense.

If the first dossier comprised materials critical to preparing Laval's defense, the second dossier reflected on serious specific charges of the indictment that Laval had "by dint of intrigues, bribery, promises and menaces" led the government of the Third Republic to be entrusted to Marshal Petain. This dossier contained Commissions Rogatoires, that is to say interrogatories under oath of members of Parliament and other notables of the Third Republic. Questions were asked about the vote of the National Assembly, the legality of the delegation to Pétain of government powers, and about any pressure that had been applied to obtain the transfer of power.

The first set of interrogatories took place in April, May and June of 1945. Needless to say, Pierre Laval and his counsel, when they were later appointed, were entirely ignorant of these inquiries. Of the thirty members of Parliament questioned, nine made no comment, ten responses were marked "Sans interet"—"without interest"—and none raised issues of illegality or pressure. To the contrary the report of Jean Niel is marked "*tres moderé concernant* Laval" and that of Yvon Delbos, Popular Front Foreign Minister records "*Ne concernant pas du tout Pierre Laval*." "Nothing about Pierre Laval."

Thirty eight others were interrogated They included such notables as Jules Jeanneney, Paul Reynaud, Albert Lebrun, and Léon Blum. These interrogatories were taken as recently as September, 1945, after Laval's defense counsel had been appointed. This time twenty responses were categorized as *"sans interet."* Again responses were tallied such as these: Jean Renaud, "Favorable à Pierre Laval"; Maurice Reclus, "Entiérement favorable à Pierre Laval"; Armand Gazel, "The judge of instruction tried without success to demonstrate by this witness a Petain-Laval plot before 1939." But there was no material evidence of illegality or undue pressure on the part of Laval.

With such evidence in hand, it was the duty of the prosecution not only to refrain from making charges they knew to be untrue, but more than that to make such exculpatory evidence available to the defense.

In the same manner, the second dossier contained ample documentation of the investigation of Laval's finances and personal affairs, the blocking of his accounts and the confiscation of his properties, but none of the financial improprieties alleged in the indictment. The third dossier contained added financial information and also documentation concerning the merchant fleet, miscellaneous correspondence and even Laval's Last Will and Testament.

The fourth dossier was replete with protests to the German authorities of varying dates against deportations and colonization in Alsace-Lorraine; against its incorporation into Germany and its subjection to German nationality and anti-Semitic statutes. All this would have been useful in combating the persistent charges of the abandonment of Alsace-Lorraine. In sum, these documents, like so many others, were suppressed by a prosecution which made charges contrary to the evidence in its hands and denied that evidence to the defense.

The fifth dossier contained a miscellany of documents which would have been helpful to the defense. There was a letter from Laval to the regional prefects suspending the labor draft. There were documents showing Laval's protection of Resistants. A letter from Pierre Taittinger, the regional prefect in Paris, warned of plots against Laval by the Paris Ultras and other documents related to Laval's last gasp August, 1945, attempt with Herriot, to reconvene the National Assembly and to restore to Parliament its powers.

The existence of this mass of exculpatory evidence is critical because of the conclusion in the sentence that France had not received any benefit from Laval's actions. It was critical because such evidence would illuminate Laval's intent. If it were admitted that France had received benefits, then it could be concluded that this was Laval's intent. Whereas had France received no benefits, the conclusion could be drawn that he intended to act solely for the benefit of Germany. The record is clear on these issues. Many Jews were deported and went to their deaths. But far more, remarkably far more among French nationals, were saved and the Vichy government had significantly helped to save them. Likewise demands for labor were frustrated; no French women and far fewer men than were demanded went to Germany. The Vichy government defended with vigor its prisoners of war and never allowed the segregation or mistreatment of Jewish prisoners. A good deal was done in the normal functioning of the organs of state, in the areas of education and social welfare under terribly adverse conditions. Perhaps Albert Camus had all of this in mind when he wrote, "We shall never know what he spared us. We shall never know what France would have been without Vichy."[12]

What were the basic goals of Laval? They were to represent France in the face of the victor, the Occupant. In 1940, the evidence of German victory was overwhelming. Germany had been victorious before, in 1870; but France had recovered and shared in the victory of 1918. It did not seem implausible that France would rise again. Indeed, that is precisely what Laval told Hitler on more than one occasion. Thus it was important to Laval and to Vichy to maintain French administration and control as far as they possibly could. If there were French commissions on Jewish affairs, it was clear that these gave men like Laval far greater latitude than had the matter been left exclusively to the Nazi hardliners. That is why Vichy wanted to control the police function. The alternative did not bear considering.

What was important to Laval was to exercise the maximum of control in defense of France, however unpopular it might be. Indeed, he undertook the most difficult tasks to preserve the image and appeal of Petain. It was important to him never to collaborate militarily with Germany, which he told Hitler as early as October 23, 1940 and, words notwithstanding, he never did.

On any detailed examination and fair assessment, Pierre Laval was a sturdy republican as befitted a poor country lad to whom the Republic had given so much, from an education to its highest offices. He was never an anti-Semite—there is no such evidence; he was surely not a Nazi. His love of the soil, of his native Auvergne, of his country were incontestable.

There was never a coup d'état against the Third Republic. As Professor Paxton has written,

> We can now see how misleading it was after the war to cloak the Third Republic's self-immolation at Vichy on July 9-10, 1940 as a coup d'état by Pierre Laval. It

became expedient to load everything on those stooped shoulders, especially after Laval was shot in the courtyard of the Fresnes prison in Paris on the morning of October 15, 1945.[13]

Paxton went further when he wrote, "What survives from genuine contemporary language suggests something very much like massive assent to the idea of building a new regime at once, even under German eyes."

Surely Pierre Laval was not the sole fountainhead of the policy of collaboration. It carried on after his dismissal in 1940 and until he returned to government in 1942. In that period, anti-Jewish legislation was passed and military collaboration with Germany pursued, both to a degree markedly higher than Pierre Laval ever countenanced. That Laval fought hard to forestall labor drafts and Jewish deportations is as incontestable as that he succeeded meaningfully in both.

Laval was a horse trader, a negotiator, a compromiser who viewed words as his only weapons in the deadly duel with Nazi Germany. It came naturally to him to promise more than he could perform, confident that he could return to fight another day. Where words would secure the ends he sought, he could be liberal with words. But he asked always to be measured, not by his words but by his acts.

Pierre Laval was far from representing one end of the political spectrum, even the Vichy spectrum. He was by nature an independent as he had always been in the Third Republic. At Vichy, he represented not an extreme but the center. To the one hand were the incense-perfumed votaries of the National Revolution whose ceremonies as much as their amateurishness in government appalled Laval. On the other hand there were always, in Paris, the Ultras, the real pro-Germans, indeed the pro-Nazis. Laval's struggle with them was as demanding as his struggle with their German masters.

Laval had to deal not simply with the Germans. He had to deal with France as it was and with the French as they were. France in the 1930s and into the 1940s was a country bitterly divided by class and culture. Its industry and economy were outdated and inefficient. As a people, the French were irresolute, their morale low, their arms, as it turned out, badly used.

Had France been united in its goals, prepared for sacrifice, sure of its ideals and its capacity to attain them, Vichy might have been a different government and Laval might have been able to follow another policy. But the French of the war years were hardly heroic. Phillippe Burrin, a distinguished French scholar gives us this picture:

They are weary of everything, the Germans, the English, the Russians; all they can think about is getting through without coming to any harm; it is as if to the great mass of this country nothing matters except survival at any price.[14]

To a mother of three children whose husband was a prisoner of war, the choices were limited and heroism was not one of them. Rather food and fuel and clothing for her family were constant preoccupations. For children, for the elderly, there were even fewer choices. The bulk of the male population of fighting age was in German prison camps. The possibilities of resistance were minimal and few sought them out in the early 1940s. It was this population Vichy had to lead and to defend. Prudence, not rebellion, seemed to be the best course.

How to combine prudence with principle was, Pierre Laval remarked in a diplomatic crisis of the 1930s, the problem of diplomacy. But what, in Vichy France, did prudence counsel and what did honor command?

In the aftermath of the French collapse of 1940 and the Allied victory of 1945, it seemed to the French that they must have been heroic and that collapse and collaboration were the work of a few evil men, chief among them Pierre Laval. Such conclusions were and remain unwarranted. But in France, a more objective analysis will probably be possible only after the World War II generation has passed from the scene.

One thing is incontestable. The trial of Pierre Laval was more than a sham, more than a travesty. It was the abandonment of almost every rule of law, every canon of ethics and every obligation of the prosecutors, the magistrates, the judges, and at the highest level the minister of justice and the head of state.

Deprived of the materials he had prepared for his defense, denied the preliminary examination which is at the heart of French criminal procedure, deprived, too, of the competent representation of well prepared lawyers, exposed to the naked hostility of the jury, which itself had been fraudulently chosen, and of the Court, deprived in open court of the right freely and fairly to defend himself, Pierre Laval knew the bitterness of the deliberate and systematic perversion of justice that characterized his trial.

And it should be noted in all of this that the trial, judgment and execution were carried out in fifteen days. In the trial of Pierre Laval, shot through with fundamental error of the most egregious kind, there was no provision for review. Court and jury could proceed with the assurance that their acts and procedures would never be examined by a competent court of appeal. The only review provided was purely political and surely did not address the issues in that thorough, impartial and professional manner which is the right of every accused person in any civilized system of justice.

The trial of Pierre Laval has left an ineffaceable stain upon the reputation of France for upholding the rule of reason and the cause of justice. Whatever question may be raised as to matters of fact, as to matters of law the verdict was and is wholly unsustainable.

It has been said that a man does not lie on his deathbed. Here is David Thompson, in *Two Frenchmen*:

> It is difficult to believe that any man who had not a deep inner conviction of his ultimate rightness of choice could have endured the long grueling ordeal of the examination and the trial which he was now to experience or that he could have put up against the highest of odds so remarkably vigorous and convincing a defense... It is only by crediting him with a sincere belief in at least most of what he professed at his trial that we can make sense of his previous actions. And it is this hidden source of strength, this fervor of confidence in what he had done that explains the vigor and effectiveness of his defense and the moral dignity of the way he died.[15]

Epilogue: The Mistress in the Shadows

One day in the 1950s, while holding a press conference, Charles de Gaulle asked the assembled journalists, "There was once someone called Pierre Laval. Whatever became of him?" The clear implication was that Laval, like Vichy, was either irrelevant or had never really existed. This was consistent with the thesis that de Gaulle was France and France was de Gaulle. And that Vichy was best forgotten.[1]

But it wasn't that simple. The life and career, public and private, of François Mitterand is emblematic of the ties between France and Vichy and of the memory of Vichy. Escaped from a prisoner of war camp, Mitterand joined the Vichy government in 1942 as a documentarist for Pétain's principal support organization, the Legion of Veterans. In 1942-43 he was a press officer for a board for the rehabilitation of prisoners of war. He publicly lauded the regime in articles he published. The first in 1942, endorsed the labor draft, the Service de Travail Obligatoire or SOL, and criticized the Legion's want of fanaticism. The second article appeared in December, 1942, in the Vichy publication *France*. It denounced France's one hundred fifty years of mistakes and was published alongside articles denouncing Jews, Masons and Gaullists. For all these services, Mitterand was awarded the Vichy decoration called the Francisque in spring, 1943.[2]

But Mitterand reached out to the Resistance in 1943, gained the confidence of de Gaulle, and in March, 1944, became the head of a single unified Resistance group of prisoners of war. This was the foundation on which he built his brilliant postwar career culminating in two terms as president of the Republic.[3]

When in 1994 a book was published detailing Mitterand's long-concealed Vichy past, it did not seem to matter that much any more and Mitterand himself cooperated in the disclosure.[4]

Mitterand died on January 8, 1996 from a prostate cancer he had also long concealed. Nor was that all. On January 11 there had been a public ceremony at Notre Dame attended by some 1,300 including many of the world's leaders. They came in flowing African robes, in Arab headdress, and in somber morning clothes. A more personal and intimate rite was celebrated in St. Peter's church in Jarnac, Mitterand's birthplace. There in the procession entering the church were Mitterand's widow Danielle and their two sons. Immediately following them were Mitterand's long-time mistress, Anne Pingeot and their daughter, Mazarine Pingeot. All three women were clad in black.

Mme. Pingeot and her daughter were there by the express invitation of Mme. Mitterand. He had shared some of his last days with them, at Christmas at Aswan in Egypt, after which he had passed the New Year with Mme. Mitterand and her sons at his country home in the southwestern French village of Latche.[5]

The picture of the mourners shown on television furnished a metaphor for Vichy's role in the history of France. History has confirmed de Gaulle as the lawfully wedded spouse of France. Vichy is the mistress who lived in the shadows, in the back streets, but who had shared bed and board, whose intimacy was as unquestioned as it was unsanctified. The TV images surely raised eyebrows and incited knowing smiles among English-speaking viewers, but at bottom it plainly showed two realities in the life of Mitterand and in the life of France.

Among the revelations of Mitterand's past was one more recent. Every year, on Armistice Day, he had, as president, sent flowers to adorn Pétain's grave. The thesis was advanced that he was honoring not Vichy but Verdun, another example of the bifurcation of historical memory.[6]

Mitterand sent no flowers to Laval's grave. It is a simple slab in the Montparnasse Cemetery in Paris bearing only the names and dates of birth and death of Laval and his wife Jeanne. Every year on October 15, the date of the execution, in their lifetimes Josée and René de Chambrun brought flowers to the grave. Their faithful housekeeper, Jeanne Daire, would clean the surface of the slab and rearrange the anonymous flowers she found there. There is no other monument to Laval in Paris. Nor is there any in Chateldon to its most famous son. But the natives there still refer to him respectfully as M. le President.

René de Chambrun achieved great success as a lawyer and in business as chairman of Cristalleries Baccarat. But the passion of his long and active life was the defense of the reputation and the memory of Pierre Laval whom he revered. He published extensively, including a three volume set of documents under the title *The Life of France Under the Occupation* and in his ninety-sixth year was active in compiling and publishing a collection of Laval's wartime speeches. In addition to his own extensive writings, the defenders Naud, Baraduc, and Jaffré all published their memoirs of the man and the trial. Indeed, on the fiftieth anniversary Jaffré published *Fifty Years Ago, The Trial That Never Was*, laying out point by point the defense that was never made. It is a venerable cliché that history is written by the winners. Losers rarely come out well; they mostly languish in the shadows like Mitterand's mistress. There are exceptions: perhaps Hannibal, surely Robert E. Lee. Pétain and Laval must inevitably be associated with a defeat that was not of their making and with the dark and dismal years of the Occupation and the roles they played in it. The French have a taste for *la gloire*, glory. There was none to be found at Vichy. In any case, glory was, like popularity, something that Laval never sought and indeed actively disdained.

A recent biography of Pétain considers the losers in history:

> But he loved his country and had a touching faith in what de Gaulle was to call the eternal France. Inadequate he may have been for the task for which he thought himself qualified, but he was not, and had never been, a traitor. In that particular at least and perhaps – dare it be said? – generally Clio, the maverick muse of History, has not played it entirely fair.[7]

Laval's biographers have tried to penetrate beneath the popular memory. Geoffrey Warner, concludes:

> In the circumstances, it is more than unfair that he had gone down in history with the reputation of a devious intriguer, for the greatest flaw in his character was not deviousness, but in a frightening tendency towards oversimplification. Perhaps the paradox can best be explained in his own words, which might also serve as his epitaph. "I have always had simple ideas in politics. People take me for a shyster, but they don't know me. What I do is so simple that it looks to those who don't understand like something very complicated."[8]

Fred Kupferman's colorful, comprehensive, and not unsympathetic account is written with great verve. It begins on the day of birth and ends at the day of death without attempting to pass final judgment. Jean-Paul Cointet takes up the challenge with this judgment:

> We end this brief review with a fascinating question: Wasn't it that he was successively betrayed by the English (in 1935), by Pétain (in December 1940), by the Germans (after April 1942), by the political world (during his trial)? A man betrayed by all must be either a naif or a saint. Perhaps the drama of Pierre Laval was that of a man too sure of himself, convinced of always being right, who pursued his logic beyond the facts, beyond that of men, and beyond even that of history. Was not Pierre Laval the victim of Pierre Laval?[9]

In March, 1940 just before the deluge, Laval met with the British Parliamentarian, Robert Boothby. Laval expressed his forebodings:

We are all agreed now that the best chance of stopping Hitler was when he sent his troops into the Rhineland; and that we failed. I know you think that the last chance was at Munich. I disagree. The last chance was at Stresa. Austria, not Czechoslovakia was the essential bastion of Central Europe.

Only one power could have saved Austria and that was Italy. We could have had Italy. But the price was Abyssinia. It was well worth paying; and believe me, it would have been a benefit, not harm, to the Abyssinians.

Laval went on to say that British prime minister MacDonald's reluctance to face facts had consequences:

It was unfortunate for all that he refused to face the unpalatable fact of Abyssinia at Stresa, because Mussolini mistook his silence for agreement instead of imbecility; and his subsequent disillusion threw him into the arms of Germany, with the result that we lost Austria and with it the whole of Central Europe.

This was Laval's essential thesis and his essential diplomacy in 1935-36. It also speaks to the first of the betrayals cited by Cointet.

With Italy, Germany could have been contained. "Not now," Laval said:

We have given most of Europe to Hitler. Let us try to hold onto what we have got left. I am a peasant from the Auvergne. I want to keep my farm, and I want to keep France. Nothing else matters now.[10]

Nothing rings truer than these words. Pierre Laval had ascended to the highest posts his nation could offer. He had been a figure of immense consequence on the world scene. More than all that, he was a peasant from the Auvergne who loved his land and the land of France. He spoke simply. He wanted to keep his land.

To "keep" is capable of many meanings. He wanted to protect his land, to defend his land. Like a good farmer, he wanted his land to flourish, to be fertile, to be productive and to sustain the lives of men and beasts for whom the land was the foundation and origin of all life. Equally simply and in a like sense he wanted to keep France. On the record, his efforts were not entirely in vain.

Notes

Prologue. The Black Plane: The Arrest of Pierre Laval

1. Fred Kupferman, *Laval, 1883-1945*, Paris: Flammarion, 478.
2. *Time*, January 4, 1932.
3. Kupferman, 478.
4. Yves Frédéric Jaffré, *Il y a 50 ans*, Paris: Albin-Michel, 1995, 270.
5. Kupferman, 481.
6. Kupferman, 481.
7. Kupferman, 481.
8. *Les Nouvelles du Matin*, August 2, 1945.
9. *New York Times*, August 2, 1945.
10. Kupferman, 481.
11. Kupferman, 481.

Chapter 1. Pierre Laval

1. For Pierre Laval's early life and education, see Geoffrey Warner, *Pierre Laval and the Eclipse of France*, New York: The Macmillan Company, 1968, 1-4 and Henri Torres, *Pierre Laval*, London: Gollancz, 1941, 12-14.
2. *New York Times*, October 23, 1931.
3. René de Chambrun, *Mes Combats pour Pierre Laval*, Paris: Perrin, 1990, 230-31.
4. Warner, 25.
5. Warner, 25.
6. Torres, 18-19.
7. Torres, 23.
8. Guy Bechtel, *Laval 20 Ans Aprés*, Paris: Laffont, 1963, 116-118.
9. Andre Francois-Poncet, *The Fateful Years*, New York: Harcourt Brace, 1949, 6.
10. Gaetano Salvemini, *Prelude to World War II*, London: Gollancz, 1953, 162.
11. The 1934-1936 diplomacy of Pierre Laval is one of the principal subjects of *The Avoidable War, Volume I, Lord Cecil and the Policy of Morality*, Transaction Publishers, New Brunswick, NJ, 1999 and *Volume 2, Pierre Laval and the Politics of Reality*, Transaction Publishers, New Brunswick, NJ, 2000 by J. Kenneth Brody.
12. *Documents on British Foreign Policy, 1919-1939. Series 2. Volume XIV*, Her Majesty's Stationery Office, London, 1947, No. 296.

Chapter 2. Preliminary Proceedings

1. Yves-Frédéric Jaffré, *Les Derniers Propos de Pierre Laval*, Paris: Editions Andre Bonne, 1953, 12-13.

2.   Jaffré, 13.
3.   Jaffré, 19-21.
4.   Jaffré, 21.
5.   Jaffré, 23, Albert Naud, "I Could Have Saved Pierre Laval," *Le Monde*, 10 June 1969.
6.   Jaffré, 23-27.
7.   Jaffré, 185-187.
8.   Jaffré, 188.
9.   Jaffré, 189.
10.   Jaffré, 189-190.
11.   Jaffré, 191.
12.   Jaffré, 190.
13.   Jaffré, 191.
14.   Jaffré, 191-192.
15.   Jaffré, 193.
16 . Jaffré, 194.
17.   Jaffré, 195.
18.   Jaffré, 194.
19.   Jaffré, 196.
20.   Jaffré, 196-197.
21.   Jaffré, 197.
22.   René de Chambrun, *Le Procés Laval*, Paris: Editions France-Empire, 1984, 19, Jaffré, 201.
23.   Jaffré, 198.
24.   Jaffré, 199-200.
25.   Jaffré, 200-201.
26.   Jaffré, 201.
27.   Jaffré, 202.
28.   Jaffré, 203.
29.   Jaffré, 205.
30.   Jaffré, 231.
31.   Jaffré, 232.
32.   Jaffré, 232-233.
33.   Jaffré, 234.
34.   Jaffré, 237.
35.   Raymond Lindon and Daniel Aronson, *La Haute Cour, 1789-1987*, Paris: puf, 108.
36.   Jaffré, 238-239.
37.   Jaffré, 240-241.

Chapter 3. The Trial, October 4, 1945[1]

1.   This chapter is based upon Le Procés Larai, Paris: Editions Albin-Michel, 1946 Procés, 7-25.
2.   Procés, 7.
3.   Jules Roy, *The Trial of Marshal Petain*, 11, New York: Harper & Row, 1968, 11.
4.   Procés, 7.
5.   Procés, 7-8.
6.   The Mongibeaux-Laval colloquy, Procés, 8.
7.   Roy, 12.
8.   Procés, 9-11.

9.   Procés, 11.
10. Procés, 11.
11. Procés, 11-12.
12. Procés, 12.
13. Procés, 13-14.
14. Procés, 15-16.
15. Procés, 17-18.
16. Procés, 19-20.
17. Procés, 21.
18. Procés, 21.
19. Procés, 21-24.
20. Procés, 24-25.
21. Kupferman, 499.

Chapter 4. The Accusation[1]

1.   This chapter is based upon Procés, 25-34.
2.   Procés, 25.
3.   Procés, 26.
4.   Procés, 27.
5.   Procés, 27.
6.   Procés, 28.
7.   Procés, 29.
8.   Procés, 29.
9.   Procés, 30.
10. Procés, 31.
11. Procés, 31-33.
12. Procés, 33.
13. Procés, 34.

Chapter 5. Pierre Laval, Prisoner[1]

1.   This chapter is based upon Jaffré, 29-40.
2.   Jaffré, 29.
3.   Jaffré, 31.
4.   Jaffré, 31.
5.   Jaffré, 31.
6.   Jaffré, 31.
7.   Jaffré, 32.
8.   Jaffré, 33-34.
9.   Jaffré, 34-35.
10. Jaffré, 35.
11. Jaffré, 35-36.
12. Jaffré, 36-37.
13. Jaffré, 37-38.
14. Jaffré, 39-40.

Chapter 6. The Trial, October 4, 1945[1]

1.   This chapter is based upon Procés, 34-61.
2.   Procés, 35.
3.   Procés, 36.
4.   Procés, 37.

5.   Procés, 38.
6.   Procés, 39.
7.   Procés, 40.
8.   Procés, 41.
9.   Procés, 42.
10.   Procés, 42.
11.   Procés, 43.
12.   Procés, 44.
13.   Procés, 44.
14.   Procés, 45.
15.   Procés, 46.
16.   Procés, 46-47.
17.   Procés, 47.
18.   Procés, 47.
19.   Procés, 48.
20.   Procés, 49.
21.   Procés, 50.
22.   Procés, 50.
23.   Procés, 50-53.
24.   Procés, 53.
25.   Procés, 55.
26.   Procés, 55.
27.   Procés, 56.
28.   Procés, 56-57.
29.   Procés, 58.
30.   Procés, 59.
31.   Procés, 59.
32.   Procés, 60.
33.   Procés, 61.

Chapter 7. Pierre Laval: A Life[1]

1.   This chapter is based upon Jaffré, 58-126.
2.   Jaffré, 58.
3.   Jaffré, 60.
4.   Jaffré, 57.
5.   Jaffré, 58.
6.   Jaffré, 41-42.
7.   Jaffré, 43.
8.   Jaffré, 46-47.
9.   Jaffré, 47.
10.   Jaffré, 51.
11.   Jaffré, 52.
12.   Jaffré, 95.
13.   Jaffré, 95.
14.   Jaffré, 96.
15.   Jaffré, 97.
16.   Jaffré, 98.
17.   Jaffré, 100.
18.   Jaffré, 102-103.
19.   Jaffré, 103.
20.   Jaffré, 108.

21. Jaffré, 109.
22. Jaffré, 113-114.
23. Jaffré, 114-115.
24. Jaffré, 115.
25. Jaffré, 117.
26. Jaffré, 118.
27. Jaffré, 122.
28. Jaffré, 123-124.
29. Jaffré, 124.
30. Jaffré, 126.

Chapter 8. The Trial, October 4, 1945[1]

1. This chapter is based upon Procés, 60-98.
2. Procés, 60.
3. Procés, 61.
4. Procés, 62.
5. Procés, 63.
6. Procés, 64.
7. Procés, 64.
8. Procés, 67.
9. Procés, 67.
10. Procés, 68.
11. Procés, 68.
12. Procés, 69.
13. Procés, 70.
14. Procés, 71.
15. Procés, 72.
16. Procés, 72.
17. Procés, 73.
18. Procés, 74.
19. Procés, 74.
20. Procés, 74.
21. Procés, 78.
22. Procés, 79.
23. Procés, 79.
24. Procés, 80.
25. Procés, 80-82.
26. Procés, 84.
27. Procés, 84-86.
28. Procés, 86.
29. Procés, 87.
30. Procés, 87-88.
31. Procés, 89.
32. Procés, 90.
33. Procés, 90.
34. Procés, 90-91.
35. Procés, 92-93.
36. Procés, 95.
37. Procés, 96.
38. Procés, 97.
39. *Figaro*, October 6, 1945.
40. *Combat*, October 6, 1945.

41.   *L'Humanité*, October 6, 1945.

Chapter 9. Pierre Laval, Republican[1]

1.   This chapter is based upon Jaffré, 65-81.
2.   Jaffré, 65.
3.   Jaffré, 66-67.
4.   Jaffré, 66.
5.   Jaffré, 67.
6.   Jaffré, 68.
7.   Jaffré, 69.
8.   Jaffré, 71.
9.   Jaffré, 71.
10.   Jaffré, 72.
11.   Jaffré, 72.
12.   Jaffré, 73.
13.   Jaffré, 74.
14.   Jaffré, 75.
15.   Jaffré, 76.
16.   Jaffré, 77.
17.   Jaffré, 78.
18.   Jaffré, 79.

Chapter 10. The Trial, October 5, 1945[1]

1.   This chapter is based upon Procés, 99-121
2.   Procés, 99.
3.   Procés, 99.
4.   Procés, 100.
5.   Procés, 100.
6.   Procés, 101.
7.   Procés, 102.
8.   Procés, 102.
9.   Procés, 103-104.
10.   Procés, 104-105.
11.   Procés, 105-107.
12.   Procés, 108-109.
13.   Procés, 109-110.
14.   Procés, 110.
15.   Procés, 112.
16.   Procés, 113.
17.   Procés, 113.
18.   Procés, 113.
19.   Procés, 115.
20.   Procés, 115.
21.   Procés, 116.
22.   Procés, 117-118.
23.   Procés, 118-120.
24.   Procés, 120-121.

Chapter 11. The Trial, October 5, 1945[1]

1.   This chapter is based upon Procés, 121-155.

2.   Procés, 121.
3.   Procés, 122.
4.   Procés, 123.
5.   Procés, 125.
6.   Procés, 126.
7.   Procés, 127.
8.   Procés, 129.
9.   Procés, 130.
10.   Procés, 129-131.
11.   Procés, 131-132.
12.   Procés, 133.
13.   Procés, 135.
14.   Procés, 136.
15.   Procés, 137.
16.   Procés, 138.
17.   Procés, 139.
18.   Procés, 140.
19.   Procés, 140.
20.   Procés, 140.
21.   Procés, 140-141.
22.   Procés, 144.
23.   Procés, 146.
24.   Procés, 146.
25.   Procés, 147.
26.   Procés, 148-149.
27.   Procés, 149.
28.   Procés, 150.
29.   Procés, 152-153.
30.   Procés, 153.
31.   Procés, 154.
32.   Procés, 154-155.

Chapter 12. The Trial, October 5, 1945[1]

1.   This chapter is based upon Procés, 156-192.
2.   Procés, 156.
3.   Procés, 157.
4.   Procés, 158.
5.   Procés, 159.
6.   Procés, 159-160.
7.   Procés, 160.
8.   Procés, 161.
9.   Procés, 162.
10.   Procés, 162.
11.   Procés, 163.
12.   Procés, 164.
13.   Procés, 165.
14.   Procés, 165.
15.   Procés, 167.
16.   Procés, 170.
17.   Procés, 170.
18.   Procés, 170.

19.   Procés, 171-173.
20.   Procés, 173.
21.   Procés, 174-179.
22.   Procés, 179.
23.   Procés, 181-183.
24.   Procés, 183.
25.   Procés, 189-192.
26.   Procés, 190.
27.   Procés, 191.
28.   Procés, 191.
29.   Procés, 192.
30.   *L'Humanité*, October 6, 1945.
31.   *Figaro*, October 6, 1945.
32.   *Combat*, October 5, 1945.

Chapter 13. Pierre Laval, Collaborator, 1

1.   *Documents on German Foreign Policy, Series D, Volume IX, 523.*
2.   Warner, 231-232.
3.   Warner, 240.
4.   Warner, 240.
5.   Robert O. Paxton, *Vichy, France, Old Guard and New Order*, New York, Alfred A. Knopf: 1972, 9.
6.   Paxton, 242.
7.   Paxton, 282.
8.   Julian Jackson, *France, the Dark Years, 1940-1945*, Oxford: Oxford University Press, 2001, 262-264.
9.   Kupferman, 1958,498.
10.   Paxton, 286.
11.   Jaffré, 220.
12.   Paxton, 294-295.
13.   Philippe Burrin, *France Under the Germans*, New York: The New Press, 1996, 26.
14.   Jacques Maritain, *France, My Country*, New York: Longmans Green & Co., 1941, 62, 85.
15.   Paxton, 111.
16.   Jaffré, 127.
17.   Jaffré, 128.
18.   Jaffré, 128.
19.   Jaffré, 128.
20.   Jaffré, 129-130.
21.   Jaffré, 130.
22.   Jaffré, 131.
23.   Jaffré, 131-132.
24.   Jaffré, 132-134.
25.   Jaffré, 134-135.
26.   Jaffré, 134.
27.   Jaffré, 134.
28.   Jaffré, 134-135.
29.   Jaffré, 135-137.
30.   Jaffré, 137.
31.   Jaffré, 136-137.

32.   Jaffré, 138.
33.   Jaffré, 167.
34.   Jaffré, 167-168.
35.   Jaffré, 168.
36.   Jaffré, 168.
37.   Jaffré, 168-169.
38.   Jaffré, 169.
39.   Jaffré, 169.
40.   Jaffré, 170.
41.   Jaffré, 170.
42.   Jaffré, 171.
43.   Jaffré, 171.
44.   Jaffré, 171-172.
45.   Jaffré, 172.
46.   Jaffré, 173.
47.   Jaffré, 159-160.
48.   Jaffré, 160-161.
49.   Jaffré, 162-163.
50.   Jaffré, 162.
51.   Jaffré, 162.
52.   Jaffré, 162-163.
53.   Jaffré, 164.
54.   Jaffré, 164.
55.   Jaffré, 165.
56.   Jaffré, 165.
57.   Jaffré, 166.
58.   Jaffré, 166.

Chapter 14. The Trial, October 6, 1945[1]

1.   This chapter is based upon Procés, 193-204.
2.   Procés, 193.
3.   Procés, 194-196.
4.   Procés, 196.
5.   Procés, 196.
6.   Procés, 197.
7.   Procés, 198.
8.   Procés, 198.
9.   Procés, 199.
10.   Procés, 200.
11.   Procés, 201.
12.   Procés, 201.
13.   Procés, 201.
14.   Procés, 202.
15.   Procés, 203.
16.   Procés, 202-204.
17.   Procés, 204.
18.   Procés, 204.

Chapter 15. Pierre Laval, Collaborator, 2[1]

1.   This chapter is based upon Jaffré, 175-183 and Jaffré 220-227.

2.   Jaffré, 175.
3.   Jaffré, 175.
4.   Jaffré, 176.
5.   Jaffré, 176.
6.   Jaffré, 177.
7.   Jaffré, 178.
8.   Jaffré, 179.
9.   Jaffré, 179.
10.   Jaffré, 180.
11.   Jaffré, 181.
12.   Jaffré, 182.
13.   Jaffré, 182-183.
14.   J. Clermont, *L'homme qu'il Fallait Tuer, Pierre Laval*, Paris: Charles de Jonquieres, 1948, 258.
15.   *La Vie de la France Sous l'Occupation*, Institut Hoover: Paris: Plon, 1957, 1433-1434.
16.   *Les Discours de Pierre Laval, 1942-1944*, Paris: Fondation Josée et Rene de Chambrun, 1999, 36.
17.   Jaffré, 220.
18.   Jaffré, 220-221.
19.   Jaffré, 220-225.
20.   Jaffré, 225.
21.   Jaffré, 226.
22.   Jaffré, 226-227.
23.   Jaffré, 227.

Chapter 16. The Trial, October 6, 1945[1]

1.   This chapter is based upon Procés, 204-209 and Jaffré, 260-267.
2.   Procés, 204.
3.   Procés, 205.
4.   Procés, 205.
5.   Procés, 205.
6.   Procés, 205.
7.   Procés, 206.
8.   Procés, 206.
9.   Procés, 207.
10.   Procés, 207.
11.   Procés, 207.
12.   Procés, 208.
13.   Procés, 208.
14.   Procés, 208.
15.   Procés, 209.
16.   Jaffré, 260.
17.   Jaffré, 261-262.
18.   Jaffré, 263.
19.   Jaffré, 264.
20.   Jaffré, 264-265.
21.   Kupferman, 503.
22.   Jaffré, 266.
23.   Jaffré, 267.
24.   Jaffré, 268.

25. *Combat*, October 7-8, 1945.
26. *Combat*, October 7-8, 1945.
27. *Figaro*, October 7, 1945.
28. *La Croix*, October 9, 1945.
29. *L'Humanité*, October 9, 1945.
30. *Figaro*, October 9, 1945.
31. *Combat*, October 9, 1945.
32. *L'Humanité*, October 9, 1945.
33. *L'Humanité*, October 9, 1945.
34. *Combat*, October 9, 1945.
35. *La Croix*, October 12, 1945.
36. *Combat*, October 10, 1945.

Chapter 17. The Trial, October 6, 8, 9, 1945[1]

1. This chapter is based upon Procés, 209-262.
2. Procés, 211.
3. Procés, 211.
4. Procés, 216.
5. Procés, 220.
6. Procés, 220.
7. Procés, 222.
8. Procés, 224-225.
9. Procés, 226-227.
10. Procés, 228-232.
11. Procés, 230-232.
12. Procés, 232.
13. Procés, 233-238.
14. Procés, 239-242.
15. Procés, 242.
16. Procés, 242.
17. Procés, 244.
18. Procés, 245.
19. Procés, 245.
20. Procés, 246.
21. Procés, 247.
22. Procés, 248.
23. Procés, 249.
24. Procés, 249-250.
25. Procés, 250.
26. Procés, 251.
27. Procés, 252.
28. Procés, 252.
29. Procés, 253.
30. Procés, 253-255.
31. Procés, 255.
32. Procés, 257-260.
33. Procés, 261-262.

Chapter 18. Pierre Laval's Decision[1]

1. This chapter is based upon Jaffré, 209-215 and Procés, 302-305.

2.   Procés, 302.
3.   Procés, 302.
4.   Procés, 303.
5.   Procés, 304.
6.   Procés, 304.
7.   Procés, 304.
8.   Procés, 305.
9.   Jaffré, 209.
10.   Jaffré, 212.
11.   Jaffré, 214.
12.   Jaffré, 214.
13.   Jaffré, 215.

Chapter 19. The Trial: October 9, 1945[1]

1.   This chapter is based upon Procés, 262-302.
2.   Procés, 262.
3.   Procés, 263.
4.   Procés, 264.
5.   Procés, 265.
6.   Procés, 265.
7.   Procés, 266.
8.   Procés, 267.
9.   Procés, 268.
10.   Procés, 269-271.
11.   Procés, 270.
12.   Procés, 273.
13.   Procés, 275.
14.   Procés, 276.
15.   Procés, 278.
16.   Procés, 279.
17.   Procés, 284.
18.   Procés, 285-288.
19.   Procés, 285-288.
20.   Procés, 290-292.
21.   Procés, 293.
22.   Procés, 295-296.
23.   Procés, 296-298.
24.   Procés, 298.
25.   Procés, 299-300.
26.   Procés, 300.
27.   Procés, 301.
28.   Procés, 301.
29.   Procés, 301-302.
30.   Procés, 302.

Chapter 20. Pierre Laval's Defense

1.   Jackson, 133.
2.   Pierre Cathala in *La Vie de la France*, Vol. 1, 106.
3.   Warner, 243.
4.   Philippe Petain, *Quatre Années an Pouvoir*, 69-71.

5.   Kupferman, 258.
6.   Kupferman, 260.
7.   Kupferman, 259-260.
8.   Jean-Paul Cointet, *Pierre Laval*, Paris: Fayard, 1993, 427.
9.   Michael O Marrus and Robert O. Paxton, *Vichy France and the Jews*, New York: Basic Books, 1986, 56 and citing Journal Oficiel, Lois et decrets, 13 November, 1938.
10. Marrus and Paxton, 70.
11. Warner, 304-305 citing *Journal Oficiel*, 18 October 1940.
12. Warner,304, Contet, 393.
13. Marrus and Paxton, 7.
14. Marrus and Paxton, xiii.
15. Marrus and Paxton 20, citing *Journal des Debats*, 25 October, 1940.
16. Marrus and Paxton, 101 citing J. O., 26 August, 1941.
17. Marrus and Paxton, 167.
18. Marrus and Paxton, 103-105.
19. Marrus and Paxton, 92, Cointet, 394.
20. Marrus and Paxton, 107.
21. Marrus and Paxton, 109 citing J.O., 2 December, 1941.
22. Marrus and Paxton, 83 citing J. O., 31 March, 1941.
23. Marrus and Paxton, 135.
24. Marrus and Paxton, 185-186.
25. Marrus and Paxton, 226.
26. Marrus and Paxton, 227.
27. Marrus and Paxton, 149 citing Jules Jeanneney, *Journal* (1), 278-287.
28. Cointet, 399.
29. Warner, 305, Kupferman, 354-355, Laval 97-98.
30. Marrus and Paxton, 267-268.
31. Eric Conan and Henry Rousso *Vichy-An Ever Present Past*, Hanover and London: University Press of New England, 1991, 20.
32. Cointet, 399-400.
33. Conan and Rousso, 20.
34. Marrus and Paxton, 351.
35. Gitta Sereny, *The German Trauma, Experience and Reflection, 1938-200*, London: Allen Lane, 2000.
36. Sereny, xv.
37. Jackson, 366.
38. Marrus and Paxton, 346 citing *Laval Parle*, 102, Pierre Laval, *The Diary of Pierre Laval*, 95.
39. Cointet, 425.
40. Cointet, 425-426.
41. Cointet, 425-426.
42. Cointet, 426-427.
43. Cointet, 426-427.
44. Warner, 306.
45. Warner, 376.
46. Warner, 376.
47. Warner, 376-377.
48. Warner, 377.
49. Marrus and Paxton, 330.
50. Jaffré 2, 156-158.
51. Cointet, 427.

52. Laqueur, 141-145
53. Davidowicz, 402
54. Dawidowicz, 403.
55. Michael Curtis, *Verdict on Vichy*, New York: Arcade Publishing, 2002, 200.
56. Curtis, 353.
57. See also Jaffré 2, 253 and Alfred Mallet, *Pierre Laval,II*, Paris: Amiot Dumont, 1954, 261.
58. Marrus and Paxton, xiv.
59. *Riverol*, May, 1986.
60. Cointet, 378-379.
61. Cointet, 379.
62. Warner, 307.
63. Warner, 307-308 citing J. O., 13 September, 1942.
64. Warner, 308.
65. Warner, 310.
66. Warner, 310 citing Cathala, I, 106.
67. Warner, 310 citing *C. E. Temoignages*, III, 231-232.
68. Cointet, 433-434.
69. Jaffré 2, 201, Cointet, 434, Kupferman, 412-413.
70. Cointet, 434, Warner, 373.
71. Jaffré 2, 201, Cointet, 434, Kupferman, 412-413.
72. Jaffré 2, 206, Cointet, 434.
73. Jaffré 2, 207.
74. Jaffré 2, 208.
75. Jaffré 2, 213.
76. Jaffré 2, 214.
77. Warner 373 citing *Laval Parle*, 125-126.
78. Warner, 373 citing Cathala, III, 1240.
79. Warner, 389-390.
80. Warner, 390-391.
81. Claude Gounelle, *Le Dossier Laval*, Paris: Plon, 1969, 371-374.
82. Warner, 210.
83. Warner, 237.
84. Warner, 293 citing Cathala, III, 1181.
85. Cointet, 409.
86. Cointet, 409, Warner, 324.
87. Warner, 324 citing *Laval Parle*, 134.
88. Kupferman, 377 citing René de Chambrun letter, Le Monde, 11 September 1971.
89. Cointet, 414.
90. Warner, 327.
91. Warner, 348-350.
92. Warner, 350-351.
93. Warner, 370-371.
94. Warner, 396-397.
95. Warner, 397-398.
96. Warner, 398-399.
97. Jaffré 2, 162.
98. Jaffré 2, 163-164.
99. Jaffré 2, 164-165.
100. Jaffré 2, 166.
101. Jaffré 2, 166.

102. Jaffré 2, 167-172.

Chapter 21. The Judgment, October 9, 1945[1]

1.   This chapter is based upon Procés, 306-309 and Jaffré, 268-272.
2.   Jaffré, 268-269.
3.   Jaffré, 269.
4.   Jaffré, 269.
5.   Jaffré, 269.
6.   Jaffré, 270.
7.   Jaffré, 270.
8.   Procés, 306.
9.   Procés, 306.
10.   Procés, 307.
11.   Procés, 307.
12.   Procés, 307-308.
13.   Procés, 308.
14.   Procés, 309.
15.   Jaffré, 270.
16.   Jaffré, 271.
17.   Jaffré, 271.
18.   Jaffré, 272.

Chapter 22. On the Eve[1]

1.   This chapter is based upon Jacques Baraduc, *Dans la Cellule de Pierre Laval*, Paris: Self, 1948, 156-186 and Jaffré, 273-306.
2.   Baraduc, 155.
3.   Jaffré, 273-274.
4.   Baraduc, 156.
5.   Baraduc, 157-158.
6.   Jaffré, 275.
7.   Jaffré, 275.
8.   Jaffré, 275.
9.   Jaffré, 276.
10.   Jaffré, 277.
11.   Jaffré, 278.
12.   Francois Mauriac, *Bloc-Notes*, Vol. 4, 436.
13.   Jaffré, 293.
14.   Baraduc, 162-163.
15.   Jaffré, 278-279.
16.   Jaffré, 279.
17.   Baraduc, 166-167, Unpublished letter, source Jaffré.
18.   Baraduc, 165.
19.   Baraduc, 169.
20.   Baraduc, 169-170.
21.   Jaffré, 288.
22.   Jaffré, 288.
23.   Jaffré, 290-291.
24.   Jaffré, 292.
25.   Baraduc, 174.
26.   Jaffré, 294.

27.   Jaffré, 295.
28.   Baraduc, 180-181.
29.   Jaffré, 300.
30.   Baraduc, 183.
31.   Baraduc, 183.
32.   Baraduc, 183.
33.   Baraduc, 184-185.
34.   Jaffré, 302.
35.   Jaffré, 303.
36.   Albert Naud, *Pourquoi je n'ai pas defendu Pierre Laval*, Paris: Fayard, 1948, 273-74.
37.   Baraduc, 186.
38.   Jaffré, 305.
39.   Jaffré, 304-306.
40.   Yves Pourcher, *Pierre Laval Vu par sa Fille*, Paris: Le Cherche Midi, 2002, 370.
41.   Pourcher, 371.

Chapter 23. Dernier Cri[1]

1.   This chapter is based upon Jaffré, 306-318 and Baraduc, 190-199.
2.   Jaffré, 306.
3.   Baraduc, 190.
4.   Baraduc, 190.
5.   Jaffré, 310.
6.   Baraduc, 191.
7.   Jaffré, 310-311.
8.   Baraduc, 192.
9.   Jaffré, 311.
10.   Baraduc, 194-195.
11.   Baraduc, 193.
12.   Jaffré, 314.
13.   Baraduc, 196.
14.   Baraduc, 195.
15.   Jaffré, 317, Baraduc, 198.
16.   Jaffré, 317.
17.   Jaffré, 317, Baraduc, 198-199.
18.   Jaffré, 317, Baraduc, 198-199.
19.   Jaffré, 318.

Chapter 24. Aftermath

1.   René de Chambrun, *Mes Combats pour Pierre Laval*, 36-42
2.   de Chambrun, 14-15, 17-29, 15 David Thompson, *Two Frenchmen*, London: The Crescent Press, 1952, 108.
3.   de Chambrun, 24.
4.   de Chambrun, 26.
5.   de Chambrun, 29.
6.   de Chambrun, 29.
7.   de Chambrun, 81.
8.   de Chambrun, 82.
9.   de Chambrun, 83.
10.   de Chambrun, 82-83.

11. The five dossiers are deposited in the archive of the Fondation Josée et René de Chambrun, Paris.
12. Roy, 253.
13. Paxton, 24-25.
14. Burrin, 188.

Epilogue

1. Guy Bechtel, *Laval 20 Ans Aprés*, Paris: Laffont, 1963.
2. Jackson, 510.
3. Jackson, 510-511.
4. Jackson, 621.
5. *New York Times*, January 14, 1996.
6. Jackson, 621.
7. Charles Williams, *Petain*, New York: Palgrave Macmillan, 2005, 4.
8. Warner, 422.
9. Cointet, 10-11.
10. Lord Boothby, (Sir Robert Boothby), Boothby, *Recollections of a Rebel*, London: Hutchinson, 1978, 305.

Bibliography

Periodicals

Combat, Paris
Ecrits de Paris, Paris
Figaro, Paris
LaCroix, Paris
L'Humanité, Paris
Les Nouvelles du Matin, Paris
New York Times, New York
Riverol, Paris

General

Aron, Robert, *The Vichy Regime, 1940-1944*, New York: The Macmillan Company, 1958.

Baraduc, Jacques, *Dans la Cellule de Pierre Laval*, Paris: Self, 1948.

Bechtel, Guy, *Laval 20 Ans Aprés*, Paris: Laffont, 1963.

Brody, J. Kenneth, *The Avoidable War, Volume One, Lord Cecil and the Policy of Morality*, New Brunswick, NJ: Transaction Publishers, 1999.

Brody, J. Kenneth, *The Avoidable War, Volume Two, Pierre Laval and the Politics of Reality*, New Brunswick, NJ: Transaction Publishers, 2000.

Burrin, Philippe, *France Under the Germans*, New York: The New Press, 1996.

Cointet, Jean-Paul, *Pierre Laval*, Paris: Fayard, 1993.

Conan, Eric and Rousso, Henry, *Vichy, An Ever Present Past*, Hanover and London: University Press of New England, 1941.

Curtis, Michael, *Verdict on Vichy*, New York: Arcade Publishing, 2002.

de Chambrun, Joseé Laval, *The Diary of Pierre Laval*, New York: Charles Scribner's Sons, 1948.

de Chambrun, René, *Le Procés Laval*, Paris: Editions France-Empire, 1984.

de Chambrun, René, *Pierre Laval Devant LHistoire*, Paris: Editions France-Empire, 1983.

de Chambrun, René, *Mes Combats Pour Pierre Laval*, Paris: Perrin, 1990.

J. Clermont, *L'Homme qü il Fallait Tuer, Pierre Laval*, Paris: Charles de Jonquieres, 1948.

Cointet, Jean-Paul, *Pierre Laval*, Paris: Fayard, 1993.

Conan, Eric and Rousso, Henry, *Vichy, An Ever-Present Past*, Hanover and London: University Press of New England, 1998.

Davidowicz, Lucy S., *The War Against the Jews*, New York: Holt, Rinehart & Winston, 1975.

Documents on British Foreign Policy, 1919-1939, Series 2, Volume XIV, London: Her Majesty's Stationery Office, 1947.

François-Pançet, André, *The Fateful Years*, New York: Harcourt, Brace, 1949.

Godechat, Jacques, *Les Constitutions de la France Depuis 1789*, Paris: G. F. Flammarion, 1995.

Gounelle, Claude, *Le Dossier Laval*, Paris: Plon, 1969.

Jackson, Julian, *France, the Dark Years, 1940-1945*, Oxford: Oxford University Press, 2001.

Jaffré, Yves Frédéric, *Il y a 50 Ans*, Paris: Albin Michel, 1995.

Jaffré, Yves Frédéric, *Les Derniers Propos de Pierre Laval*, Paris: Editions Andre Bonne, 1953.

Jacquemin, Gaston, *La Vie Publique de Pierre Laval*, Paris: Plon, 1973.

Hilberg, Raul, *The Destruction of the European Jews*, New York and London: Holmes & Meier, 1985.

Kupferman, Fred, *Laval, 1883-1945*, Paris: Flammarion, 1988.

Laqueur, Walter, editor, *The Holocaust Encyclopedia*, New Haven and London: Yale University Press, 2001.

La Vie de la France sous l'Occupation (1940-1944), Institut Hoover, Paris: Plon, 1957.

Les Discours de Pierre Laval, 1942-1944, Paris: Fondation Josée et René de Chambrun, 1999.

Le Proces Laval, Paris: Editions Albin Michel, 1946.

Lindon, Raymond and Aronson, Daniel, *La Haute Cour, 1789-1987*, Paris: puf.

Lottman, Herbert, *Petain, Hero or Traitor?* New York: William Morrow & Co., 1985.

Mallet, Alfred, *Pierre Laval, Volume 1, Des Années Obscures a la Disgrace du 13 December, 1940*, Paris: Amiot Dumont, 1954.

Mallet, Alfred, Volume II, *De la Reconquete du Pouvoir a l'Execution*, Paris: Amiot Dumont, 1955.

Maritain, Jacques, *France, My County*, New York: Longmans Green & Co., 1941.

Marrus, Michael and Paxton, Robert O., *Vichy France and the Jews*, New York: Basic Books, 1981.

Mauriac, F., *Bloc-Notes, 1952-1970*, Paris: Seuil, 1993.

Naud, Albert, "I Could Have Saved Pierre Laval," *Le Monde*, 10 June 1969.

Naud, Albert, *Pourquoi Je n'ai pas défendu Pierre Laval*, Paris: Fayard, 1948.

Paxton, Robert O., *Vichy France, Old Guard and New Order*, New York: Alfred A. Knopf, 1972.

Petain, Philippe, *Quatre Ans Au Porvoir*, Paris: La Couronne Literaire, 1949.

Pourcher, Yves, *Pierre Laval Vu par sa Fille*, Paris: Le Cherche Midi, 2002.

Riverol, May, 1986.

Roy, Jules, *The Trial of Marshal Petain*, New York: Harper & Row, 1968.

Salvemini, Gaetano, *Prelude to World War II*, London: Gollancz, 1953.

Sereny, Gitta, *The German Trauma, Experiences and Reflections, 1938-2000*, London: Allen Lane, Penguin Press, 2000.

Shirer, William, *The Collapse of the Third Republic*, New York: Simon & Schuster, 1969.

Stefani, Gaston, Levasseur, Georges and Boulot, Bernard, *Procédure Penale*, 16th edition, Paris: Editions Dalloz, 1996.

Thompson, David, *Two Frenchmen*, London: The Crescent Press, 1952.

Torres, Henri, *Pierre Laval*, London: Gollancz, 1941.

Warner, Geoffrey, *Pierre Laval and the Eclipse of France*, New York: The Macmillan Company, 1968.

Weber, Eugen, *The Hollow Years, France in the 1930s*, New York: W. W. Norton, 1994.

Werth, Alexander, *France, 1940-1945*, London: Robert Hale, Ltd. 1956.

Williams, Charles, *Petain*, New York: Palgrave Macmillan, 2005.

Index